·TOTAL· MATH & READING

Thinking Kids®
Carson-Dellosa Publishing LLC
Greensboro, North Carolina

Thinking Kids®
Carson-Dellosa Publishing LLC
P.O. Box 35665
Greensboro, NC 27425 USA

Printed in the USA • All rights reserved.   ISBN 978-1-4838-3559-4
01-339167784

Table of Contents

Math

Reading

Table of Contents

Math

NAME _____

Happy Hikers

Directions: Trace a path through the maze by counting from **1** to **10** in the correct order. Color the picture.

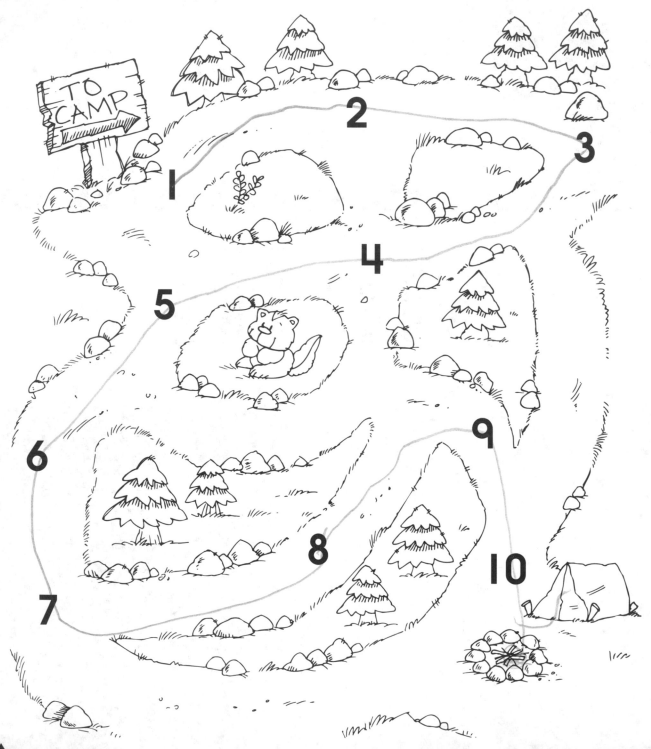

Food Favorites

Directions: Count the pictures in each group. Circle the number. Color the pictures.

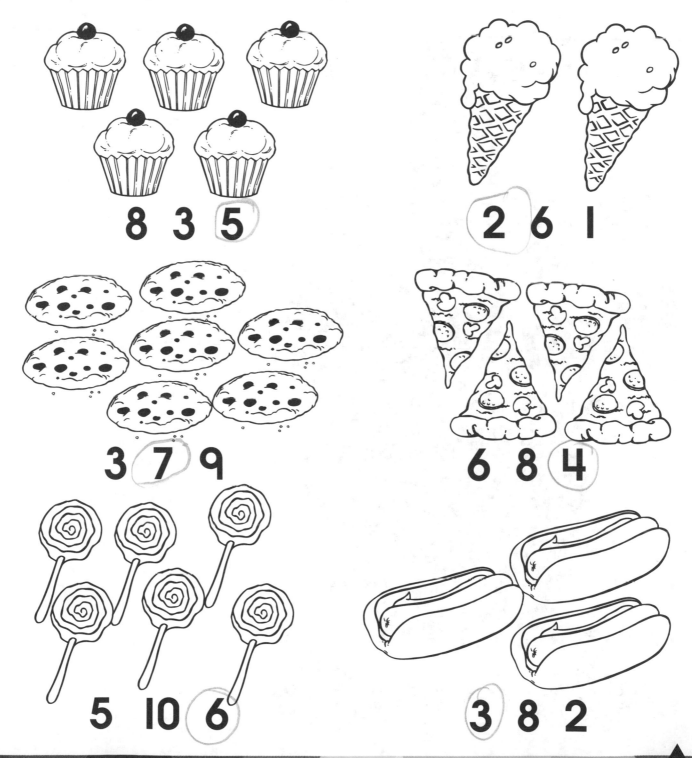

8 3 5

2 6 1

3 7 9

6 8 4

5 10 6

3 8 2

NAME _____

Clown Capers

Directions: Count the number of each thing in the picture. Write the number on the line.

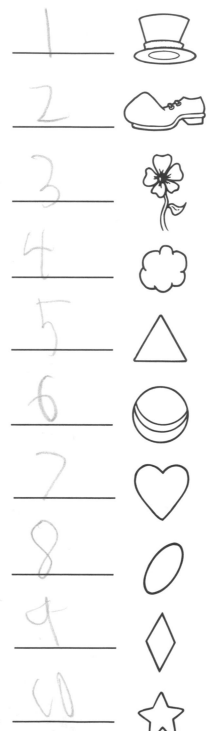

1

2

3

4

5

6

7

8

9

10

Number Words

Directions: Number the buildings from one to six.

Directions: Draw a line from the word to the number.

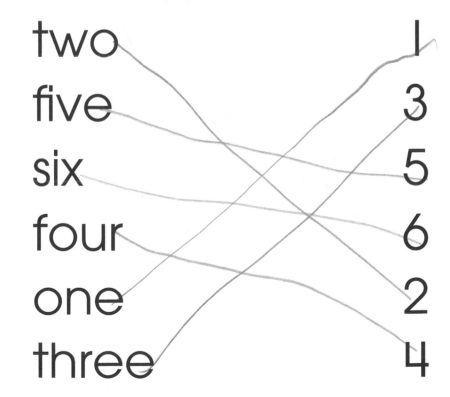

two   1

five   3

six   5

four   6

one   2

three   4

NAME _____

Number Words

Directions: Number the buildings from five to ten.

Directions: Draw a line from the word to the number.

nine   8

seven   10

five   7

eight   5

six   9

ten   6

Number Words

Directions: Write each number beside the correct picture. Then, write it again.

one	two	three	four	five	six	seven	eight	nine	ten

Example:

six   six

three   three

two   two

nine   nine

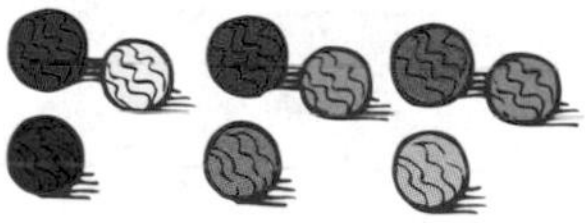

four   four

seven   seven

five   five

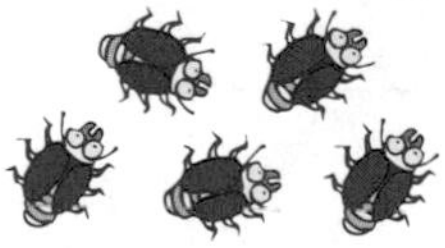

one   one

eight   eight

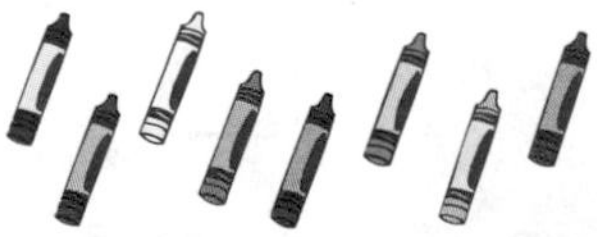

NAME _____

Sequencing Numbers

Sequencing is putting numbers in the correct order.

Directions: Write the missing numbers.

Example: 4, __**5**__, 6

3, __4__, 5   7, __8__, 9   8, __9__, 10

6, __7__, 8   __2__, 3, 4   __4__, 5, 6

5, 6, __7__   __5__, 6, 7   __2__, 3, 4

__8__, 9, 10   __6__, 7, 8   2, __3__, 4

2, 3, __4__   1, 2, __3__   7, 8, __9__

2, __3__, 4   __6__, 7, 8   4, __5__, 6

6, 7, __8__   2, 3, __4__   1, __2__, 3

7, 8, __9__   __2__, 3, 4   __8__, 9, 10

Counting

Directions: Write the numbers that are:

next in order	one less	one greater
22, 23, _24_, _25_	_15_, 16	6, _7_
674, _675_, _676_	_246_, 247	125, _126_
227, _228_, _229_	_549_, 550	499, _500_
199, _200_, _201_	_332_, 333	750, _751_
329, _340_, _341_	_861_, 862	933, _934_

Directions: Write the missing numbers.

NAME _____

Note the Count

Directions: Count the number of notes on each page of music. Write the number on the line below it. In each box, circle the greater number of notes.

_8_   _6_

_4_   _7_

_10_   _9_

_8_   _9_

Directions: Color the note in each box that is greater.

49   25

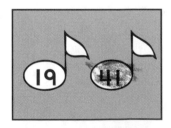

19   41

32   54

38   29

35   46

37   43

Two for the Pool

Directions: Count by **2**s. Write the numbers to **30** in the water drops. Begin at the top of the slide and go down.

NAME _____

Counting by Fives

Directions: Count by **5**s to draw the path to the playground.

I'm Counting on You

Directions: Count by **2**s. Trace and write the numbers below.

| 2 | 4 | 6 | 8 | 10 | 12 | 14 | 16 | 18 | 20 |

Directions: Count by **5**s. Trace and write the numbers below.

| 5 | 10 | 15 | 20 | 25 | 30 | 35 | 40 | 45 | 50 |

Directions: Count by **2**s.
Connect the dots.
Color the picture.

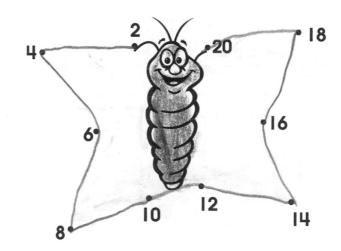

Directions: Count by **5**s.
Connect the dots.
Color the picture.

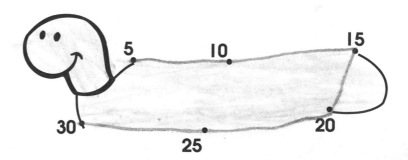

NAME _____

Desert Trek

Directions: Count by **10**s. Color each canteen with a **10** to lead the camel to the watering hole.

Critter Count

Directions: Count by **2**s, **5**s, and **10**s to find the critter count.

Each worm = 2. Count by **2**s to find the total.

= _10_

= _10_

Each turtle = 5. Count by **5**s to find the total.

= _20_

= _20_

Each ladybug = 10. Count by **10**s to find the total.

= _50_

= _60_

NAME _____

Fishing for Answers

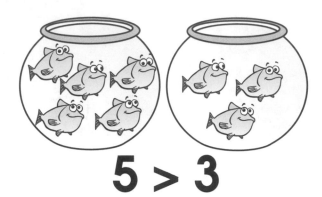

5 > 3

5 is greater than 3

3 < 5

3 is less than 5

Directions: Write the missing numbers in the number line.

1	2	3	4	5	6	7	8	9	10

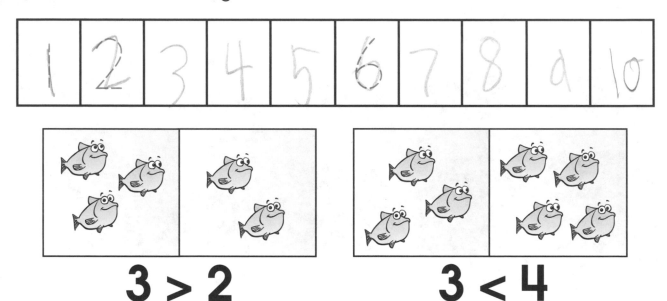

3 > 2   3 < 4

Directions: Write **>** or **<**. Use the number line to help you.

5 ⊙ 2   1 ⊙ 7   1 ⊙ 9   8 ⊙ 5

3 ⊙ 4   9 ⊙ 3   8 ⊙ 7   2 ⊙ 4

6 ⊙ 5   5 ⊙ 3   5 ⊙ 7   3 ⊙ 5

7 ⊙ 3   7 ⊙ 6   2 ⊙ 8   4 ⊙ 2

"Mouth" Math

Directions: Write **<** or **>** in each circle. Make sure the mouth is open toward the greater number!

36 (<) 49   35 (<) 53

20 (>) 18   74 (>) 21

53 (<) 76   68 (<) 80

29 (>) 26   45 (>) 19

90 (>) 89   70 (>) 67

NAME _____

Who Has the Most?

Directions: Circle the correct answer.

1. Traci has 3 🐞 s.

Bob has 4 🐞 s.

Bill has 5 🐞 s.

Who has the most 🐞 s?

Traci   Bob   (Bill)

2. Pam has 7 🐶 s.

Joe has 5 🐶 s.

Jane has 6 🐶 s.

Who has the most 🐶 s?

(Pam)   Joe   Jane

3. Jennifer has 23 🐂 s.

Sandy has 19 🐂 s.

Jack has 25 🐂 s.

Who has the most 🐂 s?

Jennifer   Sandy   (Jack)

4. Ali has 19 🐛 s.

Burt has 18 🐛 s.

Brent has 17 🐛 s.

Who has the most 🐛 s?

(Ali)   Burt   Brent

5. The boys have 14 🐱 s.

The girls have 16 🐱 s.

The teachers have 17 🐱 s.

Who has the most 🐱 s?

boys   girls   (teachers)

6. Rose has 12 🐰 s.

Betsy has 11 🐰 s.

Leslie has 13 🐰 s.

Who has the most 🐰 s?

Rose   Betsy   (Leslie)

NAME _____

Who Has the Fewest?

Directions: Circle the correct answer.

1. Pat had 4 ⚽s.

Charles had 3 ⚽s.

Andrea had 5 ⚽s.

Who had the fewest number

of ⚽s?

Pat   (Charles)   Andrea

2. Jeff has 5 🏀s.

John has 4 🏀s.

Bill has 6 🏀s.

Who has the fewest number

of 🏀s?

Jeff   (John)   Bill

3. Jane has 7 🎾s.

Susan has 9 🎾s.

Fred has 8 🎾s.

Who has the fewest number

of 🎾s?

(Jane)   Susan   Fred

4. Charles bought 12 s.

Rose bought 6 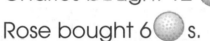s.

Dawn bought 24 s.

Who bought the fewest

number of ⚪s?

Charles   (Rose)   Dawn

5. John had 9 🏈s.

Jack had 8 🏈s.

Mark had 7 🏈s.

Who had the fewest

number of 🏈s?

John   Jack   (Mark)

6. Edith bought 12 🎾s.

Michelle bought 16 🎾s.

Marty bought 13 🎾s.

Who bought the fewest

number of 🎾s?

(Edith)   Michelle   Marty

NAME _____

Have a Ball!

Directions: Color the second ball **brown.**

Color the sixth ball yellow.

Color the fourth ball **orange.**

Color the first ball **black.**

Color the fifth ball green.

Color the seventh ball **purple.**

Orderly Ordinals

Directions: Write each word on the correct line to put the words in order.

second	fifth	seventh	first	tenth
third	eighth	sixth	fourth	ninth

1. _first_

2. _second_

3. _third_

4. _fourth_

5. _fifth_

6. _sixth_

7. _seventh_

8. _eighth_

9. _ninth_

10. _tenth_

Directions: Which picture is circled in each row? Underline the word that tells the correct number.

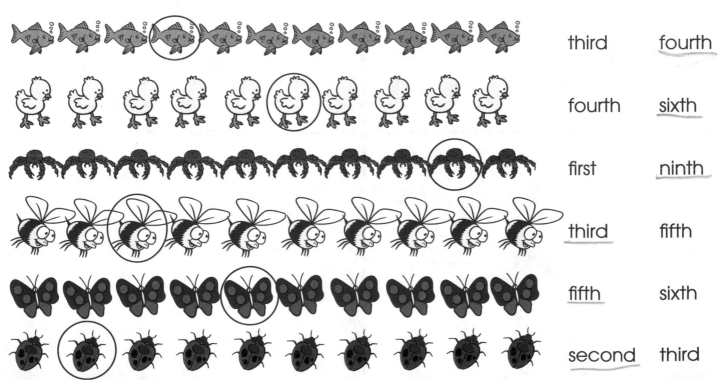

third	fourth
fourth	sixth
first	ninth
third	fifth
fifth	sixth
second	third

NAME _____

How Many Robots in All?

Directions: Look at the pictures. Complete the addition sentences.

Example:
How many s are there in all?

$2 + 4 = \underline{6}$

How many s are there in all?

$3 + 5 = \underline{8}$

How many s are there in all?

$4 + 3 = \underline{7}$

How many s are there in all?

$4 + 1 = \underline{5}$

 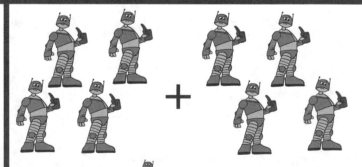

How many s are there in all?

$2 + 5 = \underline{7}$

How many s are there in all?

$4 + 4 = \underline{8}$

How Many Rabbits?

Directions: Look at the pictures. Complete the addition sentences.

Example:
How many s are there in all?

$$1 + 1 = \underline{2}$$

How many 🐰s are there in all?

$$3 + 6 = \underline{9}$$

How many 🐰s are there in all?

$$6 + 1 = \underline{7}$$

How many 🐰s are there in all?

$$3 + 4 = \underline{7}$$

How many 🐰s are there in all?

$$4 + 5 = \underline{9}$$

How many 🐰s are there in all?

$$2 + 3 = \underline{5}$$

NAME _____

The Missing Chickens

Directions: Draw the missing pictures. Complete the addition sentences.

Example:

___1___ + 2 = 3

___3___ + 3 = 6

5 + ___2___ = 7

___2___ + 3 = 5

___4___ + 4 = 8

7 + ___1___ = 8

How Many in All?

Directions: Count the number in each group and write the number on the line. Then, add the groups together and write the sum.

 _____8_____ strawberries

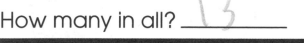 _____5_____ strawberries

How many in all? _____13_____

 _____5_____ cookies

 _____6_____ cookies

How many in all? _____11_____

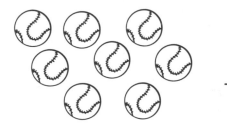 _____7_____ shoes

 _____6_____ shoes

How many in all? _____13_____

 _____3_____ balloons

 _____9_____ balloons

How many in all? _____12_____

_____8_____ balls

_____3_____ balls

How many in all? _____11_____

 _____7_____ flowers

 _____7_____ flowers

How many in all? _____14_____

NAME _____

Counting Up

Directions: Count up to get the sum. Write the missing addend in each blank.

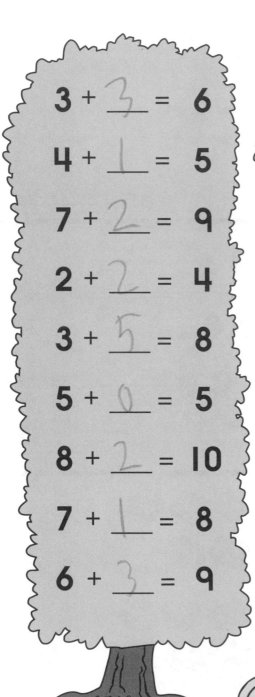

$3 + \underline{3} = 6$

$4 + \underline{1} = 5$

$7 + \underline{2} = 9$

$2 + \underline{2} = 4$

$3 + \underline{5} = 8$

$5 + \underline{0} = 5$

$8 + \underline{2} = 10$

$7 + \underline{1} = 8$

$6 + \underline{3} = 9$

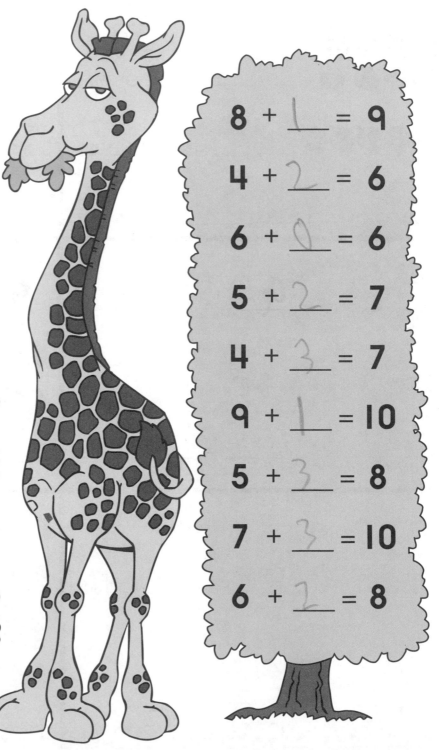

$8 + \underline{1} = 9$

$4 + \underline{2} = 6$

$6 + \underline{0} = 6$

$5 + \underline{2} = 7$

$4 + \underline{3} = 7$

$9 + \underline{1} = 10$

$5 + \underline{3} = 8$

$7 + \underline{3} = 10$

$6 + \underline{2} = 8$

It's All the Same

Directions: Count the objects and fill in the blanks. Then, switch the addends and write another addition sentence.

Example:

 +

If __3__ + __8__ = __11__ , so does __8__ + __3__ .

If __8__ + __9__ = __17__ , so does __9__ + __8__ .

If __7__ + __8__ = __15__ , so does __8__ + __7__ .

If __4__ + __6__ = __10__ , so does __6__ + __4__ .

If __6__ + __7__ = __13__ , so does __7__ + __6__ .

NAME _____

Target Practice

Directions: Add the numbers from the inside out. The first one has been done for you.

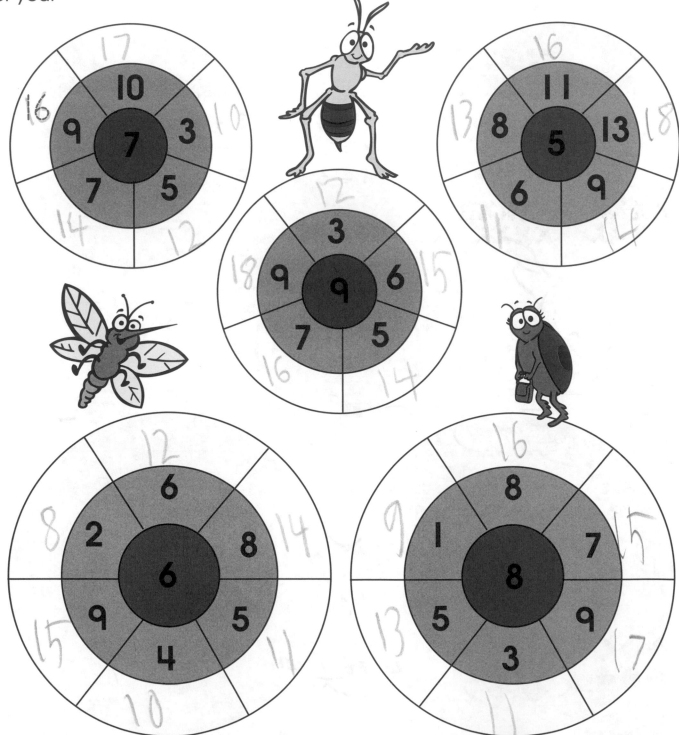

Ride the Rapids

Directions: Write each problem on the life jacket with the correct answer.

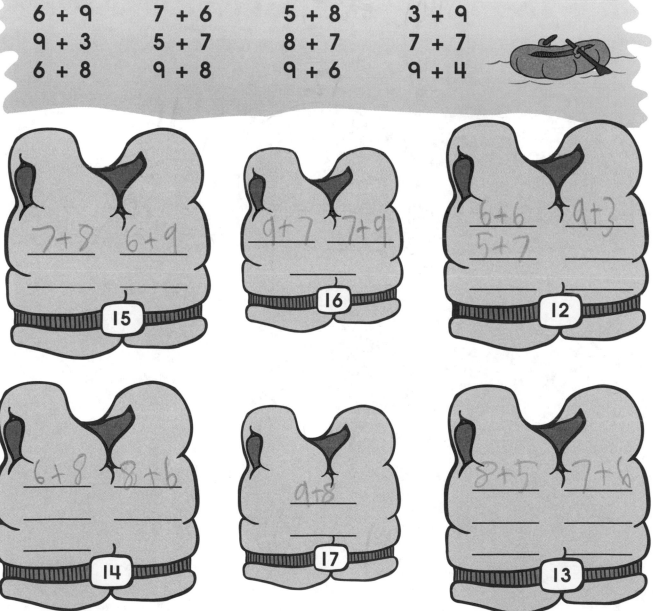

8 + 5   8 + 6   7 + 5   8 + 4   4 + 9
6 + 6   9 + 7   9 + 5   6 + 7   5 + 9
7 + 8   7 + 9   8 + 9   8 + 8
6 + 9   7 + 6   5 + 8   3 + 9
9 + 3   5 + 7   8 + 7   7 + 7
6 + 8   9 + 8   9 + 6   9 + 4

Life jacket 15: 7 + 8   6 + 9

Life jacket 16: 9 + 7   7 + 9

Life jacket 12: 6 + 6   9 + 3   5 + 7

Life jacket 14: 6 + 8   8 + 6

Life jacket 17: 9 + 8

Life jacket 13: 8 + 5   7 + 6

NAME _____

Lots of Number Partners

Directions: Connect as many pairs as you can to make each sum.

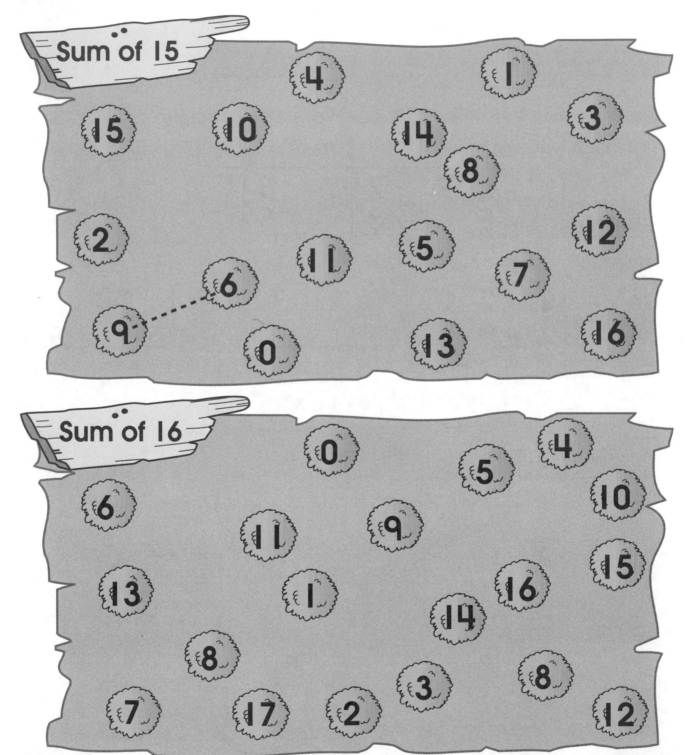

Solve the Riddle

Directions: Add to find the sums. Connect the dots in order. Use the sums and letters from the boxes to answer the riddle.

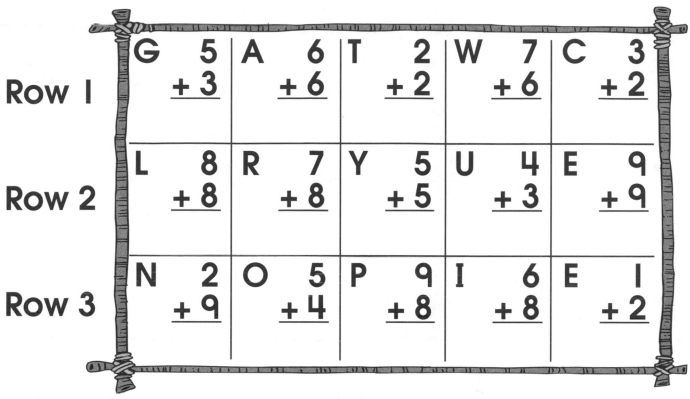

Row 1	G 5 + 3	A 6 + 6	T 2 + 2	W 7 + 6	C 3 + 2
Row 2	L 8 + 8	R 7 + 8	Y 5 + 5	U 4 + 3	E 9 + 9
Row 3	N 2 + 9	O 5 + 4	P 9 + 8	I 6 + 8	E 1 + 2

RIDDLE: What will you get when you cross an eel and a goat?

___ ___ ___ ___ ___ ___ ___
10 9 7   13 14 16 16

___ ___ ___ ___ ___
 8 18 4   12 11

___ ___ ___ ___ ___ ___ ___ ___
 3 16 18 5 4 15 14 5

___ ___ ___
 5 12 11

___ ___ ___ ___ ___ ___
 9 17 18 11 18 15

NAME _____

Coloring by Number

Directions: Find each sum.
If the sum is **13**, color the space **brown.**
If the sum is **14**, color the space yellow.
If the sum is **16**, color the space **red.**
If the sum is **17**, color the space **blue.**

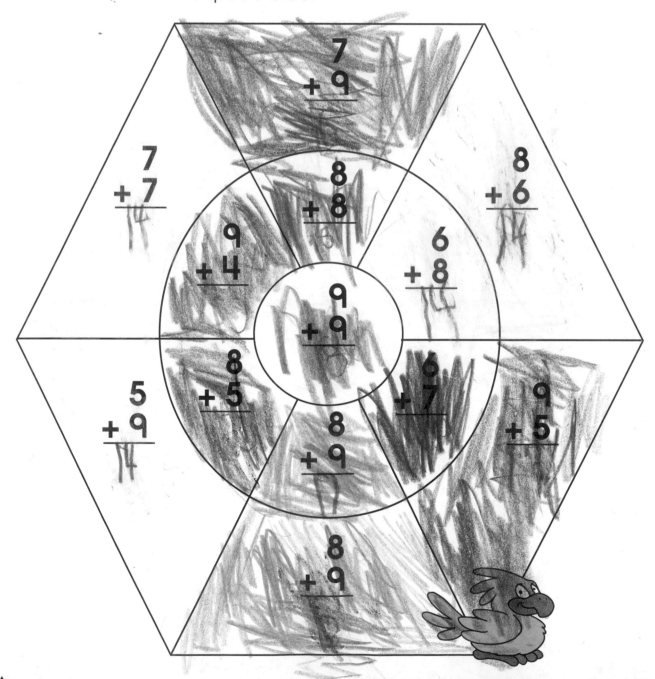

NAME _____

Counting Up the Coins

Directions: Solve the problem on each bag. Write the answer on the coin below it. Color the odd sums yellow.

$9 + 2$

$6 + 7$

$4 + 7$

$8 + 8$

$6 + 9$

$7 + 5$

$5 + 8$

$9 + 9$

$7 + 4$

$8 + 3$

$8 + 9$

$6 + 5$

$8 + 7$

$7 + 9$

$6 + 6$

NAME

Problem Solving

Directions: Solve each problem.

Example:

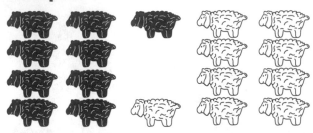

$$9$$
$$+ 9$$

____ black sheep

____ white sheep

____ sheep in all

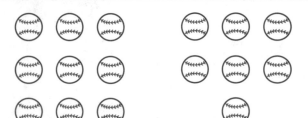

____ softballs

____ baseballs

____ balls in all

____ glasses of juice

____ empty glasses

____ glasses in all

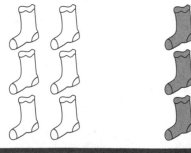

____ white socks

____ gray socks

____ socks in all

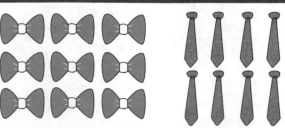

____ bow ties

____ regular ties

____ ties in all

NAME _____

Hop Along Numbers

Directions: Use the number line to count back.

Example: 8, __7__, __6__

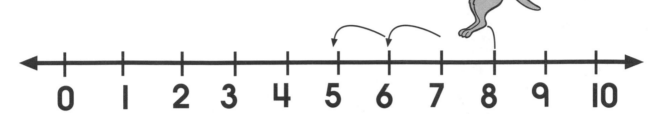

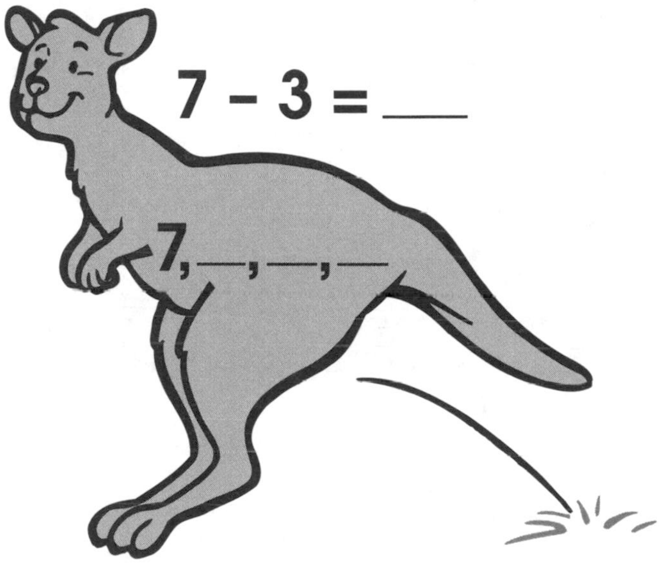

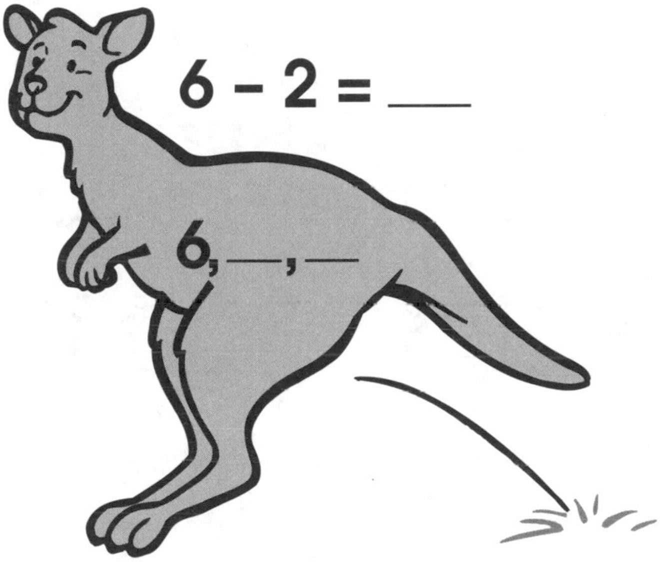

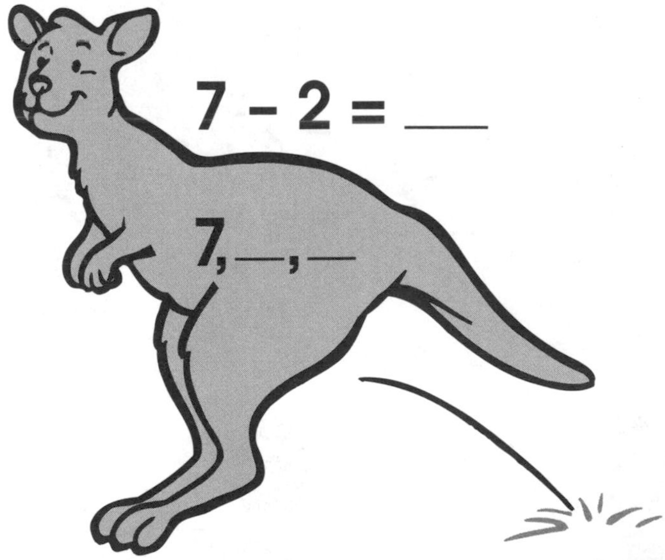

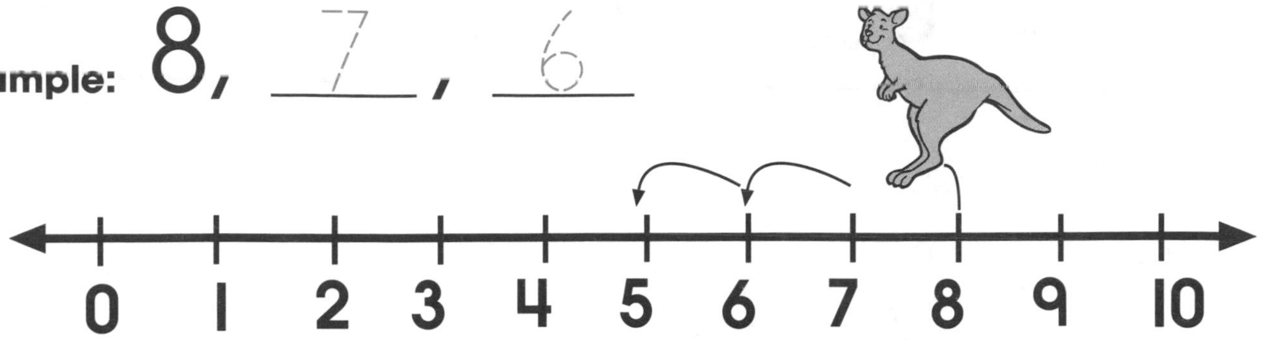

7 – 3 = ___

7,___,___,___

6 – 2 = ___

6,___,___

8 – 1 = ___

8,___

7 – 2 = ___

7,___,___

NAME _____

Leaves Leaving the Limb

Directions: Subtract to find the difference. Use the code to color the leaves.

Code: **0 = green**   **1 = red**   **2 = yellow**   **3 = brown**

$$\begin{array}{r} 1 \\ -0 \\ \hline \end{array}$$

$$\begin{array}{r} 5 \\ -2 \\ \hline \end{array}$$

$$\begin{array}{r} 3 \\ -3 \\ \hline \end{array}$$

$$\begin{array}{r} 2 \\ -1 \\ \hline \end{array}$$

$$\begin{array}{r} 3 \\ -1 \\ \hline \end{array}$$

$$\begin{array}{r} 2 \\ -2 \\ \hline \end{array}$$

$$\begin{array}{r} 4 \\ -2 \\ \hline \end{array}$$

$$\begin{array}{r} 5 \\ -3 \\ \hline \end{array}$$

$$\begin{array}{r} 3 \\ -0 \\ \hline \end{array}$$

$$\begin{array}{r} 5 \\ -4 \\ \hline \end{array}$$

$$\begin{array}{r} 1 \\ -1 \\ \hline \end{array}$$

$$\begin{array}{r} 2 \\ -1 \\ \hline \end{array}$$

How many of each color?

 _____    _____   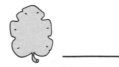 _____    _____

NAME _____

Secrets of Subtraction

Directions: Solve the subtraction problems. Use the code to find the secret message.

Code:

7	5	2	6	4	3
K	T	Y	E	W	A

PLEASE, DON'T EVER

8 -3	10 - 7	9 -2	10 - 4		9 -6	6 -2	7 -4	8 -6
___	___	___	___		___	___	___	___

MY MATH

NAME _____

Differences in Boxes

Directions: Color the two numbers in each box that show the given difference.

Difference of 1

6	4		3	1		4	0
3	8		5	6		1	7

Difference of 1

3	7		2	3		6	3
1	8		5	7		9	7

Difference of 2

3	0		3	8		7	1
7	1		6	9		4	6

Difference of 2

3	4		7	4		10	8
8	2		10	5		5	4

Difference of 0

2	1		7	3		5	6
4	2		8	3		5	4

Looping Differences

Directions: Circle the two numbers next to each other that make the given difference. Find as many as you can in each row.

Difference of 1

2	3	0	(8	7)	2	9	10	6	5	1	4	4	3

Difference of 1

8	4	5	3	7	1	2	4	9	8	0	1	7	6

Difference of 2

5	4	2	3	1	0	3	5	8	9	3	6	8	5

Difference of 2

7	5	10	8	1	4	6	3	2	6	7	9	2	0

Difference of 3

1	6	3	2	8	4	7	6	10	0	3	9	5	2

NAME _____

Hidden Differences of 2

Directions: Circle the pairs that have a difference of **2**.

Hidden Differences of 3

Directions: Circle the pairs that have a difference of **3**.

NAME _____

Hidden Differences

Directions: Find the shape with the correct difference. Copy the numbers that make that difference.

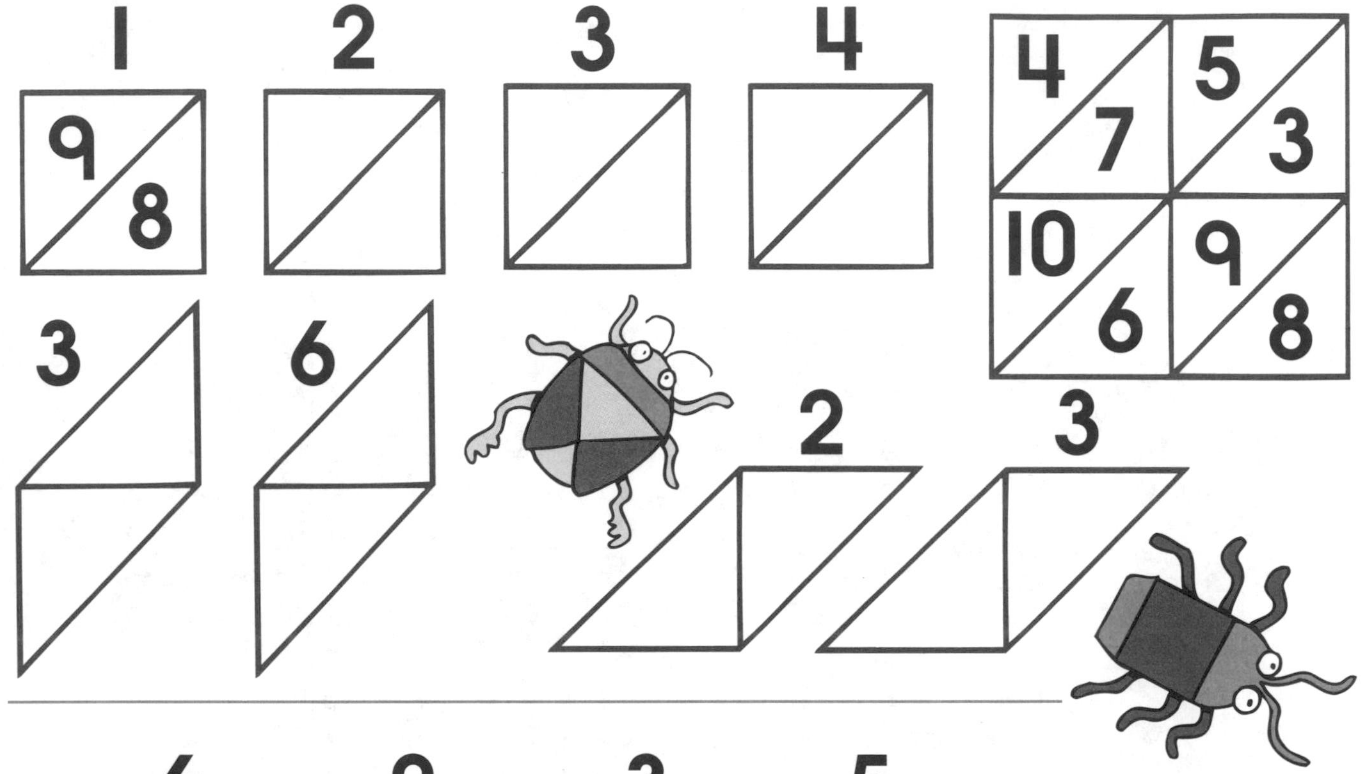

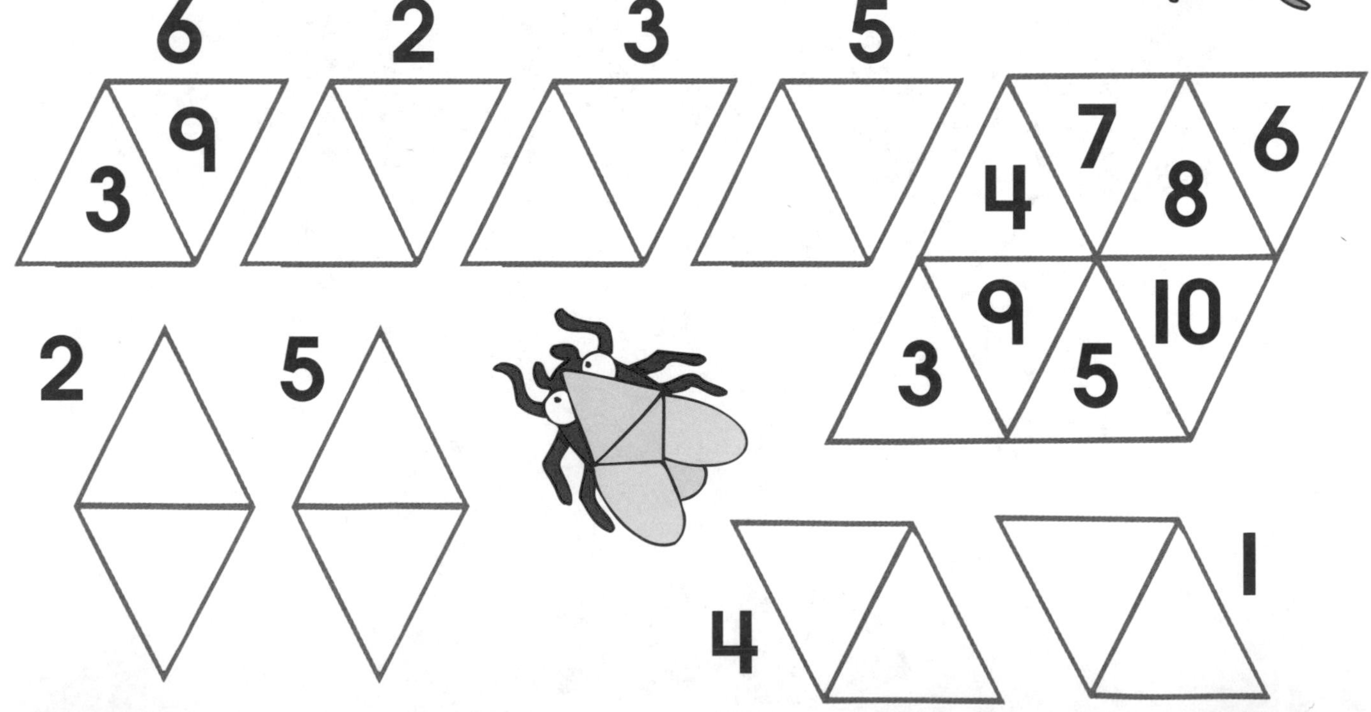

1   2   3   4

9
8

4   5
7   3
10   9
6   8

3   6   2   3

6   2   3   5

9
3

7   6
4   8
9   10
3   5

2   5   4   1

NAME _____

Gone Fishing

Directions: Complete the subtraction sentences to make each problem correct.

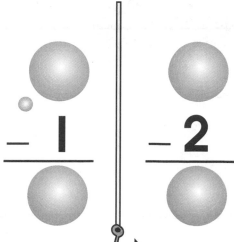

$$-\ \underline{1}$$

$$-\ \underline{2}$$

$$-\ \underline{3}$$

$$-\ \underline{4}$$

$$-\ \underline{5}$$

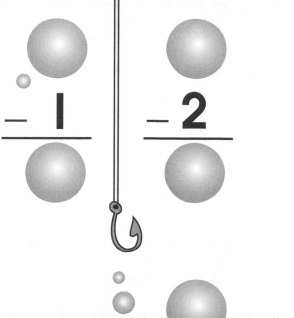

$$-\ \underline{}\ 2$$

$$-\ \underline{}\ 4$$

$$-\ \underline{}\ 0$$

$$-\ \underline{}\ 3$$

$$5 \quad -\ \underline{}$$

$$6 \quad -\ \underline{}$$

$$7 \quad -\ \underline{}$$

$$8 \quad -\ \underline{}$$

$$9 \quad -\ \underline{}$$

NAME _____

Subtraction Facts Through 12

Directions: Subtract.

11 − 9		11 − 2	11 − 8 11 − 3
11 − 6		11 − 5	11 − 7 11 − 4
12 − 8		12 − 4	12 − 7  12 − 5
12 − 9		12 − 3	12 − 6 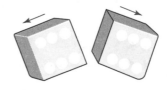

Directions: Subtract.

11	11	12	11	12	12
− 3	− 6	− 3	− 8	− 7	− 9

11	12	12	12	11	12
− 7	− 4	− 5	− 6	− 2	− 8

Subtraction Facts Through 14

Directions: Subtract.
Examples:

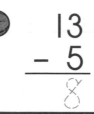

$$13 - 5 = 8$$

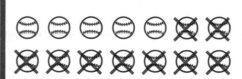

$$14 - 9 = 5$$

$$14 - 8$$

$$13 - 4$$

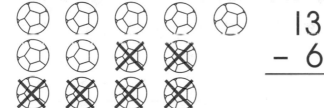

$$13 - 6$$

$$14 - 5$$

Directions: Subtract.

12 − 7	10 − 2	13 − 4	14 − 9	11 − 8	14 − 5
14 − 6	12 − 8	13 − 5	10 − 6	13 − 6	13 − 7
11 − 6	13 − 9	14 − 8	12 − 3	14 − 7	13 − 8

NAME _____

Subtraction Facts Through 18

Directions: Subtract.
Example:

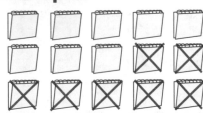

$$\begin{array}{r} 15 \\ -\ 7 \\ \hline 8 \end{array}$$

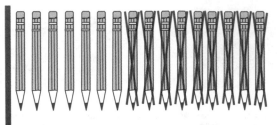

$$\begin{array}{r} 16 \\ -\ 9 \\ \hline \end{array}$$

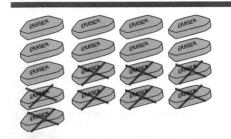

$$\begin{array}{r} 17 \\ -\ 8 \\ \hline \end{array}$$

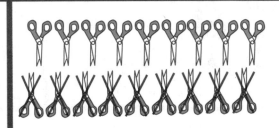

$$\begin{array}{r} 18 \\ -\ 9 \\ \hline \end{array}$$

Directions: Subtract.

18 − 9	13 − 5	16 − 8	17 − 9	14 − 6	13 − 9
17 − 8	15 − 9	14 − 5	13 − 6	16 − 7	12 − 4
14 − 7	15 − 8	16 − 9	12 − 7	15 − 7	13 − 4
15 − 6	14 − 8	12 − 3	13 − 9	14 − 9	11 − 3

NAME _____

"Grrreat" Picture

Directions: Subtract. Write the answer in the space. Then, color the spaces according to the answers.

I = white	2 = purple	3 = black	4 = green	5 = yellow
6 = blue	7 = pink	8 = gray	9 = orange	10 = red

NAME _____

Crayon Count

Directions: Count the crayons. Write the number on the blank. Circle the problems that equal the answer.

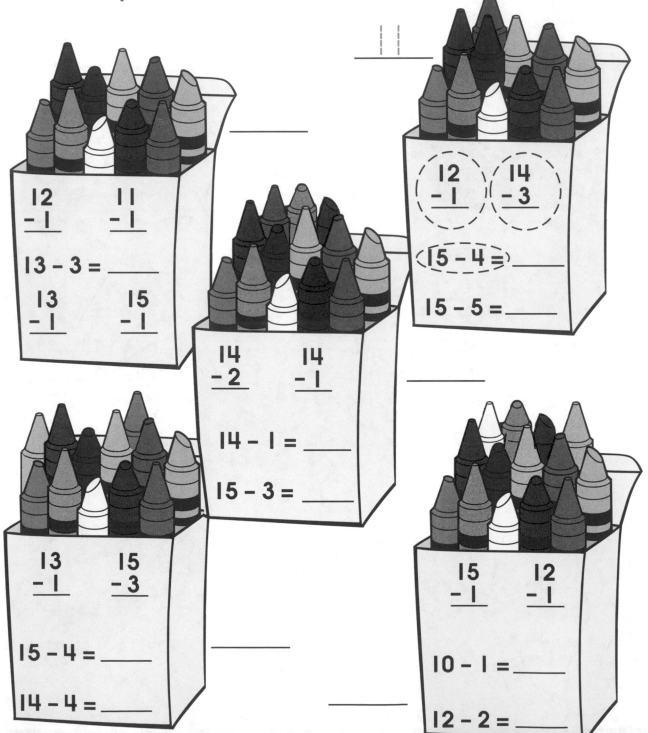

_11_

_____

$$\begin{array}{r} 12 \\ -1 \\ \hline \end{array}$$ $$\begin{array}{r} 11 \\ -1 \\ \hline \end{array}$$

$13 - 3 =$ _____

$$\begin{array}{r} 13 \\ -1 \\ \hline \end{array}$$ $$\begin{array}{r} 15 \\ -1 \\ \hline \end{array}$$

$$\begin{array}{r} 12 \\ -1 \\ \hline \end{array}$$ $$\begin{array}{r} 14 \\ -3 \\ \hline \end{array}$$

$15 - 4 =$ _____

$15 - 5 =$ _____

$$\begin{array}{r} 14 \\ -2 \\ \hline \end{array}$$ $$\begin{array}{r} 14 \\ -1 \\ \hline \end{array}$$

$14 - 1 =$ _____

$15 - 3 =$ _____

$$\begin{array}{r} 13 \\ -1 \\ \hline \end{array}$$ $$\begin{array}{r} 15 \\ -3 \\ \hline \end{array}$$

$15 - 4 =$ _____

$14 - 4 =$ _____

$$\begin{array}{r} 15 \\ -1 \\ \hline \end{array}$$ $$\begin{array}{r} 12 \\ -1 \\ \hline \end{array}$$

$10 - 1 =$ _____

$12 - 2 =$ _____

Facts Through 5

Directions: Add or subtract.

Examples:

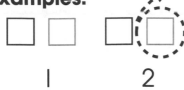

$$\begin{array}{r} 1 \\ +1 \\ \hline 2 \end{array}$$
$$\begin{array}{r} 2 \\ -1 \\ \hline 1 \end{array}$$
$$\begin{array}{r} 2 \\ +1 \\ \hline \end{array}$$
$$\begin{array}{r} 1 \\ +2 \\ \hline \end{array}$$
$$\begin{array}{r} 3 \\ -1 \\ \hline \end{array}$$
$$\begin{array}{r} 3 \\ -2 \\ \hline \end{array}$$

$$\begin{array}{r} 3 \\ +1 \\ \hline \end{array} \qquad \begin{array}{r} 1 \\ +3 \\ \hline \end{array}$$

$$\begin{array}{r} 2 \\ +2 \\ \hline \end{array}$$

$$\begin{array}{r} 4 \\ +0 \\ \hline \end{array} \qquad \begin{array}{r} 0 \\ +4 \\ \hline \end{array}$$

$$\begin{array}{r} 4 \\ -1 \\ \hline \end{array} \qquad \begin{array}{r} 4 \\ -3 \\ \hline \end{array}$$

$$\begin{array}{r} 4 \\ -2 \\ \hline \end{array}$$

$$\begin{array}{r} 4 \\ -0 \\ \hline \end{array} \qquad \begin{array}{r} 4 \\ -4 \\ \hline \end{array}$$

$$\begin{array}{r} 3 \\ +2 \\ \hline \end{array} \qquad \begin{array}{r} 2 \\ +3 \\ \hline \end{array}$$

$$\begin{array}{r} 4 \\ +1 \\ \hline \end{array} \qquad \begin{array}{r} 1 \\ +4 \\ \hline \end{array}$$

$$\begin{array}{r} 5 \\ +0 \\ \hline \end{array} \qquad \begin{array}{r} 0 \\ +5 \\ \hline \end{array}$$

$$\begin{array}{r} 5 \\ -2 \\ \hline \end{array} \qquad \begin{array}{r} 5 \\ -3 \\ \hline \end{array}$$

$$\begin{array}{r} 5 \\ -1 \\ \hline \end{array} \qquad \begin{array}{r} 5 \\ -4 \\ \hline \end{array}$$

$$\begin{array}{r} 5 \\ -0 \\ \hline \end{array} \qquad \begin{array}{r} 5 \\ -5 \\ \hline \end{array}$$

NAME _____

Facts for 6 and 7

Directions: Add or subtract.

Examples:

$$\begin{array}{r} 5 \\ +1 \\ \hline 6 \end{array}$$
$$\begin{array}{r} 1 \\ +5 \\ \hline \end{array}$$
$$\begin{array}{r} 6 \\ -1 \\ \hline 5 \end{array}$$
$$\begin{array}{r} 6 \\ -5 \\ \hline \end{array}$$

$$\begin{array}{r} 3 \\ +3 \\ \hline \end{array}$$
$$\begin{array}{r} 6 \\ -3 \\ \hline \end{array}$$
$$\begin{array}{r} 4 \\ +2 \\ \hline \end{array}$$
$$\begin{array}{r} 2 \\ +4 \\ \hline \end{array}$$
$$\begin{array}{r} 6 \\ -2 \\ \hline \end{array}$$
$$\begin{array}{r} 6 \\ -4 \\ \hline \end{array}$$

$$\begin{array}{r} 4 \\ +3 \\ \hline \end{array}$$
$$\begin{array}{r} 3 \\ +4 \\ \hline \end{array}$$
$$\begin{array}{r} 5 \\ +2 \\ \hline \end{array}$$
$$\begin{array}{r} 2 \\ +5 \\ \hline \end{array}$$
$$\begin{array}{r} 6 \\ +1 \\ \hline \end{array}$$
$$\begin{array}{r} 1 \\ +6 \\ \hline \end{array}$$

$$\begin{array}{r} 7 \\ -3 \\ \hline \end{array}$$
$$\begin{array}{r} 7 \\ -4 \\ \hline \end{array}$$
$$\begin{array}{r} 7 \\ -2 \\ \hline \end{array}$$
$$\begin{array}{r} 7 \\ -5 \\ \hline \end{array}$$
$$\begin{array}{r} 7 \\ -1 \\ \hline \end{array}$$
$$\begin{array}{r} 7 \\ -6 \\ \hline \end{array}$$

$$\begin{array}{r} 3 \\ +3 \\ \hline \end{array}$$
$$\begin{array}{r} 5 \\ +2 \\ \hline \end{array}$$
$$\begin{array}{r} 6 \\ +0 \\ \hline \end{array}$$
$$\begin{array}{r} 7 \\ -7 \\ \hline \end{array}$$
$$\begin{array}{r} 7 \\ -4 \\ \hline \end{array}$$
$$\begin{array}{r} 6 \\ -2 \\ \hline \end{array}$$

Facts for 8

Directions: Add or subtract.

Examples:

$$\begin{array}{r} 5 \\ + 3 \\ \hline 8 \end{array} \qquad \begin{array}{r} 3 \\ + 5 \\ \hline \end{array} \qquad \begin{array}{r} 8 \\ - 3 \\ \hline 5 \end{array} \qquad \begin{array}{r} 8 \\ - 5 \\ \hline \end{array}$$

$$\begin{array}{r} 4 \\ + 4 \\ \hline \end{array} \qquad \begin{array}{r} 6 \\ + 2 \\ \hline \end{array} \qquad \begin{array}{r} 2 \\ + 6 \\ \hline \end{array} \qquad \begin{array}{r} 7 \\ + 1 \\ \hline \end{array} \qquad \begin{array}{r} 1 \\ + 7 \\ \hline \end{array}$$

$$\begin{array}{r} 8 \\ - 4 \\ \hline \end{array} \qquad \begin{array}{r} 8 \\ - 2 \\ \hline \end{array} \qquad \begin{array}{r} 8 \\ - 6 \\ \hline \end{array} \qquad \begin{array}{r} 8 \\ - 1 \\ \hline \end{array} \qquad \begin{array}{r} 8 \\ - 7 \\ \hline \end{array}$$

$$\begin{array}{r} 2 \\ + 6 \\ \hline \end{array} \qquad \begin{array}{r} 4 \\ + 3 \\ \hline \end{array} \qquad \begin{array}{r} 5 \\ + 1 \\ \hline \end{array} \qquad \begin{array}{r} 3 \\ + 5 \\ \hline \end{array} \qquad \begin{array}{r} 7 \\ + 1 \\ \hline \end{array} \qquad \begin{array}{r} 0 \\ + 8 \\ \hline \end{array}$$

$$\begin{array}{r} 8 \\ - 1 \\ \hline \end{array} \qquad \begin{array}{r} 7 \\ - 6 \\ \hline \end{array} \qquad \begin{array}{r} 8 \\ - 5 \\ \hline \end{array} \qquad \begin{array}{r} 6 \\ - 3 \\ \hline \end{array} \qquad \begin{array}{r} 8 \\ - 0 \\ \hline \end{array} \qquad \begin{array}{r} 8 \\ - 2 \\ \hline \end{array}$$

NAME _____

Facts for 9

Directions: Add or subtract.

Examples:

$$\begin{array}{r} 5 \\ +4 \\ \hline 9 \end{array}$$
$$\begin{array}{r} 4 \\ +5 \\ \hline \end{array}$$
$$\begin{array}{r} 9 \\ -4 \\ \hline 5 \end{array}$$
$$\begin{array}{r} 9 \\ -5 \\ \hline \end{array}$$

$$\begin{array}{r} 6 \\ +3 \\ \hline \end{array}$$
$$\begin{array}{r} 3 \\ +6 \\ \hline \end{array}$$
$$\begin{array}{r} 7 \\ +2 \\ \hline \end{array}$$
$$\begin{array}{r} 2 \\ +7 \\ \hline \end{array}$$
$$\begin{array}{r} 8 \\ +1 \\ \hline \end{array}$$
$$\begin{array}{r} 1 \\ +8 \\ \hline \end{array}$$

$$\begin{array}{r} 9 \\ -3 \\ \hline \end{array}$$
$$\begin{array}{r} 9 \\ -6 \\ \hline \end{array}$$
$$\begin{array}{r} 9 \\ -2 \\ \hline \end{array}$$
$$\begin{array}{r} 9 \\ -7 \\ \hline \end{array}$$
$$\begin{array}{r} 9 \\ -1 \\ \hline \end{array}$$
$$\begin{array}{r} 9 \\ -8 \\ \hline \end{array}$$

$$\begin{array}{r} 5 \\ +4 \\ \hline \end{array}$$
$$\begin{array}{r} 2 \\ +7 \\ \hline \end{array}$$
$$\begin{array}{r} 6 \\ +1 \\ \hline \end{array}$$
$$\begin{array}{r} 9 \\ +0 \\ \hline \end{array}$$
$$\begin{array}{r} 1 \\ +8 \\ \hline \end{array}$$
$$\begin{array}{r} 4 \\ +4 \\ \hline \end{array}$$

$$\begin{array}{r} 9 \\ -5 \\ \hline \end{array}$$
$$\begin{array}{r} 7 \\ -3 \\ \hline \end{array}$$
$$\begin{array}{r} 9 \\ -8 \\ \hline \end{array}$$
$$\begin{array}{r} 9 \\ -3 \\ \hline \end{array}$$
$$\begin{array}{r} 9 \\ -9 \\ \hline \end{array}$$
$$\begin{array}{r} 9 \\ -0 \\ \hline \end{array}$$

Facts for 10

Directions: Add or subtract.

Examples:

$$\begin{array}{r} 5 \\ +5 \\ \hline 10 \end{array}$$

$$\begin{array}{r} 10 \\ -5 \\ \hline 5 \end{array}$$

$$\begin{array}{r} 6 \\ +4 \\ \hline \end{array} \qquad \begin{array}{r} 4 \\ +6 \\ \hline \end{array}$$

$$\begin{array}{r} 10 \\ -4 \\ \hline \end{array} \qquad \begin{array}{r} 10 \\ -6 \\ \hline \end{array}$$

$$\begin{array}{r} 7 \\ +3 \\ \hline \end{array} \qquad \begin{array}{r} 3 \\ +7 \\ \hline \end{array}$$

$$\begin{array}{r} 10 \\ -3 \\ \hline \end{array} \qquad \begin{array}{r} 10 \\ -7 \\ \hline \end{array}$$

$$\begin{array}{r} 8 \\ +2 \\ \hline \end{array} \qquad \begin{array}{r} 2 \\ +8 \\ \hline \end{array}$$

$$\begin{array}{r} 10 \\ -2 \\ \hline \end{array} \qquad \begin{array}{r} 10 \\ -8 \\ \hline \end{array}$$

$$\begin{array}{r} 9 \\ +1 \\ \hline \end{array} \qquad \begin{array}{r} 1 \\ +9 \\ \hline \end{array}$$

$$\begin{array}{r} 10 \\ -1 \\ \hline \end{array} \qquad \begin{array}{r} 10 \\ -9 \\ \hline \end{array}$$

$$\begin{array}{r} 4 \\ +6 \\ \hline \end{array} \quad \begin{array}{r} 5 \\ +5 \\ \hline \end{array} \quad \begin{array}{r} 9 \\ +1 \\ \hline \end{array} \quad \begin{array}{r} 10 \\ -8 \\ \hline \end{array} \quad \begin{array}{r} 10 \\ -3 \\ \hline \end{array} \quad \begin{array}{r} 10 \\ -0 \\ \hline \end{array}$$

NAME _____

Facts Through 10

Directions: Add.

Example:

$$\begin{array}{r} 5 \\ +4 \\ \hline 9 \end{array} \qquad \begin{array}{r} 4 \\ +3 \\ \hline \end{array} \qquad \begin{array}{r} 1 \\ +2 \\ \hline \end{array} \qquad \begin{array}{r} 5 \\ +3 \\ \hline \end{array} \qquad \begin{array}{r} 4 \\ +6 \\ \hline \end{array} \qquad \begin{array}{r} 4 \\ +4 \\ \hline \end{array}$$

$$\begin{array}{r} 0 \\ +6 \\ \hline \end{array} \qquad \begin{array}{r} 4 \\ +1 \\ \hline \end{array} \qquad \begin{array}{r} 8 \\ +1 \\ \hline \end{array} \qquad \begin{array}{r} 9 \\ +1 \\ \hline \end{array} \qquad \begin{array}{r} 8 \\ +2 \\ \hline \end{array} \qquad \begin{array}{r} 2 \\ +2 \\ \hline \end{array}$$

$$\begin{array}{r} 2 \\ +7 \\ \hline \end{array} \qquad \begin{array}{r} 5 \\ +2 \\ \hline \end{array} \qquad \begin{array}{r} 1 \\ +6 \\ \hline \end{array} \qquad \begin{array}{r} 5 \\ +5 \\ \hline \end{array} \qquad \begin{array}{r} 4 \\ +5 \\ \hline \end{array} \qquad \begin{array}{r} 6 \\ +2 \\ \hline \end{array}$$

Directions: Subtract.

Example:

$$\begin{array}{r} 10 \\ -6 \\ \hline 4 \end{array} \qquad \begin{array}{r} 8 \\ -2 \\ \hline \end{array} \qquad \begin{array}{r} 5 \\ -3 \\ \hline \end{array} \qquad \begin{array}{r} 7 \\ -6 \\ \hline \end{array} \qquad \begin{array}{r} 4 \\ -3 \\ \hline \end{array} \qquad \begin{array}{r} 10 \\ -5 \\ \hline \end{array}$$

$$\begin{array}{r} 9 \\ -3 \\ \hline \end{array} \qquad \begin{array}{r} 10 \\ -2 \\ \hline \end{array} \qquad \begin{array}{r} 7 \\ -2 \\ \hline \end{array} \qquad \begin{array}{r} 8 \\ -6 \\ \hline \end{array} \qquad \begin{array}{r} 10 \\ -9 \\ \hline \end{array} \qquad \begin{array}{r} 8 \\ -8 \\ \hline \end{array}$$

$$\begin{array}{r} 10 \\ -4 \\ \hline \end{array} \qquad \begin{array}{r} 9 \\ -6 \\ \hline \end{array} \qquad \begin{array}{r} 9 \\ -8 \\ \hline \end{array} \qquad \begin{array}{r} 8 \\ -1 \\ \hline \end{array} \qquad \begin{array}{r} 10 \\ -7 \\ \hline \end{array} \qquad \begin{array}{r} 7 \\ -4 \\ \hline \end{array}$$

Problem Solving

Directions: Solve each problem.

Example:

$$\begin{array}{r} 4 \\ + \ 3 \\ \hline 7 \end{array}$$

leaves on the ground
leaves falling
leaves in all

$$-\ \rule{1cm}{0.4pt}$$

balls in all
balls falling
balls not falling

$$+\ \rule{1cm}{0.4pt}$$

fish by a rock
more fish coming
fish in all

$$-\ \rule{1cm}{0.4pt}$$

pencils in all
pencils taken
pencils not taken

$$+\ \rule{1cm}{0.4pt}$$

puppies on a rug
more puppies coming
puppies in all

NAME _____

Checkup

Directions: Add.

2 +4	7 +3	4 +5	6 +2	2 +3	0 +4
4 +3	1 +5	2 +8	3 +3	6 +4	2 +1
3 +1	7 +0	8 +1	5 +2	3 +6	5 +5

Directions: Subtract.

3 -3	5 -2	10 -6	9 -2	7 -3	10 -5
9 -1	8 -7	1 -0	6 -4	8 -5	10 -8
9 -6	4 -3	6 -3	7 -5	10 -9	8 -4

Addition and Subtraction Fun

Directions: Solve the number problem under each picture. Write **+** or **−** to show if you should add or subtract.

Example:
How many  s in all?

4 + 5 = _____

How many s in all?

7 ___ 5 = _____

Example:
How many s are left?

12 − 3 = _____

How many s are left?

15 ___ 8 = _____

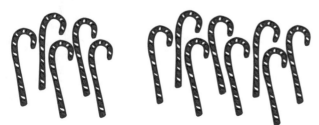

How many s in all?

5 ___ 8 = _____

How many s are left?

11 ___ 4 = _____

NAME _____

Hopping Around

Directions: Write the number sentence on the line below each number line.

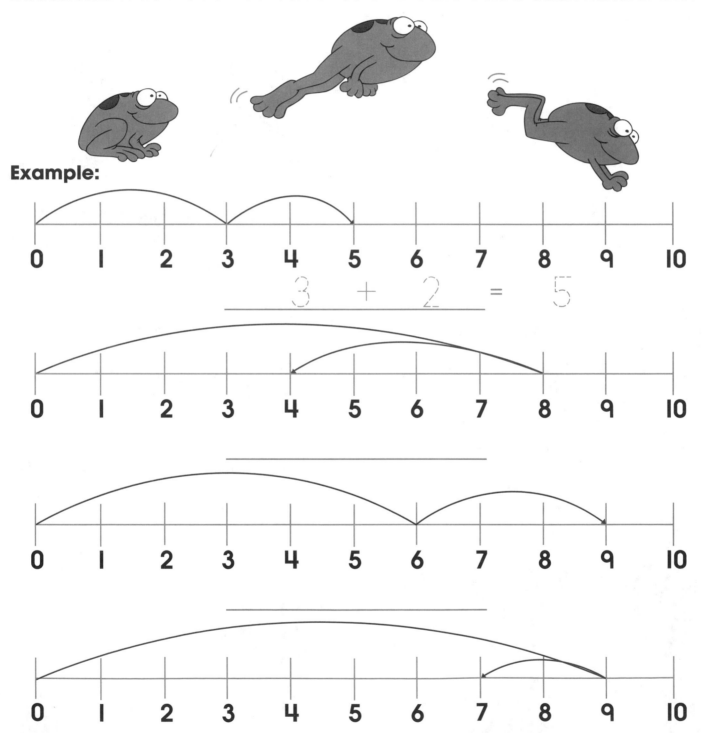

Example:

```
0  1  2  3  4  5  6  7  8  9  10
        3  +  2  =  5
```

Total Math & Reading Grade 2

Big Families

Directions: Complete each number sentence in each number family.

2
$0 +$ ___ $= 2$
$2 + 0 =$ ___
___ $- 0 = 2$
$2 - 2 =$ ___

3
$1 + 2 =$ ___
___ $+ 1 = 3$
$3 -$ ___ $= 2$
$3 - 2 =$ ___

4
___ $+ 3 = 4$
$3 + 1 =$ ___
$4 -$ ___ $= 3$
___ $- 3 = 1$

5
$2 + 3 =$ ___
___ $+ 2 = 5$
$5 -$ ___ $= 3$
___ $- 3 = 2$

6
$2 +$ ___ $= 6$
$4 + 2 =$ ___
$6 -$ ___ $= 4$
$6 - 4 =$ ___

6
$5 +$ ___ $= 6$
___ $+$ ___ $=$ ___
$6 -$ ___ $= 5$
___ $- 5 =$ ___

NAME _____

Sums and Differences

Directions: Color two numbers in each box to show the given sum or difference.

Sum of 8

3	7
1	4

3	6
7	2

6	5
4	4

3	8
1	5

Difference of 1

6	3
1	5

5	9
10	7

8	5
3	2

5	2
4	0

Sum of 9

0	5
6	4

4	3
6	2

8	3
1	2

5	5
7	2

Difference of 2

6	9
1	4

4	10
7	5

5	8
1	10

0	2
7	3

Bigger Families

Directions: Complete each number sentence in the families.

7

___ + 4 = 7

4 + 3 = ___

___ − 3 = 4

7 − ___ = 3

8

3 + ___ = 8

5 + 3 = ___

8 − ___ = 5

___ − 5 = 3

9

4 + 5 = ___

___ + 4 = 9

9 − ___ = 5

___ − 5 = 4

10

___ + 6 = 10

6 + 4 = ___

10 − 4 = ___

___ − ___ = ___

11

3 + ___ = ___

___ + ___ = ___

11 − ___ = 8

___ − ___ = ___

12

5 + ___ = 12

___ + ___ = ___

12 − ___ = ___

___ − ___ = ___

Place Value: Ones, Tens

The **place value** of a digit or numeral is shown by where it is in the number. For example, in the number **23**, **2** has the place value of **tens**, and **3** is **ones**.

Directions: Add the tens and ones and write your answers in the blanks.

Example:

+   = 33

3 tens   +   3 ones = 33

	tens ones			tens ones
7 tens + 5 ones	= _____	4 tens + 0 ones	= _____
2 tens + 3 ones	= _____	8 tens + 1 one	= _____
5 tens + 2 ones	= _____	1 ten + 1 one	= _____
5 tens + 4 ones	= _____	6 tens + 3 ones	= _____
9 tens + 5 ones	= _____		

Directions: Draw a line to the correct number.

6 tens + 7 ones	73
4 tens + 2 ones	67
8 tens + 0 ones	51
7 tens + 3 ones	80
5 tens + 1 one	42

NAME _____

Finding Place Value: Ones and Tens

Directions: Write the numbers for the tens and ones. Then, add.

Example:

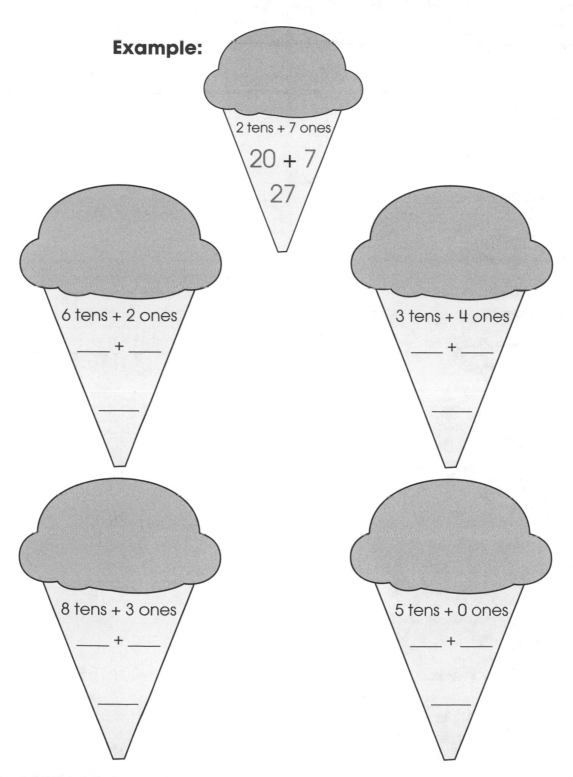

2 tens + 7 ones

20 + 7

27

6 tens + 2 ones

___ + ___

___

3 tens + 4 ones

___ + ___

___

8 tens + 3 ones

___ + ___

___

5 tens + 0 ones

___ + ___

___

NAME _____

Numbers 11 through 18

1¢   **10¢**   **10¢**

Directions: Complete the problems.

Example:

   ____ten____one = ____

   ____ten____ones = ____

  ____ten____ones = ____

  ____ten____ones = ____

  ____ten____ones = ____

  ____ten____ones = ____

  ____ten____ones = ____

  ____ten____ones = ____

NAME _____

Numbers 19 through 39

Directions: Complete the problems.

Example:

__2__ tens = __20__

____ tens ____ ones = ____

____ tens ____ ones = ____

____ tens ____ ones = ____

____ tens = ____

____ tens ____ ones = ____

____ tens ____ ones = ____

____ tens ____ ones = ____

NAME _____

Numbers 40 through 99

Directions: Complete the problems.

Example:

____4____ tens = ____40____

_____tens_____ ones =_____

_____tens_____ ones =_____

_____tens_____ ones =_____

_____ tens = _____

_____tens_____ ones =_____

_____tens_____ ones =_____

_____tens_____ ones =_____

NAME _____

Numbers through 99

Directions: Complete the problems.

Example:

4 tens   6 ones = __46__   2 tens   1 one = _____

1 ten   2 ones = _____   5 tens   7 ones = _____

3 tens   7 ones = _____   1 ten   9 ones = _____

2 tens   4 ones = _____   8 tens   8 ones = _____

9 tens   = _____   6 tens   7 ones = _____

6 tens   = _____   7 tens   2 ones = _____

5 tens   3 ones = _____   9 tens   5 ones = _____

7 tens   8 ones = _____   4 tens   1 one = _____

1 ten   1 one = _____   3 tens   4 ones = _____

8 tens   4 ones = _____   6 tens   6 ones = _____

3 tens   5 ones = _____   8 tens   9 ones = _____

4 tens   9 ones = _____   2 tens   = _____

9 tens   6 ones = _____   5 tens   = _____

NAME _____

Hundreds, Tens, and Ones

Directions: Count the groups of crayons. Write the number of hundreds, tens, and ones.

Example:

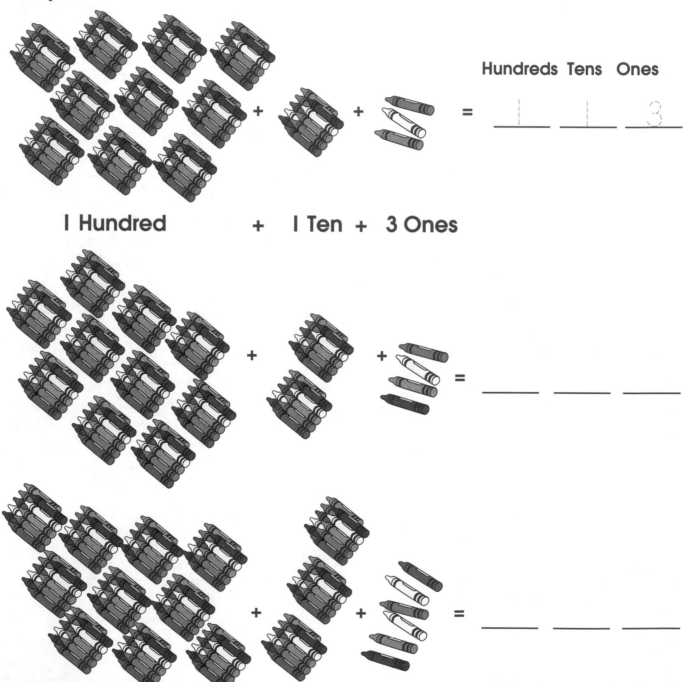

Hundreds Tens Ones

_1_ _1_ _3_

1 Hundred   +   1 Ten + 3 Ones

= ___ ___ ___

= ___ ___ ___

What Big Numbers!

Directions: Write each number.

Example:

Hundreds	Tens	Ones
■	|||	●●

__1__ hundreds
__3__ tens
__2__ ones = __132__

Hundreds	Tens	Ones
■	||||	●●● ●●● ●

___ hundreds
___ tens
___ ones = _____

Hundreds	Tens	Ones
■ ■ ■	|||	●●● ●●● ●●●

___ hundreds
___ tens
___ ones = _____

Hundreds	Tens	Ones
■ ■ ■ ■ ■			●

___ hundreds
___ tens
___ ones = _____

Hundreds	Tens	Ones
■ ■		●●● ●●● ●●●

___ hundreds
___ tens
___ ones = _____

Hundreds	Tens	Ones
■ ■ ■ ■ ■ ■	||||||		●●●

___ hundreds
___ tens
___ ones = _____

Hundreds	Tens	Ones
■ ■ ■	|||||	●●● ●●

___ hundreds
___ tens
___ ones = _____

Hundreds	Tens	Ones
■ ■	|||||| |||	●●● ●●● ●

___ hundreds
___ tens
___ ones = _____

NAME _____

Count 'Em Up!

Directions: Look at the example. Then, write the missing numbers in the blanks.

Example:

2 hundreds + 3 tens + 6 ones =

hundreds	tens	ones
2	3	6

= 236

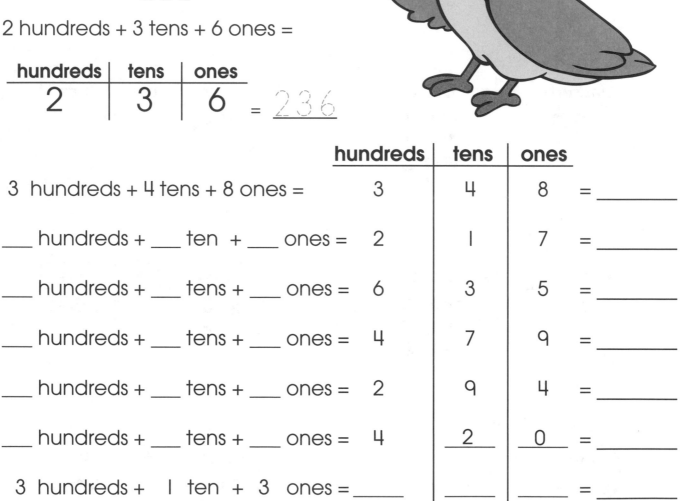

	hundreds	tens	ones	
3 hundreds + 4 tens + 8 ones =	3	4	8	= _____
___ hundreds + ___ ten + ___ ones =	2	1	7	= _____
___ hundreds + ___ tens + ___ ones =	6	3	5	= _____
___ hundreds + ___ tens + ___ ones =	4	7	9	= _____
___ hundreds + ___ tens + ___ ones =	2	9	4	= _____
___ hundreds + ___ tens + ___ ones =	4	2	0	= _____
3 hundreds + 1 ten + 3 ones = _____	____	____	= _____
3 hundreds + ___ tens + 7 ones = _____	5	____	= _____
6 hundreds + 2 tens + ___ ones = _____	____	8	= _____

Up, Up, and Away

Directions: Use the code to color the balloons. If the answer has:

7 hundreds, color it **red.**
6 hundreds, color it **green.**
5 hundreds, color it **orange.**
8 tens, color it **yellow.**
3 tens, color it **brown.**

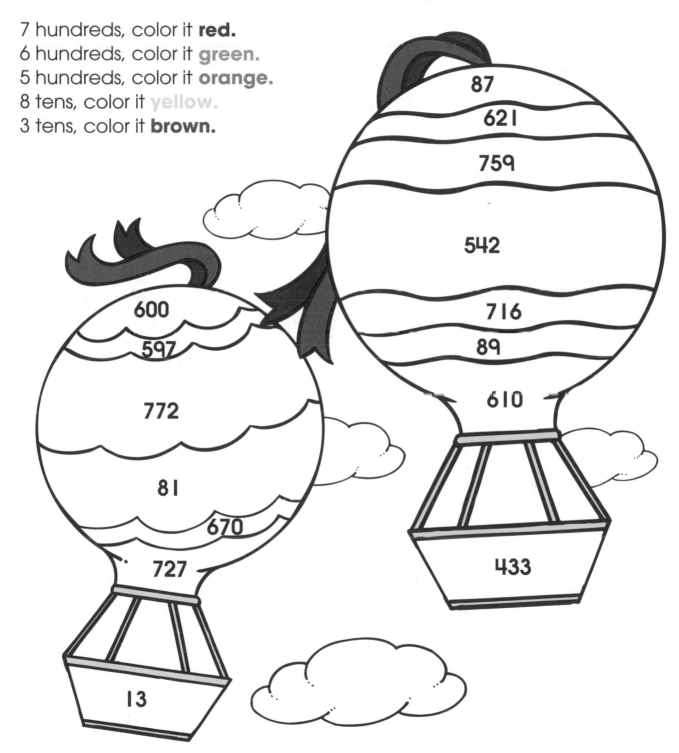

NAME _____

Place Value: Thousands

Directions: Study the example. Write the missing numbers.

Example:

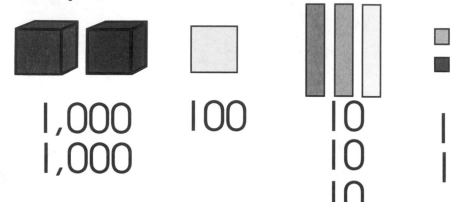

2 thousands + 1 hundred + __3__ tens + 2 ones = __2,132__

5,286 = ____ thousands + ____ hundreds + ____ tens + ____ ones

1,831 = ____ thousand + ____ hundreds + ____ tens + ____ one

8,972 = ____ thousands + ____ hundreds + ____ tens + ____ ones

4,528 = ____ thousands + ____ hundreds + ____ tens + ____ ones

3,177 = ____ thousands + ____ hundred + ____ tens + ____ ones

Directions: Draw a line to the number that has:

8 hundreds	7,103
5 ones	2,862
9 tens	5,996
7 thousands	1,485

Place Value: Thousands

$$6 , 4 \; 3 \; 1$$

thousands | hundreds | tens | ones

Directions: Tell which number is in each place.

 Thousands place:

2,456   4,621   3,456

_____   _____   _____

 Tens place:

4,286   1,234   5,678

_____   _____   _____

 Hundreds place:

6,321   3,210   7,871

_____   _____   _____

 Ones place:

5,432   6,531   9,980

_____   _____   _____

NAME _____

2-Digit Addition

Directions: Study the example. Follow the steps to add.

Example:

$$\begin{array}{r} 33 \\ +41 \\ \hline \end{array}$$

Step 1: Add the ones.

tens	ones
3	3
+4	1
	4

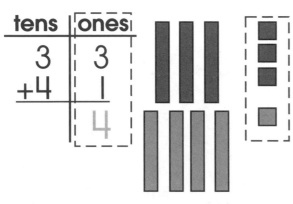

Step 2: Add the tens.

tens	ones
3	3
+4	1
7	4

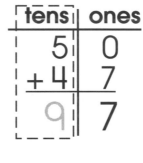

tens	ones
4	2
+2	4
6	6

tens	ones
5	0
+4	7
9	7

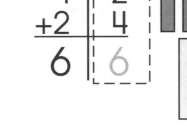

$$\begin{array}{r} 24 \\ +62 \\ \hline \end{array}$$
$$\begin{array}{r} 15 \\ +23 \\ \hline \end{array}$$
$$\begin{array}{r} 38 \\ +61 \\ \hline \end{array}$$
$$\begin{array}{r} 11 \\ +26 \\ \hline \end{array}$$
$$\begin{array}{r} 37 \\ +42 \\ \hline \end{array}$$
$$\begin{array}{r} 72 \\ +11 \\ \hline \end{array}$$
$$\begin{array}{r} 33 \\ +51 \\ \hline \end{array}$$
$$\begin{array}{r} 10 \\ +30 \\ \hline \end{array}$$

$$\begin{array}{r} 25 \\ +42 \\ \hline \end{array}$$
$$\begin{array}{r} 62 \\ +14 \\ \hline \end{array}$$
$$\begin{array}{r} 32 \\ +44 \\ \hline \end{array}$$
$$\begin{array}{r} 25 \\ +13 \\ \hline \end{array}$$
$$\begin{array}{r} 82 \\ + 6 \\ \hline \end{array}$$
$$\begin{array}{r} 91 \\ + 5 \\ \hline \end{array}$$
$$\begin{array}{r} 16 \\ +71 \\ \hline \end{array}$$
$$\begin{array}{r} 55 \\ + 3 \\ \hline \end{array}$$

2-Digit Addition

Directions: Add the total points scored in each game. Remember to add **ones** first and **tens** second.

Example:

Total __**39**__

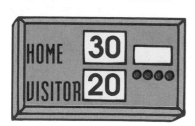

Total _____

Total _____

Total _____

Total _____

Total _____

Total _____

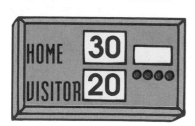

Total _____

Total _____

Total _____

NAME _____

Adding Tens

3 tens	30		6 tens	60
+ 4 tens	+40		+ 2 tens	+20
7 tens	70		8 tens	80

Directions: Add.

2 tens	20		6 tens	60
+ 4 tens	+40		+ 2 tens	+20
tens			tens	

20	10	40	30	50
+20	+50	+20	+40	+30

30	60	20	70	10
+20	+10	+50	+10	+10

10	40	80	60	20
+20	+40	+10	+30	+60

70	40	30	50	30
+20	+10	+10	+40	+30

Problem Solving

Directions: Solve each problem.

Example:

There are 20 men in the plane.

30 women get in the plane.

How many men and women are in the plane?

Jill buys 10 apples.

Carol buys 20 apples.

How many apples in all?

There are 30 ears of corn in one pile.

There are 50 ears of corn in another pile.

How many ears of corn in all?

Henry cut 40 pieces of wood.

Art cut 20 pieces of wood.

How many pieces of wood were cut?

Adolpho had 60 baseball cards.

Maria had 30 baseball cards.

How many baseball cards in all?

NAME _____

Digital Addition

Add the ones.

tens	ones
2	4
+3	2
	6

Then, add the tens.

tens	ones
2	4
+3	2
5	6

Directions: Solve the addition problems below.

tens	ones
1	7
+2	1

tens	ones
3	4
+5	2

tens	ones
	5
+6	2

tens	ones
	6
+5	2

tens	ones
2	0
+4	0

tens	ones
5	1
+	8

tens	ones
7	2
+1	7

tens	ones
4	7
+2	1

tens	ones
2	5
+6	2

tens	ones
4	2
+2	4

tens	ones
8	3
+1	4

tens	ones
3	2
+2	5

Scoreboard Sums

Directions: Add the total points scored in each game. Remember to add the ones first, then the tens.

Example:

HOME   22
VISITOR   17

Total ___39___

HOME   27
VISITOR 40

Total _____

HOME   44
VISITOR 22

Total _____

HOME   24
VISITOR 43

Total _____

HOME   35
VISITOR 23

Total _____

HOME   56
VISITOR 41

Total _____

HOME   73
VISITOR 26

Total _____

HOME   50
VISITOR 40

Total _____

HOME   28
VISITOR 51

Total _____

HOME   34
VISITOR 55

Total _____

NAME _____

Anchors Away

Directions: Solve the addition problems. Use the code to find the answer to this riddle:

What did the pirate have to do before every trip out to sea?

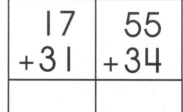

48	36	58	96	69	75	89	29
O	H	G	B	T	E	N	A

Example:

42 +16	34 +41	60 + 9
58		
G		

17 +31	55 +34

26 +43	14 +22	52 +23

83 +13	24 +24	5 +24	52 +17
			!

Two-Digit Subtraction

Directions: Look at the example.
Follow the steps to subtract.

Examples:

$$\begin{array}{r} 28 \\ -14 \\ \hline \end{array} \qquad \begin{array}{r} 24 \\ -12 \\ \hline \end{array}$$

Step 1: Subtract the ones.

tens	ones
2	8
– 1	4
	4

Step 2: Subtract the tens.

tens	ones
2	8
– 1	4
1	4

Step 1: Subtract the ones.

tens	ones
2	4
– 1	2
	2

Step 2: Subtract the tens.

tens	ones
2	4
– 1	2
1	2

$$\begin{array}{r} 24 \\ -12 \\ \hline \end{array} \quad \begin{array}{r} 61 \\ -30 \\ \hline \end{array} \quad \begin{array}{r} 77 \\ -44 \\ \hline \end{array} \quad \begin{array}{r} 85 \\ -24 \\ \hline \end{array} \quad \begin{array}{r} 57 \\ -23 \\ \hline \end{array} \quad \begin{array}{r} 87 \\ -33 \\ \hline \end{array}$$

NAME _____

Subtracting Tens

Examples:

6 tens	60		8 tens	80
− 3 tens	− 30		− 2 tens	− 20
3 tens	30		6 tens	60

Directions: Subtract.

7 tens	70		4 tens	40
− 5 tens	− 50		− 2 tens	− 20
tens			tens	

50	60	20	80	40
− 30	− 20	− 10	− 40	− 40

90	80	70	30	50
− 50	− 20	− 30	− 20	− 40

60	40	80	90	70
− 30	− 10	− 30	− 20	− 50

80	90	70	60	50
− 70	− 80	− 40	− 40	− 20

Problem Solving

Directions: Solve each problem.

Example:

Mr. Cobb counts 70 s.

He sells 30 s.

How many s are left?

$$\begin{array}{r} 70 \\ -\ 30 \\ \hline 40 \end{array}$$

Keith has 20 s.

Leon has 10 s.

How many more s does Keith have than Leon?

Tina plants 60 s.

Melody plants 30 s.

How many more s did Tina plant than Melody?

Link has 80 s.

Jessica has 50 s.

How many more s does Link have than Jessica?

Maranda hits 40 s.

Harold hits 30 s.

How many more s does Maranda hit than Harold?

NAME _____

All Aboard

Directions: Count the tens and ones and write the numbers. Then, subtract to solve the problems.

tens	ones
4 2	2 1

tens	ones

tens	ones

tens	ones

tens	ones

tens	ones

Cookie Mania

There are 46 cookies.
Bill eats 22 cookies.
How many are left?

$$\begin{array}{r} 46 \\ -22 \\ \hline \end{array}$$

1. Subtract the ones.

tens	ones
4	6
-2	2
	4

2. Subtract the tens.

tens	ones
4	6
-2	2
2	4

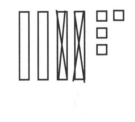

Directions: Subtract the ones first. Then, subtract the tens.

tens	ones
7	8
-2	5

tens	ones
5	9
-3	6

tens	ones
8	3
-6	1

tens	ones
6	7
-4	3

tens	ones
9	7
-1	4

tens	ones
5	4
-3	0

tens	ones
4	2
-3	1

tens	ones
2	8
-1	8

NAME _____

Prehistoric Problems

Directions: Solve the subtraction problems. Use the code to color the picture.

Code:　**25** = blue　**57** = green
　　　　　31 = yellow　**14** = orange
　　　　　21 = brown　**11** = red

$$\begin{array}{r} 52 \\ -\ 21 \\ \hline \end{array}$$

$$\begin{array}{r} 47 \\ -\ 22 \\ \hline \end{array}$$

$$\begin{array}{r} 25 \\ -\ 11 \\ \hline \end{array}$$

$$\begin{array}{r} 62 \\ -\ 31 \\ \hline \end{array}$$

$$\begin{array}{r} 77 \\ -\ 20 \\ \hline \end{array}$$

$$\begin{array}{r} 51 \\ -\ 40 \\ \hline \end{array}$$

$$\begin{array}{r} 69 \\ -\ 12 \\ \hline \end{array}$$

$$\begin{array}{r} 98 \\ -\ 41 \\ \hline \end{array}$$

$$\begin{array}{r} 55 \\ -\ 34 \\ \hline \end{array}$$

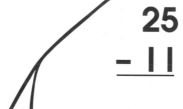

2-Digit Addition: Regrouping

Addition is "putting together" or adding two or more numbers to find the sum. Regrouping is using **ten ones** to form **one ten**, **ten tens** to form **one 100**, **fifteen ones** to form **one ten** and **five ones**, and so on.

Directions: Study the examples. Follow the steps to add.

Example:

$$\begin{array}{r} 14 \\ +\ 8 \\ \hline \end{array}$$

Step 1:
Add the ones.

tens	ones
1	4
+	8
	12

Step 2:
Regroup the tens.

tens	ones
1	4
+	8
	2

Step 3:
Add the tens.

tens	ones
1	4
+	8
2	2

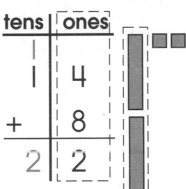

tens	ones
1	6
+3	7
5	3

tens	ones
3	8
+5	3
9	1

tens	ones
2	4
+4	7
7	1

$$\begin{array}{r} 28 \\ +17 \\ \hline \end{array} \qquad \begin{array}{r} 32 \\ +38 \\ \hline \end{array} \qquad \begin{array}{r} 54 \\ +25 \\ \hline \end{array} \qquad \begin{array}{r} 19 \\ +55 \\ \hline \end{array} \qquad \begin{array}{r} 44 \\ +48 \\ \hline \end{array} \qquad \begin{array}{r} 25 \\ +64 \\ \hline \end{array} \qquad \begin{array}{r} 29 \\ +33 \\ \hline \end{array} \qquad \begin{array}{r} 79 \\ +15 \\ \hline \end{array}$$

NAME _____

2-Digit Addition: Regrouping

Directions: Add the total points scored in the game. Remember to add the ones, regroup, and then add the tens.

Example:

Total __**85**__

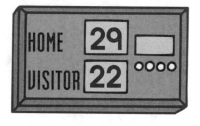

Total _____

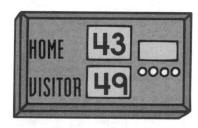

Total _____

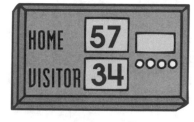

Total _____

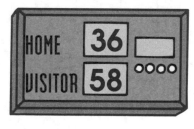

Total _____

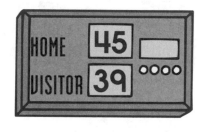

Total _____

Total _____

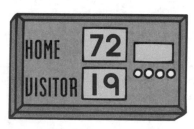

Total _____

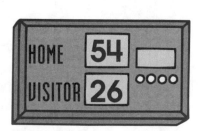

Total _____

2-Digit Addition

Directions: Add the ones.   Rename 11 as 10 + 1.   Add the tens.

```
  3 8              8                        1              1
+ 4 3          + 3                      3 8          3 8
                                      + 4 3        + 4 3
              11 or 10 + 1                   1        8 1
```

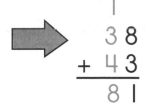

Directions: Add.

Example:

```
  1 7          2 6          4 7          6 8          3 7
+ 3 4        + 4 7        + 3 5        + 2 4        + 2 8
  5 1
```

```
  2 9          5 8          6 9          7 8          1 9
+ 4 8        + 2 7        + 1 7        + 1 3        + 4 4
```

```
  5 5          2 7          3 9          5 7          3 8
+ 2 8        + 3 5        + 5 2        + 2 7        + 3 6
```

```
  4 9          6 5          2 3          6 4          4 6
+ 4 3        + 1 8        + 1 8        + 1 8        + 3 9
```

```
  5 4          3 8          6 6          2 8          1 9
+ 2 7        + 4 4        + 2 6        + 3 4        + 5 6
```

NAME _____

Problem Solving

Directions: Solve each problem.

Example:

16 boys ride their bikes to school.

18 girls ride their bikes to school.

How many bikes are ridden to school?

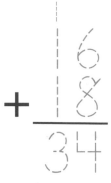

Dad reads 26 pages.

Mike reads 37 pages.

How many pages did Dad and Mike read?

Tiffany counts 46 stars.

Mike counts 39 stars.

How many stars did they count?

Mom has 29 golf balls.

Dad has 43 golf balls.

How many golf balls do they have?

Vicki ran in 26 races.

Kay ran in 14 races.

How many races did they run?

2-Digit Subtraction: Regrouping

Subtraction is taking away or subtracting one number from another to find the difference. Regrouping is using **one ten** to form **ten ones, one 100** to form **ten tens,** and so on.

Directions: Study the examples. Follow the steps to subtract.

Example:
$$37$$
$$-19$$

Step 1:
Regroup.

tens	ones
2	17
~~3~~	~~7~~
-1	9

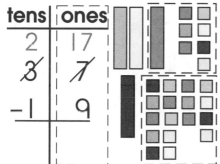

tens	ones
0	12
~~1~~	~~2~~
-	9
	3

Step 2:
Subtract the ones.

tens	ones
2	17
~~3~~	~~7~~
-1	9
	8

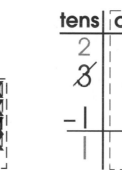

tens	ones
2	14
~~3~~	~~4~~
-1	6
1	8

Step 3:
Subtract the tens.

tens	ones
2	17
~~3~~	~~7~~
-1	9
1	8

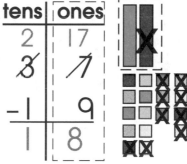

tens	ones
3	15
~~4~~	~~5~~
-2	9
1	6

28	46	12	30	52	47	21	45
- 19	- 18	- 8	- 12	- 25	- 35	- 13	- 25

Subtraction With Regrouping

Directions: Subtract to find the difference. Regroup as needed. Color the spaces with differences of:

10-19 = red **50-59** = brown **30-39** = green
40-49 = yellow **20-29** = blue **60-69** = orange

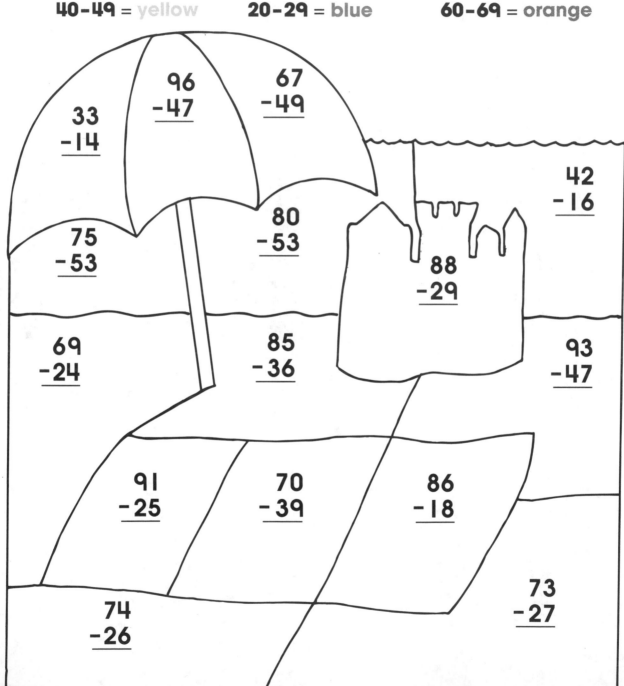

2-Digit Subtraction

Directions: Rename 73 as 6 tens and 13 ones.

6 13
$$\begin{array}{r} 7\!\!\!/3 \\ -\ 4\ 8 \\ \hline \end{array}$$

$$\begin{array}{r} 7\ 3 \\ -\ 4\ 8 \\ \hline \end{array}$$

Subtract the ones.

6 13
$$\begin{array}{r} 7\!\!\!/3 \\ -\ 4\ 8 \\ \hline 5 \end{array}$$

Subtract the tens.

6 13
$$\begin{array}{r} 7\!\!\!/3 \\ -\ 4\ 8 \\ \hline 2\ 5 \end{array}$$

Directions: Subtract.

Example:

5 13
$$\begin{array}{r} 6\!\!\!/3 \\ -\ 4\ 8 \\ \hline 1\ 5 \end{array}$$

$$\begin{array}{r} 8\ 3 \\ -\ 4\ 5 \\ \hline \end{array}$$

$$\begin{array}{r} 7\ 4 \\ -\ 2\ 9 \\ \hline \end{array}$$

$$\begin{array}{r} 9\ 4 \\ -\ 4\ 8 \\ \hline \end{array}$$

$$\begin{array}{r} 6\ 2 \\ -\ 2\ 5 \\ \hline \end{array}$$

$$\begin{array}{r} 4\ 5 \\ -\ 2\ 7 \\ \hline \end{array}$$

$$\begin{array}{r} 3\ 3 \\ -\ 2\ 4 \\ \hline \end{array}$$

$$\begin{array}{r} 2\ 4 \\ -\ \ \ 8 \\ \hline \end{array}$$

$$\begin{array}{r} 8\ 6 \\ -\ 3\ 7 \\ \hline \end{array}$$

$$\begin{array}{r} 7\ 2 \\ -\ 4\ 8 \\ \hline \end{array}$$

$$\begin{array}{r} 3\ 6 \\ -\ 1\ 7 \\ \hline \end{array}$$

$$\begin{array}{r} 2\ 6 \\ -\ 1\ 8 \\ \hline \end{array}$$

$$\begin{array}{r} 4\ 3 \\ -\ 1\ 9 \\ \hline \end{array}$$

$$\begin{array}{r} 6\ 3 \\ -\ 4\ 8 \\ \hline \end{array}$$

$$\begin{array}{r} 9\ 3 \\ -\ 1\ 8 \\ \hline \end{array}$$

$$\begin{array}{r} 8\ 2 \\ -\ 2\ 6 \\ \hline \end{array}$$

$$\begin{array}{r} 7\ 3 \\ -\ 2\ 8 \\ \hline \end{array}$$

$$\begin{array}{r} 9\ 5 \\ -\ 6\ 9 \\ \hline \end{array}$$

$$\begin{array}{r} 5\ 7 \\ -\ 3\ 8 \\ \hline \end{array}$$

$$\begin{array}{r} 4\ 1 \\ -\ 2\ 5 \\ \hline \end{array}$$

$$\begin{array}{r} 5\ 4 \\ -\ 1\ 8 \\ \hline \end{array}$$

$$\begin{array}{r} 6\ 1 \\ -\ 3\ 4 \\ \hline \end{array}$$

$$\begin{array}{r} 9\ 1 \\ -\ 3\ 7 \\ \hline \end{array}$$

$$\begin{array}{r} 8\ 1 \\ -\ 4\ 4 \\ \hline \end{array}$$

$$\begin{array}{r} 3\ 2 \\ -\ 1\ 5 \\ \hline \end{array}$$

Problem Solving

Directions: Solve each problem.

Example:

Dad cooks 23 potatoes.

He uses 19 potatoes in the potato salad.

How many potatoes are left?

Susan draws 32 butterflies.

She colored 15 of them brown.

How many butterflies does she have left to color?

A book has 66 pages.

Pedro reads 39 pages.

How many pages are left to read?

Jerry picks up 34 sea shells.

He puts 15 of them in a box.

How many does he have left?

Beth buys 72 sheets of paper.

She uses 44 sheets for her school work.

How many sheets of paper are left?

Addition and Subtraction Review

Directions: Add.

4	8	9	7	5	6
+ 9	+ 6	+ 8	+ 6	+ 7	+ 5

9	5	7	9	8	7
+ 6	+ 8	+ 4	+ 9	+ 7	+ 9

30	20	45	52	60	83
+ 40	+ 30	+ 23	+ 23	+ 25	+ 15

Directions: Subtract.

16	15	13	12	11	17
− 7	− 9	− 4	− 7	− 9	− 8

18	17	16	15	14	16
− 9	− 9	− 8	− 8	− 7	− 9

40	60	85	73	96	54
− 30	− 10	− 23	− 41	− 43	− 44

NAME _____

Addition and Subtraction Review

Directions: Add.

```
   4        9        5        6        7        9
 + 8      + 2      + 9      + 6      + 5      + 4
```

```
   8        7        3        7        6        6
 + 8      + 6      + 9      + 7      + 9      + 5
```

```
  40       50       75       66       47       34
+ 20     + 30     + 20     + 31     + 51     + 23
```

Directions: Subtract.

```
  17       15       12       13       14       16
 - 9      - 6      - 3      - 7      - 6      - 8
```

```
  15       14       13       15       12       11
 - 7      - 9      - 6      - 7      - 9      - 8
```

```
  30       50       65       87       75       66
- 10     - 30     - 30     - 34     - 23     - 43
```

Review: 2-Digit Addition

Directions: Add.

3 6	1 4	5 7	4 4	3 3
+ 5 5	+ 2 8	+ 3 8	+ 4 8	+ 2 9

2 3	2 7	6 8	2 3	4 2
+ 1 8	+ 2 7	+ 2 5	+ 1 9	+ 1 9

5 6	4 9	3 8	3 6	4 9
+ 2 8	+ 2 7	+ 4 9	+ 1 8	+ 2 4

1 8	5 1	7 4	3 5	5 2
+ 5 4	+ 3 9	+ 1 7	+ 2 8	+ 1 9

4 8	2 5	3 9	2 9	5 4
+ 2 6	+ 2 8	+ 3 3	+ 4 4	+ 2 7

NAME _____

Problem Solving

Directions: Solve each problem.

Example:

Simon sees 36 birds flying.

Julie sees 28 birds flying.

How many birds do they see flying?

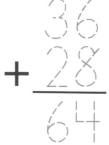

$$+\ \begin{array}{r} 36 \\ 28 \\ \hline 64 \end{array}$$

Brandon ran the race in 35 seconds.

Ryan ran the race in 28 seconds.

How many seconds did they run?

Tom has 63 nickels.

Connie has 29 nickels.

How many nickels do they have?

Pam sees 48 monkeys at the zoo.

Brenda sees 35 different monkeys.

How many monkeys did they see?

There are 29 cows in one pen.

There are 47 cows in the other pen.

How many cows in all?

Shoot for the Stars

Directions: Add the total points scored in the game. Remember to add the ones first and regroup. Then, add the tens.

Example:

HOME 53
VISITOR 27

Total _____80_____

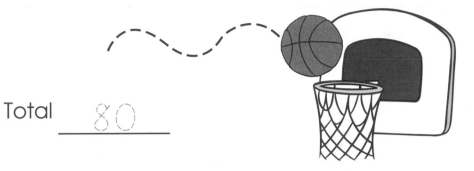

HOME 29
VISITOR 45

HOME 57
VISITOR 39

HOME 63
VISITOR 19

Total _____

Total _____

Total _____

HOME 66
VISITOR 28

HOME 47
VISITOR 49

HOME 36
VISITOR 45

Total _____

Total _____

Total _____

HOME 27
VISITOR 38

HOME 54
VISITOR 39

HOME 37
VISITOR 59

Total _____

Total _____

Total _____

NAME _____

Review: 2-Digit Subtraction

Directions: Subtract.

$$\begin{array}{r} 85 \\ -\ 16 \\ \hline \end{array} \qquad \begin{array}{r} 93 \\ -\ 48 \\ \hline \end{array} \qquad \begin{array}{r} 72 \\ -\ 35 \\ \hline \end{array} \qquad \begin{array}{r} 63 \\ -\ 27 \\ \hline \end{array} \qquad \begin{array}{r} 43 \\ -\ 38 \\ \hline \end{array}$$

$$\begin{array}{r} 56 \\ -\ 29 \\ \hline \end{array} \qquad \begin{array}{r} 75 \\ -\ 49 \\ \hline \end{array} \qquad \begin{array}{r} 84 \\ -\ 38 \\ \hline \end{array} \qquad \begin{array}{r} 91 \\ -\ 65 \\ \hline \end{array} \qquad \begin{array}{r} 37 \\ -\ 18 \\ \hline \end{array}$$

$$\begin{array}{r} 21 \\ -\ 14 \\ \hline \end{array} \qquad \begin{array}{r} 35 \\ -\ 18 \\ \hline \end{array} \qquad \begin{array}{r} 42 \\ -\ 29 \\ \hline \end{array} \qquad \begin{array}{r} 72 \\ -\ 47 \\ \hline \end{array} \qquad \begin{array}{r} 81 \\ -\ 54 \\ \hline \end{array}$$

$$\begin{array}{r} 64 \\ -\ 38 \\ \hline \end{array} \qquad \begin{array}{r} 53 \\ -\ 28 \\ \hline \end{array} \qquad \begin{array}{r} 94 \\ -\ 57 \\ \hline \end{array} \qquad \begin{array}{r} 48 \\ -\ 39 \\ \hline \end{array} \qquad \begin{array}{r} 23 \\ -\ 18 \\ \hline \end{array}$$

$$\begin{array}{r} 74 \\ -\ 58 \\ \hline \end{array} \qquad \begin{array}{r} 83 \\ -\ 36 \\ \hline \end{array} \qquad \begin{array}{r} 62 \\ -\ 26 \\ \hline \end{array} \qquad \begin{array}{r} 54 \\ -\ 28 \\ \hline \end{array} \qquad \begin{array}{r} 32 \\ -\ 17 \\ \hline \end{array}$$

Go "Fore" It!

Directions: Add or subtract using regrouping.

```
tens  ones
  2    15
  3     5
 -2     7
        8
```

$$\begin{array}{r} 56 \\ -\ 27 \\ \hline \end{array}$$

$$\begin{array}{r} 40 \\ -\ 16 \\ \hline \end{array}$$

$$\begin{array}{r} 35 \\ +27 \\ \hline \end{array}$$

$$\begin{array}{r} 44 \\ +28 \\ \hline \end{array}$$

$$\begin{array}{r} 93 \\ -\ 39 \\ \hline \end{array}$$

$$\begin{array}{r} 42 \\ -\ 14 \\ \hline \end{array}$$

$$\begin{array}{r} 97 \\ -\ 48 \\ \hline \end{array}$$

$$\begin{array}{r} 33 \\ +18 \\ \hline \end{array}$$

$$\begin{array}{r} 73 \\ -\ 24 \\ \hline \end{array}$$

$$\begin{array}{r} 56 \\ -\ 17 \\ \hline \end{array}$$

$$\begin{array}{r} 68 \\ -\ 49 \\ \hline \end{array}$$

$$\begin{array}{r} 49 \\ +32 \\ \hline \end{array}$$

$$\begin{array}{r} 77 \\ -\ 68 \\ \hline \end{array}$$

$$\begin{array}{r} 27 \\ +19 \\ \hline \end{array}$$

NAME _____

Adding Hundreds

Examples:

5 hundreds	5 0 0	4 hundreds	4 0 0
+ 3 hundreds	+ 3 0 0	+ 5 hundreds	+ 5 0 0
8 hundreds	8 0 0	9 hundreds	9 0 0

Directions: Add.

3 hundreds	3 0 0	6 hundreds	6 0 0
+ 1 hundreds	+ 1 0 0	+ 2 hundreds	+ 2 0 0
4 hundreds	4 0 0	hundreds	

```
  2 0 0        1 0 0        6 0 0        4 0 0
+ 2 0 0      + 7 0 0      + 3 0 0      + 5 0 0
```

```
  3 0 0        8 0 0        4 0 0        7 0 0
+ 4 0 0      + 1 0 0      + 4 0 0      + 2 0 0
```

```
  5 0 0        1 0 0        5 0 0        3 0 0
+ 1 0 0      + 6 0 0      + 2 0 0      + 2 0 0
```

```
  3 0 0        4 0 0        3 0 0        2 0 0
+ 3 0 0      + 2 0 0      + 5 0 0      + 1 0 0
```

Problem Solving

Directions: Solve each problem.

Example:

Ria packed 300 boxes.

Melvin packed 200 boxes.

How many boxes did Ria and Melvin pack?

$$+\frac{\begin{array}{r}300\\200\end{array}}{500}$$

Santo typed 500 letters.

Hale typed 400 letters.

How many letters did they type?

Paula used 100 paper clips.

Milton used 600 paper clips.

How many paper clips did they use?

The grocery store sold 400 red apples.

The grocery store also sold 100 yellow apples.

How many apples did the grocery store sell in all?

Miles worked 200 days.

Julia worked 500 days.

How many days did they work?

NAME _____

3-Digit Addition

```
  2 4 5          2 4 5          2 4 5
+ 2 5 3        + 2 5 3        + 2 5 3
------         ------         ------
      8          9 8          4 9 8
```

Directions: Add.

Example:

```
  7 4 5              6 2 3
+   2 3            + 1 5 6
------            ------
  7 6 8
```

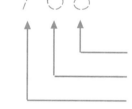 Add the ones.
Add the tens.
Add the hundreds.

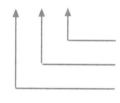 Add the ones.
Add the tens.
Add the hundreds.

```
  4 1 5        5 6 6        3 7 3          1 6 0
+ 3 4 2      +   3 3      + 2 2 1        + 3 3 4
------       ------       ------         ------
```

```
  8 3 5        6 4 2        2 8 7          7 2 3
+   4 2      + 2 5 1      + 4 1 2        +   4 5
------       ------       ------         ------
```

```
  1 3 3        4 5 4        3 1 4          6 5 4
+ 5 2 2      + 3 2 4      + 6 0 2        + 2 3 5
------       ------       ------         ------
```

Problem Solving

Directions: Solve each problem.

Example:

Gene collected 342 rocks.

Lester collected 201 rocks.

How many rocks did they collect?

Tina jumped the rope 403 times.

Henry jumped the rope 426 times.

How many times did they jump?

There are 210 people wearing blue hats.

There are 432 people wearing red hats.

How many hats in all?

Asta used 135 paper plates.

Clyde used 143 paper plates.

How many paper plates did they use in all?

Aunt Mary had 536 dollars.

Uncle Lewis had 423 dollars.

How many dollars did they have in all?

NAME _____

Problem Solving

Directions: Solve each problem.

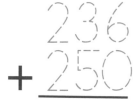

There are 236 boys in school.

There are 250 girls in school.

How many boys and girls are in school?

Mary saw 131 cars.

Marvin saw 268 trucks.

How many cars and trucks did they see in all?

Jack has 427 pennies.

Jill has 370 pennies.

How many pennies do they have in all?

There are 582 red apples.

There are 206 yellow apples.

How many apples are there in all?

Ann found 122 shells.

Pedro found 76 shells.

How many shells did they find?

Subtracting Hundreds

8 hundreds	8 0 0	6 hundreds	6 0 0
− 3 hundreds	− 3 0 0	− 2 hundreds	− 2 0 0
5 hundreds	5 0 0	4 hundreds	4 0 0

Directions: Subtract.

Example:

9 hundreds	9 0 0	3 hundreds	3 0 0
− 7 hundreds	− 7 0 0	− 1 hundreds	− 1 0 0
2 hundreds	2 0 0	hundreds	

7 0 0	5 0 0	9 0 0	8 0 0
− 3 0 0	− 4 0 0	− 4 0 0	− 5 0 0

6 0 0	3 0 0	5 0 0	4 0 0
− 5 0 0	− 2 0 0	− 1 0 0	− 2 0 0

9 0 0	8 0 0	6 0 0	5 0 0
− 1 0 0	− 4 0 0	− 2 0 0	− 3 0 0

4 0 0	7 0 0	8 0 0	9 0 0
− 1 0 0	− 6 0 0	− 2 0 0	− 6 0 0

NAME _____

Problem Solving

Directions: Solve each problem.

Example:

There were 400 apples in a box.

Jesse took 100 apples from the box.

How many apples are still in the box?

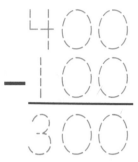

Tommy bought 300 golf balls.

He gave Irene 200 golf balls.

How many golf balls does he have left?

The black horse ran 900 feet.

The brown horse ran 700 feet.

How many more feet did the black horse run?

The paint store has 800 gallons of paint.

It sells 300 gallons of paint.

How many gallons of paint are left?

There are 700 children.

There are 200 boys.

How many girls are there?

NAME _____

3-Digit Subtraction

Directions: Subtract the ones.

```
  7 4 6
- 4 2 4
------
      2
```

Subtract the tens.

```
  7 4 6
- 4 2 4
------
    2 2
```

Subtract the hundreds.

```
  7 4 6
- 4 2 4
------
  3 2 2
```

Directions: Subtract.

Example:

```
  8 7 9
-   4 6
------
  8 3 3
```

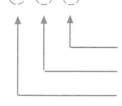

— Subtract the ones.
— Subtract the tens.
— Subtract the hundreds.

```
  5 8 6
- 1 4 2
```

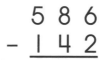

— Subtract the ones.
— Subtract the tens.
— Subtract the hundreds.

```
  6 3 5        4 7 8        3 3 8        9 5 7
- 4 2 3      - 2 4 1      -   2 7      - 7 3 4
```

```
  2 9 7        8 4 6        7 6 9        6 5 3
- 1 4 5      - 3 2 5      - 5 1 4      - 1 4 2
```

```
  5 6 9        3 6 5        8 1 8        9 3 6
- 3 3 3      - 2 1 3      - 6 1 8      - 4 2 4
```

NAME _____

Problem Solving

Directions: Solve each problem.

Example:

The grocery store buys 568 cans of beans.

It sells 345 cans of beans.

How many cans of beans are left?

$$
\begin{array}{r}
568 \\
- 345 \\
\hline
223
\end{array}
$$

The cooler holds 732 gallons of milk.

It has 412 gallons of milk in it.

How many more gallons of milk
will it take to fill the cooler?

Ann does 635 push-ups.

Carl does 421 push-ups.

How many more push-ups does Ann do?

Kurt has 386 pennies.

Neal has 32 pennies.

How many more pennies does Kurt have?

It takes 874 nails to build a tree house.

Jillian has 532 nails.

How many more nails does she need?

Review: Addition and Subtraction

Directions: Add.

$$
\begin{array}{r} 124 \\ +\ 323 \\ \hline \end{array}
\qquad
\begin{array}{r} 520 \\ +\ 407 \\ \hline \end{array}
\qquad
\begin{array}{r} 739 \\ +\ 150 \\ \hline \end{array}
\qquad
\begin{array}{r} 861 \\ +\ \ \ \ 6 \\ \hline \end{array}
$$

Directions: Subtract.

$$
\begin{array}{r} 900 \\ -\ 600 \\ \hline \end{array}
\qquad
\begin{array}{r} 800 \\ -\ 200 \\ \hline \end{array}
\qquad
\begin{array}{r} 974 \\ -\ 564 \\ \hline \end{array}
\qquad
\begin{array}{r} 508 \\ -\ \ \ \ 7 \\ \hline \end{array}
$$

$$
\begin{array}{r} 728 \\ -\ 326 \\ \hline \end{array}
\qquad
\begin{array}{r} 657 \\ -\ \ \ 45 \\ \hline \end{array}
\qquad
\begin{array}{r} 894 \\ -\ 464 \\ \hline \end{array}
\qquad
\begin{array}{r} 596 \\ -\ 352 \\ \hline \end{array}
$$

Directions: Solve each problem.

There are 275 nails in a box.

123 nails are taken out of the box.

How many nails are still in the box?

Gerald peeled 212 apples.

Anna peeled 84 apples.

How many apples did they peel in all?

NAME _____

Review: 3-Digit Addition

Directions: Add.

Example:

```
   3 4 0        7 5 4        8 2 6        6 3 2
 + 2 2 5      +   3 2      +     3      + 3 2 2
   5 6 5        7 8 6
```

```
   1 9 8        4 5 6        5 4 1        2 7 3
 + 2 0 0      +   3 1      + 3 3 3      + 4 1 5
```

```
   9 0 0        8 4 7        7 2 1        4 0 2
 +   3 4      + 1 3 1      + 1 7 6      + 3 8 3
```

```
   1 5 6        6 4 4        2 1 5        3 7 2
 + 4 2 3      + 2 5 1      + 5 4 2      + 4 1 7
```

```
   5 1 8        7 8 3        6 8 4        7 1 0
 + 3 5 1      +     5      +   1 4      + 2 6 0
```

Review: 3-Digit Subtraction

Directions: Subtract.

Example:

```
   8 5 6        4 3 2        5 9 8        7 6 9
 - 3 5 2      -   2 1      - 4 1 6      - 3 4 5
   5 0 4        4 1 1
```

```
   3 1 9        9 5 4        2 7 5        6 4 3
 -     6      - 7 3 1      -     3      - 3 1 3
```

```
   7 7 5        8 3 4        9 4 2        4 7 8
 - 2 6 1      -   1 2      - 1 1 1      - 3 2 4
```

```
   5 6 2        4 4 4        3 8 5        7 5 4
 - 4 3 1      - 2 1 2      - 1 5 2      -     3
```

```
   8 6 8        9 4 3        6 8 9        5 7 7
 - 2 3 4      - 8 4 3      - 4 1 7      -   3 7
```

NAME _____

Multiplication

Multiplication is a short way to find the sum of adding the same number a certain amount of times. For example, 7 × 4 = 28 instead of 7 + 7 + 7 + 7 = 28.

Directions: Study the example. Solve the problems.

Example:

3 + 3 + 3 = 9
3 threes = 9
3 × 3 = 9

7 + 7 = ____
2 sevens = ____
2 × 7 = ____

4 + 4 + 4 + 4 = ____
4 fours = ____
4 × ____ = ____

5 + 5 = ____
2 fives = ____
2 × ____ = ____

2 + 2 + 2 + 2 = ____
4 twos = ____
4 × ____ = ____

6 + 6 = ____
2 sixes = ____
2 × ____ = ____

Multiplication

Multiplication is repeated addition.

Directions: Draw a picture for each problem.
Then, write the missing numbers.

Example:

Draw 2 groups of three apples.

$3 + 3 = 6$

or $2 \times 3 = 6$

Draw 3 groups of four hearts.

$4 + 4 + 4 =$ _____

or $3 \times$ _____ $=$ _____

Draw 2 groups of five boxes.

$5 +$ _____ $=$ _____

or $2 \times$ _____ $=$ _____

Draw 6 groups of two circles.

$2 +$ _____ $+$ _____ $+$ _____ $+$ _____ $+$ _____ $=$ _____

or $6 \times$ _____ $=$ _____

Draw 7 groups of three triangles.

$3 +$ _____ $+$ _____ $+$ _____ $+$ _____ $+$ _____ $+$ _____ $=$ _____

or _____ $\times$ _____ $=$ _____

NAME _____

Multiplication

Directions: Study the example. Draw the groups and write the total.

Example:

3×2

$2 + 2 + 2 = $ ____ 6 ____

3×4

___ + ___ + ___ = _____

2×5

___ + ___ = _____

5×3

___ + ___ + ___ + ___ + ___ = _____

Multiplication

Directions: Solve the problems.

9 + 9 = ____   7 + 7 = ____

2 nines = ____   2 sevens = ____

2 × 9 = ____   2 × ____ = ____

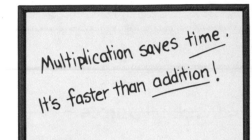

4 + 4 + 4 + 4 = ____   8 + 8 + 8 + 8 + 8 = ____

____ fours = ____   ____ eights = ____

____ × 4 = ____   ____ × 8 = ____

5 + 5 + 5 = ____   9 + 9 = ____   6 + 6 + 6 = ____

____ fives = ____   ____ nines = ____   ____ sixes = ____

____ × 5 = ____   ____ × 9 = ____   ____ × 6 = ____

3 + 3 = ____   7 + 7 + 7 + 7 = ____   2 + 2 = ____

____ threes = ____ ____ sevens = ____   ____ twos = ____

____ × 3 = ____   ____ × 7 = ____   ____ × 2 = ____

NAME _____

Multiplication

Directions: Use the code to color the rainbow.

If the answer is:

6, color it **green**.

8, color it **purple**.

9, color it **red**.

16, color it **pink**.

18, color it **white**.

21, color it **brown**.

25, color it **orange**.

27, color it **blue**.

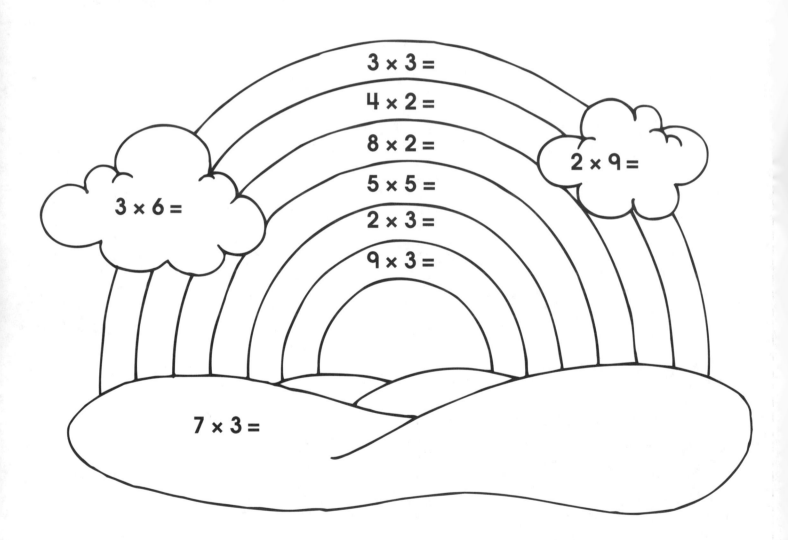

3 × 3 =

4 × 2 =

8 × 2 =

5 × 5 =

2 × 3 =

9 × 3 =

2 × 9 =

3 × 6 =

7 × 3 =

NAME _____

Problem Solving

Directions: Tell if you add, subtract, or multiply. Then, write the answers. Hint: **In all** means to add. **Left** means to subtract. Groups with the same number in each means to multiply.

Example:

There are 6 red birds and 7 blue birds.
How many birds in all?

____add____   ___13___ birds

The pet store had 25 goldfish, but 10 were sold.
How many goldfish are left?

_____ _____ goldfish

There are 5 cages of bunnies. There are 2 bunnies in each cage.
How many bunnies are there in the store?

_____ _____ bunnies

The store had 18 puppies this morning. It sold 7 puppies today.
How many puppies are left?

puppies

NAME _____

Circle

A **circle** is a shape that is round. This is a circle: ◯

Directions: Find the circles and draw squares around them.

Directions: Trace the word. Then, write the word.

c¡rcle

Square

A **square** is a shape with four corners and four sides of the same length. This is a square: ☐

Directions: Find the squares and draw circles around them.

Directions: Trace the word. Then, write the word.

square

NAME _____

Rectangle

A **rectangle** is a shape with four corners and four sides. The sides opposite each other are the same length. This is a rectangle: ☐

Directions: Find the rectangles and draw circles around them.

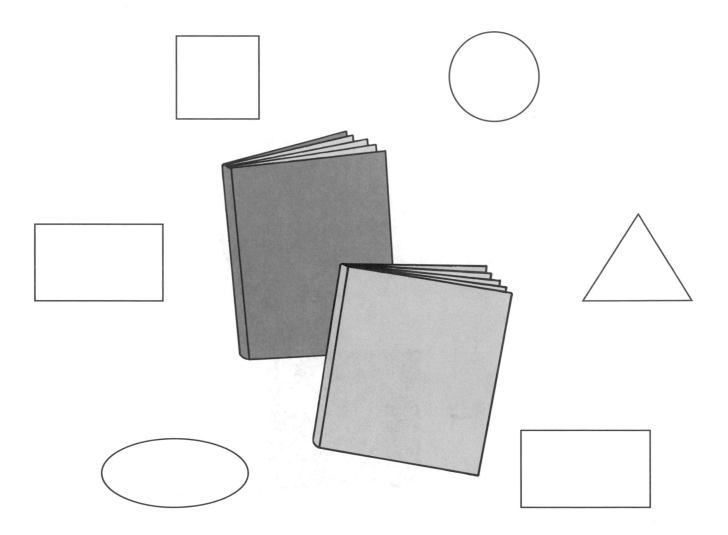

Directions: Trace the word. Then, write the word.

rectangle

Triangle

A **triangle** is a shape with three corners and three sides. This is a triangle:

Directions: Find the triangles and draw circles around them.

Directions: Trace the word. Then, write the word.

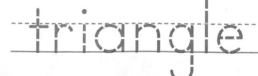

NAME _____

Oval and Rhombus

An **oval** is egg-shaped. This is an oval: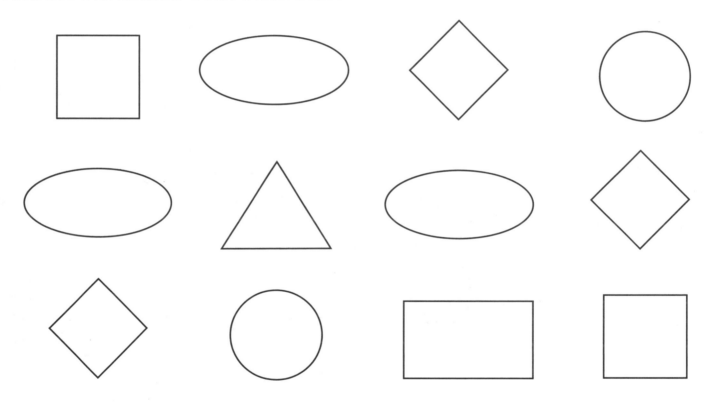

A **rhombus** is a shape with four sides of the same length. Its corners form points at the top, sides, and bottom. This is a rhombus:

Directions: Find the ovals. Color them **red.**
Find the rhombuses. Color them **blue.**

Directions: Trace the word. Then, write the word.

oval

rhombus

Shapes

Directions: Some shapes have sides. How many sides does each shape below have? Write the number of sides inside each shape.

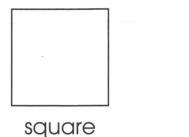

square

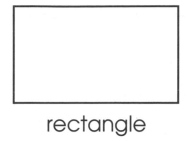

rectangle

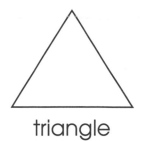

triangle

Directions: Help Robbie get to his space car by tracing the path that has only squares, rectangles, and triangles.

Hint: You may want to draw an **X** on all the other shapes. This will help you see the path more clearly.

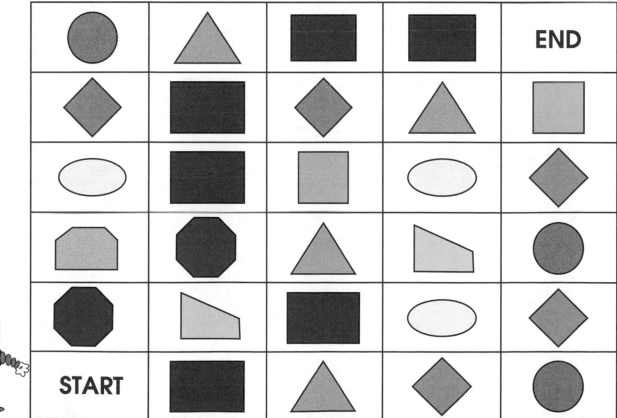

Shapes

Directions: Look at the grid below. All the shapes have straight sides, like a square.

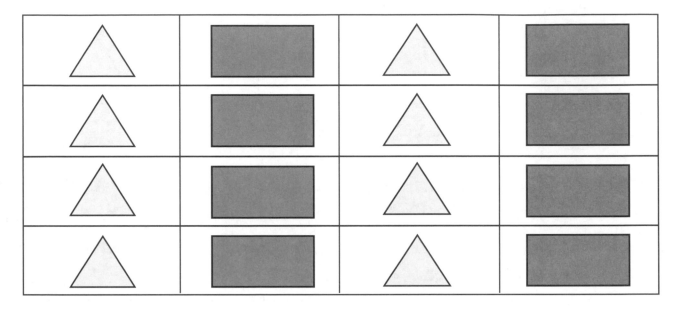

Directions: Now, make your own pattern grid. Use only shapes with straight sides like the grid above. The grid has been started for you.

Measurement: Inches

Directions: Cut out the ruler. Measure each object to the nearest inch.

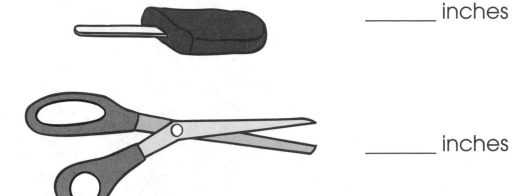

_____ inches

_____ inches

_____ inch

Directions: Measure objects around your house. Write the measurement to the nearest inch.

can of soup   _____ inches

pen   _____ inches

toothbrush   _____ inches

paper clip   _____ inches

small toy   _____ inches

cut out

8 — 7 — 6 — 5 — 4 — 3 — 2 — 1

Page is blank for cutting exercise on previous page.

Measurement: Inches

Directions: Use the ruler from page 131 to measure the fish to the nearest inch.

about _____ inches

about _____ inch

about _____ inches

about _____ inch

about _____ inches

about _____ inches

NAME _____

How Big Are You?

Directions: How big are you? **Estimate**, or guess, how long some of your body parts are. Write your estimates below. Then, have a friend use an inch ruler to measure you. Write the numbers below. How close were your estimates?

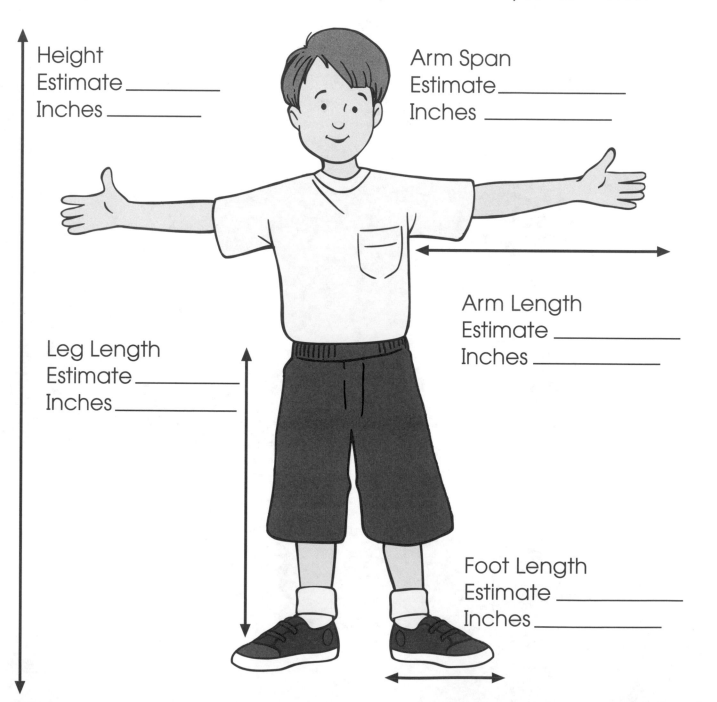

Height
Estimate _____
Inches _____

Arm Span
Estimate _____
Inches _____

Arm Length
Estimate _____
Inches _____

Leg Length
Estimate _____
Inches _____

Foot Length
Estimate _____
Inches _____

NAME _____

Measurement: Inches

An **inch** is a unit of length in the standard measurement system.

Directions: Use the ruler on page 131 to measure each object to the nearest inch.

Example: The paper clip is about 1 inch long.

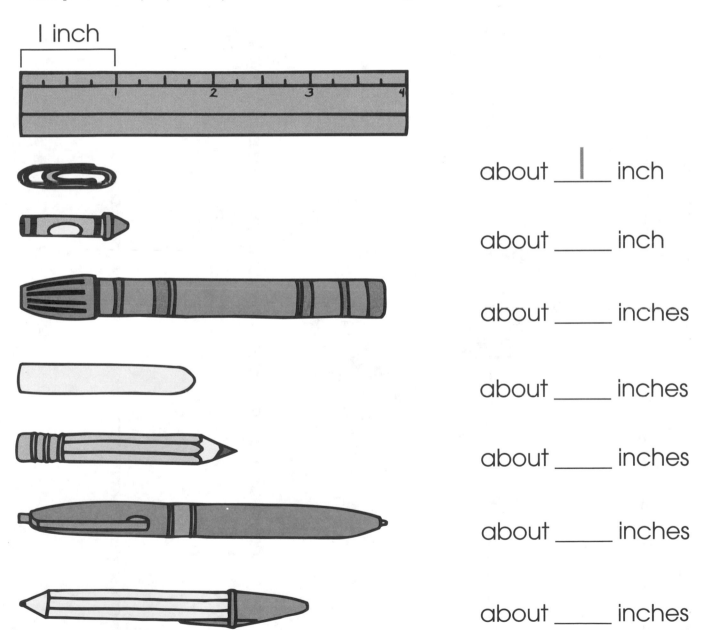

about ___1___ inch

about _____ inch

about _____ inches

about _____ inches

about _____ inches

about _____ inches

about _____ inches

NAME _____

Measuring Monkeys

Directions: Use the inch ruler on page 131 to measure the length of each rope. Write the answer in each blank.

Measurement: Centimeters

A **centimeter** is a unit of length in the metric system. There are 2.54 centimeters in an inch.

Directions: Use a centimeter ruler to measure the crayons to the nearest centimeter.

Example: The first crayon is about 7 centimeters long.

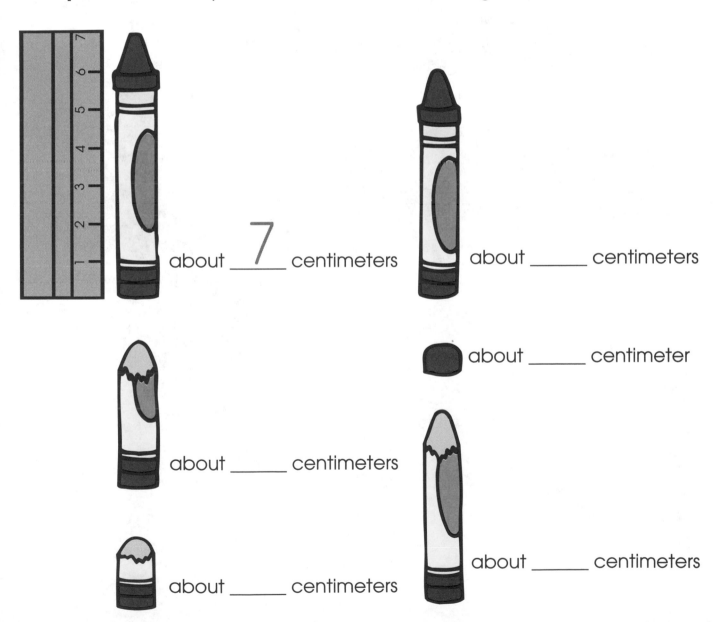

about __7__ centimeters

about _____ centimeters

about _____ centimeter

about _____ centimeters

about _____ centimeters

about _____ centimeters

NAME _____

Measuring in Centimeters

Directions: Use a centimeter ruler to find the height or the length of the objects below. Write the answer in each blank.

Example:

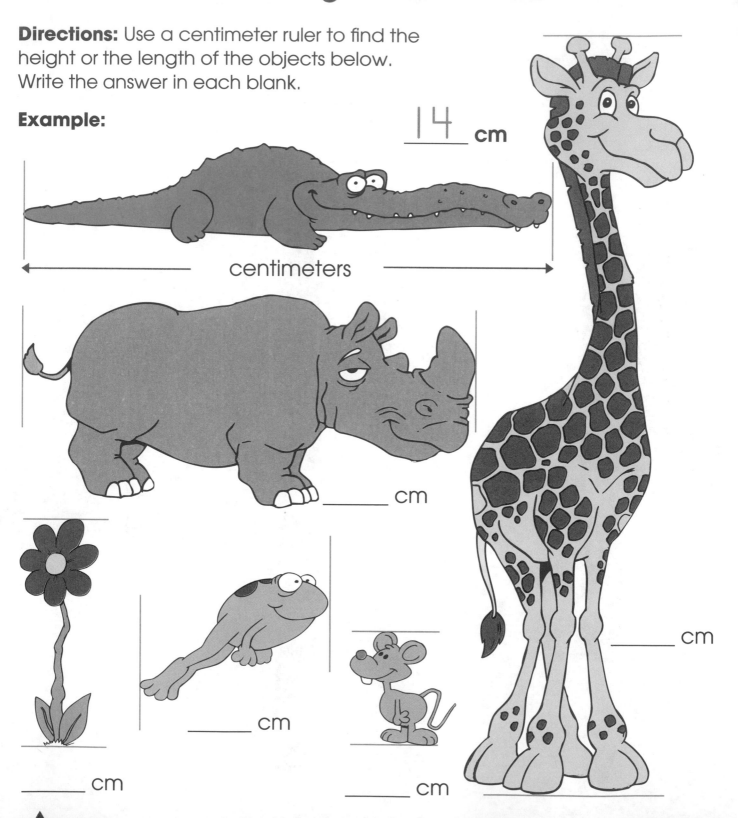

14 cm

centimeters

_____ cm

_____ cm

_____ cm

_____ cm

_____ cm

Centimeter Sharpening

Directions: Use a centimeter ruler to measure each pencil. Subtract to find how many centimeters were lost when sharpening each pencil.

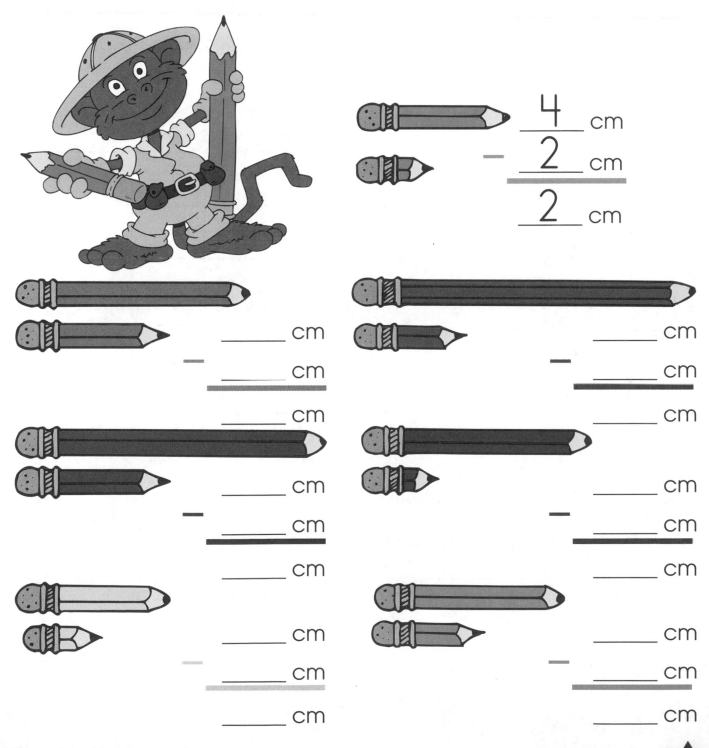

$$\frac{\begin{array}{r} 4 \text{ cm} \\ -\ 2 \text{ cm} \end{array}}{2 \text{ cm}}$$

_____ cm

_____ cm

_____ cm

_____ cm

_____ cm

_____ cm

_____ cm

_____ cm

_____ cm

_____ cm

_____ cm

_____ cm

_____ cm

_____ cm

_____ cm

_____ cm

NAME _____

Good Morning

Directions: Make your own bar graph. List 5 kinds of cereal on the graph below. Ask 5 people to vote for one cereal. Record the votes on the graph by coloring in 1 space for each vote. Use the information to answer the questions.

Favorite Cereal

Cereals

| | 1 | 2 | 3 | 4 | 5 |

Number of People

1. Which cereal was the favorite? _____

2. Which cereal had the fewest votes?_____

3. How many more voted for _____ than for
        (name of cereal)

_____? _____
        (name of cereal)

4. How many people chose _____ and
        (name of cereal)

_____ altogether? _____
        (name of cereal)

NAME _____

Jungle Weather

Directions: The pictures show the weather for one month. Count the number of sunny, cloudy, and rainy days.

Directions: Complete the pictograph using the tallies above.

NAME _____

What a Meal!

Directions: Use the pictograph to complete each sentence below.

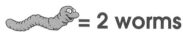 = 2 worms

Grace Goldfish	🪱 🪱 🪱 🪱 🪱
Willie Walleye	🪱 🪱 🪱 🪱 🪱 🪱 🪱
Calvin Catfish	🪱 🪱 🪱 🪱 🪱
Benny Bluegill	🪱 🪱
Beth Bass	🪱 🪱 🪱 🪱 🪱 🪱 🪱
Patty Perch	🪱 🪱 🪱

1. _____ got the fewest worms.

2. _____ got the most worms.

3. _____ and _____ got the same number of worms.

4. Benny and Patty together caught the same number of worms

   as _____ .

5. Write the number of worms that each fish ate.

   ____   ____   ____   ____   ____   ____
   Grace   **Willie**   **Calvin**   **Benny**   **Beth**   **Patty**

Graphs

A **graph** is a drawing that shows information about numbers.

Directions: Count the apples in each row. Color the boxes to show how many apples have bites taken out of them.

Example:

1	2	3	4	5	6	7	8

NAME _____

Graphs

Directions: Count the fish. Color the bowls to make a graph that shows the number of fish.

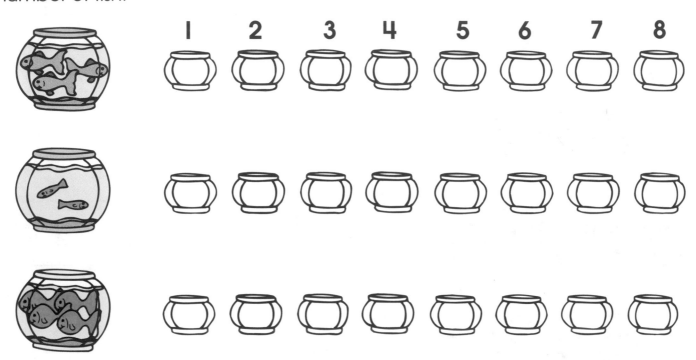

Directions: Use your fishbowl graphs to find the answers to the following questions. Draw a line to the correct bowl.

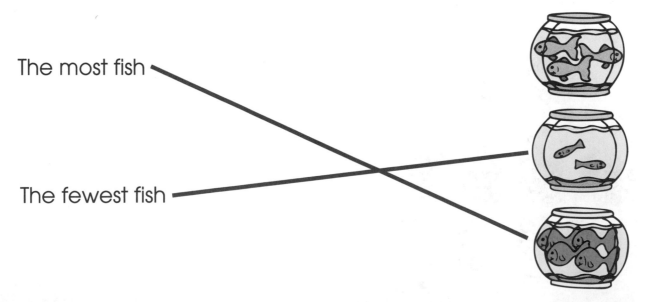

The most fish

The fewest fish

NAME _____

Treasure Quest

Directions: Read the directions. Draw the pictures where they belong on the grid. Start at 0 and go . . .

over 2, up 5. Draw a

over 9, up 3. Draw a

over 8, up 6. Draw a

over 5, up 2. Draw a

over 1, up 7. Draw a

over 7, up 1. Draw a

over 6, up 4. Draw a

over 2, up 3. Draw a

over 3, up 1. Draw a

over 4, up 6. Draw a

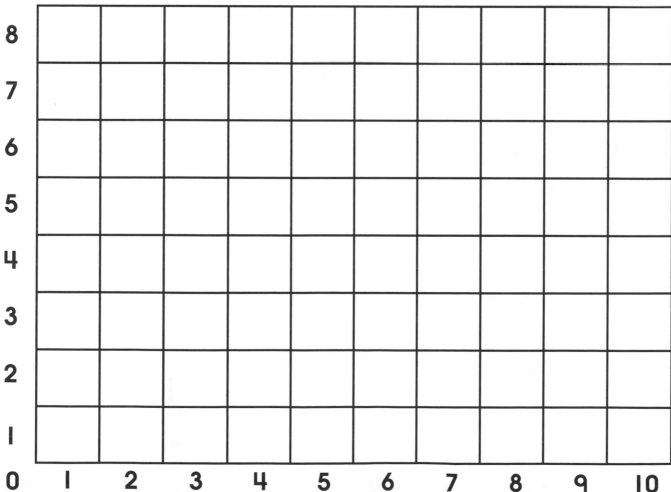

NAME _____

Let's Get Things in Order!

Directions: Help Mrs. Brown pick flowers in her garden. The flowers she wants are listed in the chart. Use the descriptions to color the flowers in her garden.

↓	→	Color it:
1st row	6th flower	red
2nd row	4th flower	blue
3rd row	1st flower	yellow
4th row	9th flower	pink
5th row	10th flower	orange
6th row	2nd flower	green
7th row	5th flower	black
8th row	7th flower	grey
9th row	8th flower	purple
10th row	3rd flower	brown

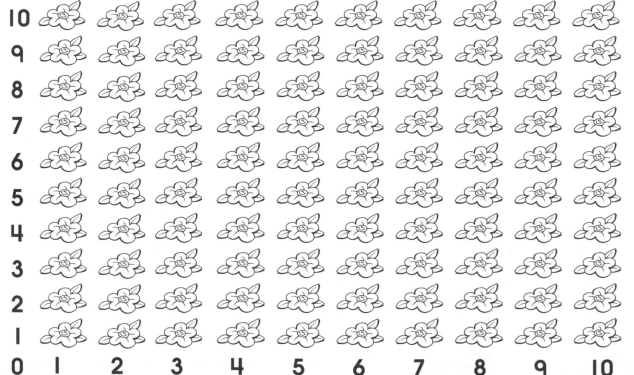

Whole and Half

A **fraction** is a number that names part of a whole, such as $\frac{1}{2}$.

Directions: Color half of each thing.

Example: whole apple    half an apple

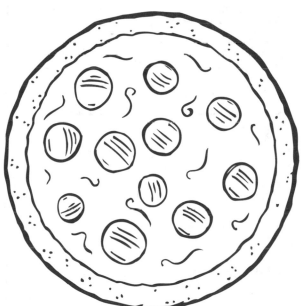

NAME _____

One Third

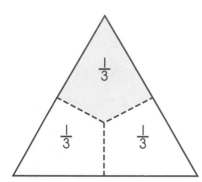

 part is blue.

The [3] parts are the same size.

$\frac{1}{3}$ of the inside is blue.

Directions: Complete the fraction statements.

Example:

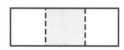

 part is blue.

_____ parts are the same size.

_____ of the inside is blue.

_____ part is blue.

_____ parts are the same size.

_____ of the inside is blue.

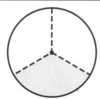

_____ part is blue.

_____ parts are the same size.

_____ of the inside is blue.

_____ part is blue.

_____ parts are the same size.

_____ of the inside is blue.

_____ of the inside is blue.

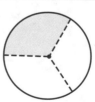

_____ of the inside is blue.

One Fourth

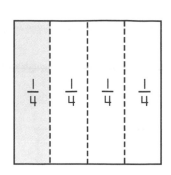

$\frac{1}{4}$ $\frac{1}{4}$ $\frac{1}{4}$ $\frac{1}{4}$

part is blue.

The  parts are the same size.

of the inside is blue.

Directions: Complete the fraction statements.

Example:

_____ part is blue.

_____ parts are the same size.

_____ of the inside is blue.

_____ part is blue.

_____ parts are the same size.

_____ of the inside is blue.

_____ part is blue.

_____ parts are the same size.

_____ of the inside is blue.

_____ part is blue.

_____ parts are the same size.

_____ of the inside is blue.

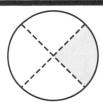

_____ of the inside is blue.

_____ of the inside is blue.

NAME _____

Thirds and Fourths

Directions: Each shape has **3** equal parts. Color one section, or $\frac{1}{3}$, of each shape.

Directions: Each shape has **4** equal parts. Color one section, or $\frac{1}{4}$, of each shape.

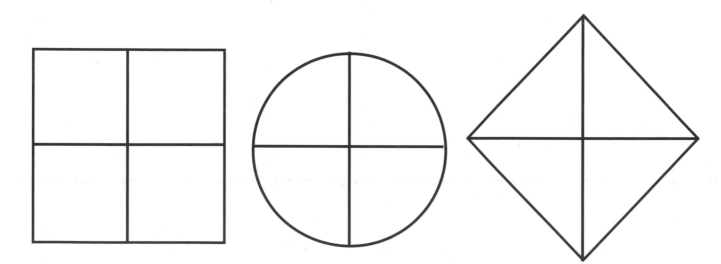

NAME _____

Fractions: Half, Third, Fourth

Directions: Color the correct fraction of each shape.

Examples:

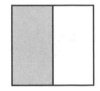

shaded part   1
equal parts   2
$\frac{1}{2}$ (one-half) shaded

shaded part   1
equal parts   3
$\frac{1}{3}$ (one-third) shaded

shaded part   1
equal parts   4
$\frac{1}{4}$ (one-fourth) shaded

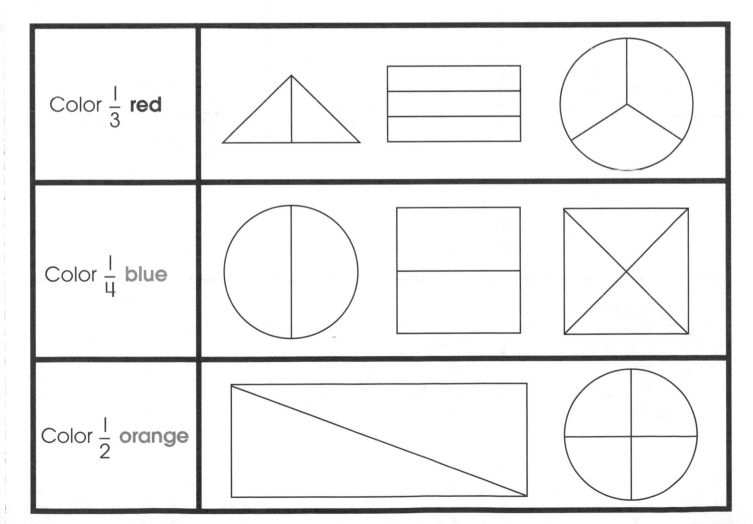

Color $\frac{1}{3}$ **red**

Color $\frac{1}{4}$ **blue**

Color $\frac{1}{2}$ **orange**

NAME _____

Fraction Food

Directions: Count the equal parts. Circle the fraction that names one of the parts.

$\dfrac{1}{2}$ $\dfrac{1}{3}$ $\dfrac{1}{4}$

$\dfrac{1}{2}$ $\dfrac{1}{3}$ $\dfrac{1}{4}$

$\dfrac{1}{2}$ $\dfrac{1}{3}$ $\dfrac{1}{4}$

$\dfrac{1}{2}$ $\dfrac{1}{3}$ $\dfrac{1}{4}$

$\dfrac{1}{2}$ $\dfrac{1}{3}$ $\dfrac{1}{4}$

$\dfrac{1}{2}$ $\dfrac{1}{3}$ $\dfrac{1}{4}$

$\dfrac{1}{2}$ $\dfrac{1}{3}$ $\dfrac{1}{4}$

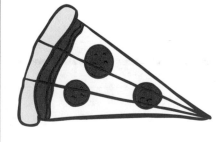

$\dfrac{1}{2}$ $\dfrac{1}{3}$ $\dfrac{1}{4}$

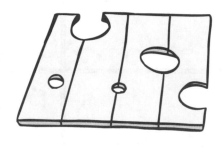

$\dfrac{1}{2}$ $\dfrac{1}{3}$ $\dfrac{1}{4}$

NAME _____

Shaded Shapes

Directions: Draw a line to match each fraction with its correct shape.

$\frac{1}{3}$ shaded

$\frac{2}{4}$ shaded

$\frac{1}{4}$ shaded

$\frac{1}{2}$ shaded

$\frac{3}{4}$ shaded

$\frac{2}{3}$ shaded

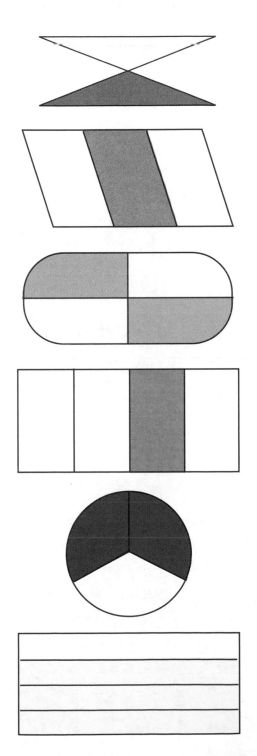

NAME _____

Mean Monster's Diet

Directions: Help Mean Monster choose the right piece of food.

1. Mean Monster may have $\frac{1}{4}$ of this chocolate pie. Color in $\frac{1}{4}$ of the pie.

2. For a snack, he wants $\frac{1}{3}$ of this chocolate cake. Color in $\frac{1}{3}$ of the cake.

3. For an evening snack, he can have $\frac{1}{4}$ of the candy bar. Color in $\frac{1}{4}$ of the candy bar.

4. Mean Monster may eat $\frac{1}{3}$ of this pizza. Color in $\frac{1}{3}$ of the pizza.

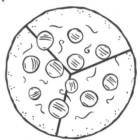

5. For lunch, Mean Monster gets $\frac{1}{2}$ of the sandwich. Color in $\frac{1}{2}$ of the sandwich.

6. He ate $\frac{1}{2}$ of the apple for lunch. Color in $\frac{1}{2}$ of the apple.

Clocks: Identifying Parts

Directions: A clock face has numbers. Trace the numbers on the clock.

NAME _____

Writing the Time

An hour is sixty minutes long. It takes an hour for the big hand to go around the clock. When the big hand is on 12, and the little hand points to a number, that is the hour!

Directions: The **big hand** is on the **12**. Color it **red**. The **little hand** is on the **8**. Color it **blue**.

The **big hand** is on _____ .

The **little hand** is on _____ .

It is _____ o clock.

Writing the Time

Directions: Color the little hour hand **red**. Fill in the blanks.

The **big hand** is on _____ .

The **little hand** is on _____ .

It is _____ o clock.

The **big hand** is on _____ .

The **little hand** is on _____ .

It is _____ o clock.

The **big hand** is on _____ .

The **little hand** is on _____ .

It is _____ o clock.

The **big hand** is on _____ .

The **little hand** is on _____ .

It is _____ o clock.

NAME _____

Practice

Directions: What is the time?

_____ o clock

_____ o clock

_____ o clock

_____ o clock

_____ o clock

_____ o clock

_____ o clock

_____ o clock

_____ o clock

_____ o clock

_____ o clock

_____ o clock

Matching Digital and Face Clocks

Long ago, there were only wind-up clocks. Today, we also have electric and battery clocks.

Directions: Match the digital and face clocks that show the same time.

NAME _____

Writing Time on the Half-Hour

Directions: Write the times.

_____

_____ minutes past

_____ o clock

_____

_____ minutes past

_____ o clock

What is your dinner time?

Directions: Circle the time you eat.

NAME _____

Writing Time on the Half-Hour

Directions: What time is it?

_____

_____

_____

_____

_____

_____

NAME _____

Time to the Quarter-Hour: Introduction

Each **hour** has **60** minutes. An **hour** has **4 quarter-hours**. A **quarter-hour** is **15 minutes**.

This clock face shows a quarter of an hour.

From the **12** to the **3** is **15 minutes**.

From the 12 to the 3 is 15 minutes.

_____15_____ minutes after _____8_____ o clock

is _____8:15_____

Writing Time on the Half-Hour

Directions: Draw the hands. Write the times.

5:15

__15__ minutes after

__5__ o clock

10:15

_____ minutes after

_____ o clock

2:15

_____ minutes after

_____ o clock

9:15

_____ minutes after

_____ o clock

NAME _____

Time to the Minute Intervals: Introduction

Each **number** on the clock face stands for **5** minutes.

Directions: Count by **5s** beginning at the **12**.
Write the numbers here:

__00__ 05 10 15 20 25

It is __25__ minutes after __8__
o clock. It is written 8:25.

Directions: Count by **5s**.

__00__ ___ ___ ___ ___ ___ ___

It is _____ minutes after _____ o clock.

_____ : _____

Drawing the Minute Hand

Directions: Draw the hands on these fish clocks.

7:45

8:05

11:15

3:20

5:55

1:50

12:10

10:25

4:40

NAME _____

Counting Pennies

Directions: Count the pennies.
How many cents?

Example:

    = **4¢**

        = ☐

       = ☐

         = ☐

   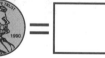 = ☐

        = ☐

       = ☐

  = ☐

          = ☐

NAME _____

Counting Pennies

Directions: Count the pennies in each triangle.

_____ ¢   _____ ¢

_____ ¢

NAME _____

Nickels: Introduction

Directions: Look at the two sides of a nickel. Color the nickels **silver**.

front   back

_____ nickel = ____5____ pennies

_____ nickel = ____5____ cents

_____ nickel = ____5____ ¢

Directions: Write the number of cents in a nickel.

5¢ = ____¢ + ____¢ + ____¢ + ____¢ + ____¢

Nickels: Counting by Fives

Directions: Count the nickels by 5s. Write the amount.

Example:

 PICKLES 5¢ each

5 cents = 1 nickel

  15 ¢

  ☐ ¢

Count __5__, __10__, __15__.

Count ___, ___.

  ☐ ¢

    ☐ ¢

Count ___, ___, ___,

___, ___.

Count ___, ___, ___, ___,

___, ___, ___.

   ☐ ¢

    ☐ ¢

Count ___, ___, ___,

___.

Count ___, ___, ___,

___, ___, ___.

NAME _____

Dimes: Introduction

A dime is small, but quite strong. It can buy more than a penny or a nickel.

front    back

Directions: Each side of a dime is different. It has ridges on its edge. Color the dime **silver**.

Directions: Write the number of cents in a dime.

_____ dime   =   _____ pennies

_____ dime   =   _____ cents

_____ dime   =   _____ ¢

NAME _____

Dimes: Counting by Tens

Directions: Count by 10s. Write the number. Circle the group with more.

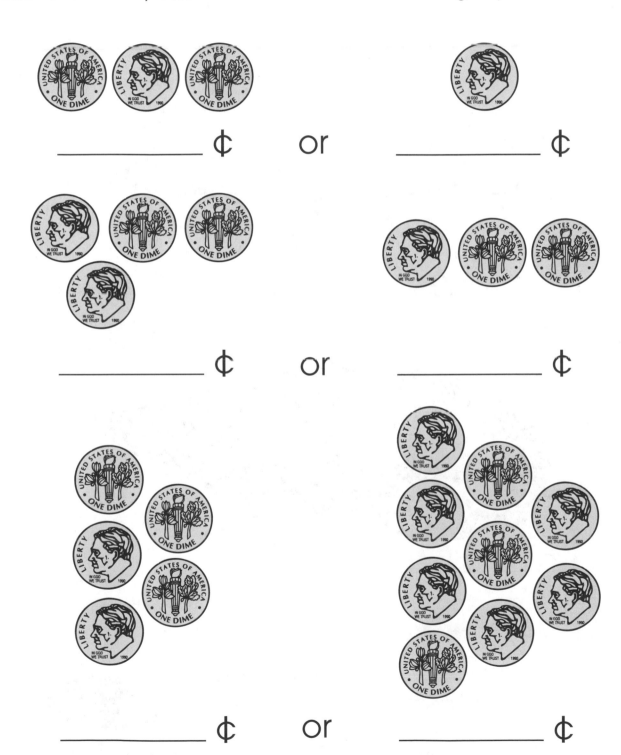

_____ ¢   or   _____ ¢

_____ ¢   or   _____ ¢

_____ ¢   or   _____ ¢

NAME _____

Counting with Dimes, Nickels, and Pennies

Directions: Count the money. Start with the dime. Write the amount.

1.

_____ ¢

2.

_____ ¢

3. Circle the answer.
   Who has more money?

Quarters: Introduction

Our first president, George Washington, is on the front. The American eagle is on the back.

front   back

Directions: Write the number of cents in a quarter.

_____ quarter = _____ pennies

_____ quarter = _____ cents

_____ quarter = _____ ¢

Directions: Count these nickels by 5s. Is this another way to make 25¢?

yes   no

Counting with Quarters

These are some machines that use quarters.

Directions: Color each machine you have to put quarters into. Circle the number of quarters you need.

I need _____ quarters to wash clothes.

I need _____ quarter(s) to make a phone call.

NAME ______________________________

Counting with Quarters, Dimes, Nickels, and Pennies

Directions: Match the money with the amount.

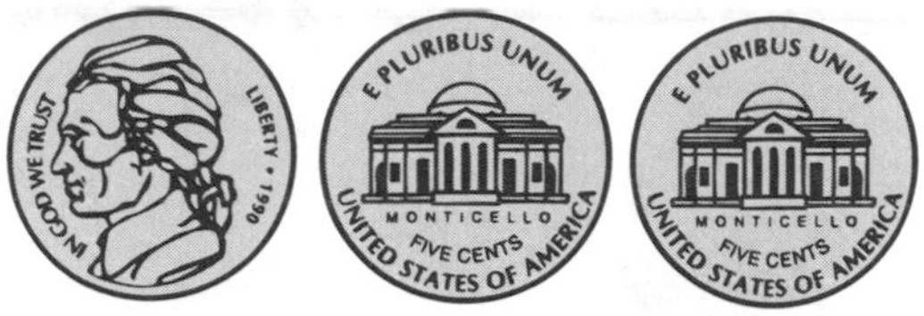

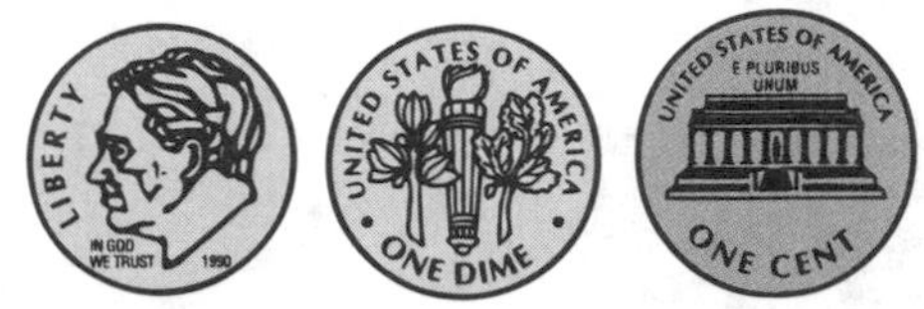

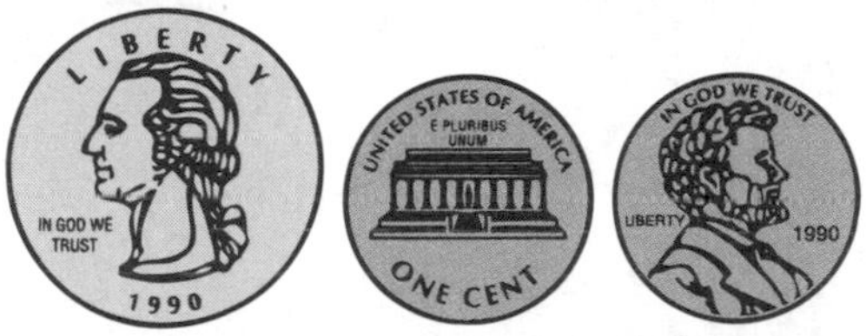

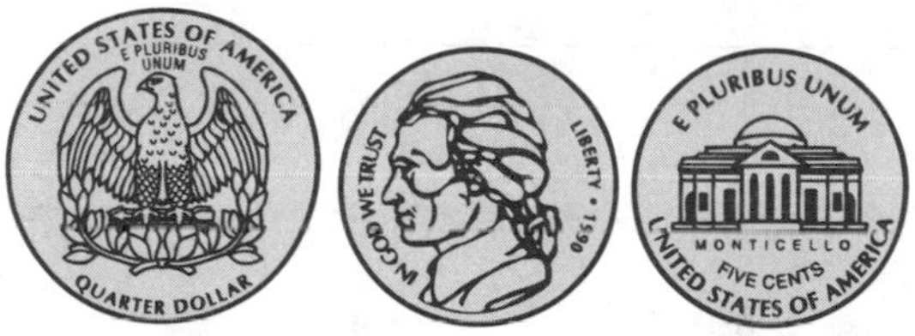

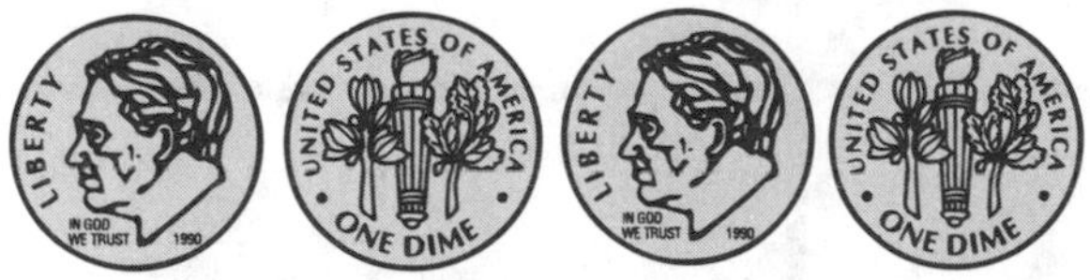

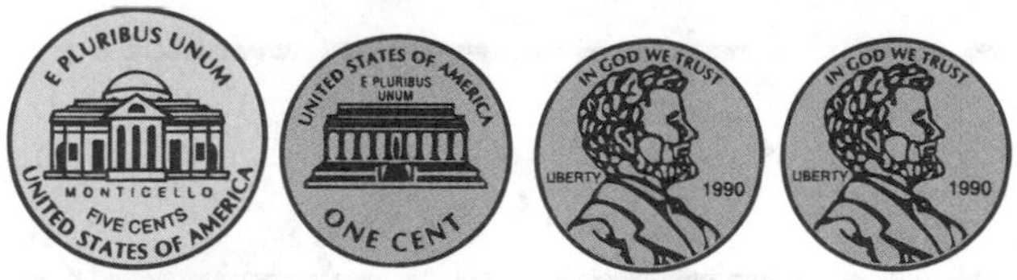

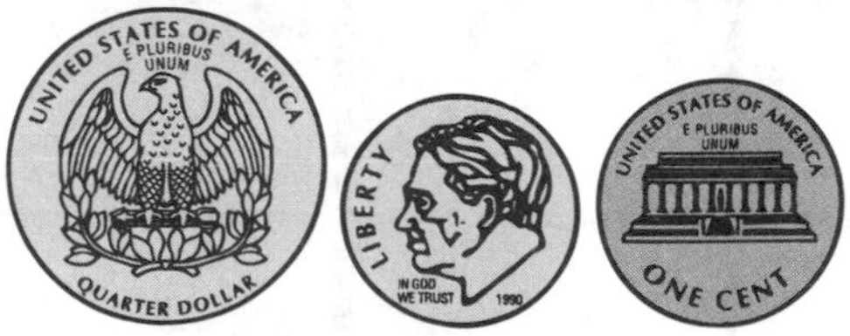

35 ¢

36 ¢

40 ¢

27 ¢

15 ¢

21 ¢

8 ¢

NAME _____

Counting with Quarters, Dimes, Nickels, and Pennies

Here are things to buy for your hair.

Directions: How many of each coin do you need?
Write 1, 2, 3, or 4.

	Quarters	Dimes	Nickels	Pennies
(flower headband)				
(brush)				
(headband)				
(bow headband)				
(comb)				

Subtracting for Change

Adam wanted to know how much change he would have left when he bought things. He made this picture to help him subtract.

4 dimes – 1 dime 3 dimes	40 ¢ – 10 ¢ 30 ¢

Directions: Cross out and subtract.

6 dimes – 4 dimes _____ dimes	60 ¢ – 40 ¢ _____ ¢

NAME _____

Problem-Solving with Money

Directions: Draw the coins you use. Write the number of coins on each blank.

1.

9¢

_____ dimes

_____ nickels

_____ pennies

2.

11¢

_____ dimes

_____ nickels

_____ pennies

3.

14¢

_____ dimes

_____ nickels

_____ pennies

4. Find another way to pay for the

14¢

_____ dimes

_____ nickels

_____ pennies

Problem-Solving with Money

Directions: Draw the coins you use. Write the number of coins on each blank.

1.

 (35¢)

_____ quarters

_____ dimes

_____ nickels

_____ pennies

2.

 (29¢)

_____ quarters

_____ dimes

_____ nickels

_____ pennies

3.

 (43¢)

_____ quarters

_____ dimes

_____ nickels

_____ pennies

4. Find another way to pay for the

 (43¢)

_____ quarters

_____ dimes

_____ nickels

_____ pennies

NAME _____

Making Exact Amounts of Money: How Much More?

Directions: Count the coins. Find out how much more money you need to pay the exact amount.

How much money do you have? _____ ¢

How much more money do you need? _____ ¢

How much money do you have? _____ ¢

How much more money do you need? _____ ¢

Directions: Solve this puzzle.

How much more money
does Monkey need?

_____ ¢

Reading

NAME

Batter Up!

What did Bobby yell to the batter?

Directions: To find out, say the name of each picture. On the line, write the letter that you hear at the beginning of each picture.

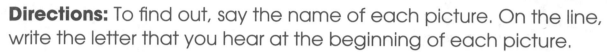

!

NAME _____

Bats and Balls

Directions: Look at the baseball words below. Use the letters from the word box to make new words. **Hint:** Some letters can be used for both sets of words.

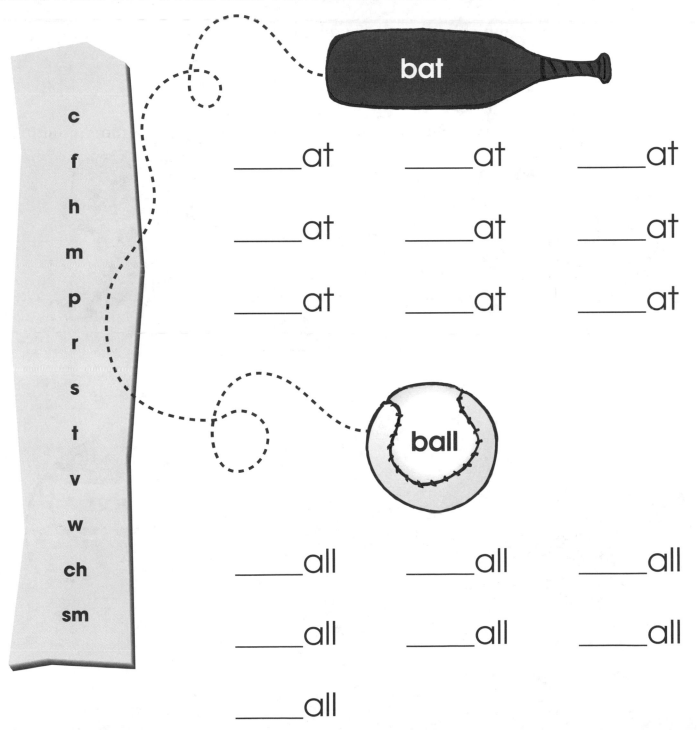

bat

c
f
h
m
p
r
s
t
v
w
ch
sm

___at   ___at   ___at

___at   ___at   ___at

___at   ___at   ___at

ball

___all   ___all   ___all

___all   ___all   ___all

___all

NAME _____

What Does That Spell?

Directions: Write the letters from the word box to make new words. Some letters can be used for both sets of words.

f b c n p sk s t fl

win

____in   ____in

____in   ____in

____in   ____in

game

____ame   ____ame

____ame   ____ame

____ame   ____ame

Sounds the Same

Different words may begin with the same sound.

Example: Box and **boy** begin with the same sound.
Cat and **dog** do not.

Directions: Say each picture's name. Color the pictures in the box if their names begin with the same sound.

NAME _____

Tic-Tac-Toe

Directions: Find the three pictures in each game whose names begin with the same sound. Draw a line through them.

Beginning Consonants: *b, c, d, f, g, h, j*

Directions: Fill in the beginning consonant for each word.

Example: __c__ at

___ox

___acket

___oat

___ouse

___og

___ire

NAME _____

Beginning Consonants: *k, l, m, n, p, q, r*

Directions: Write the letter that makes the beginning sound for each picture.

_____ _____ _____ _____

_____ _____ _____ _____

_____ _____ _____ _____

_____ _____ _____ _____

Beginning Consonants: *k, l, m, n, p, q, r*

Directions: Fill in the beginning consonant for each word.

Example: __r__ose

___oney

___uilt

___ion

___an

___ey

___ose

NAME _____

Beginning Consonants: *s, t, v, w, x, y, z*

Directions: Write the letter under each picture that makes the beginning sound.

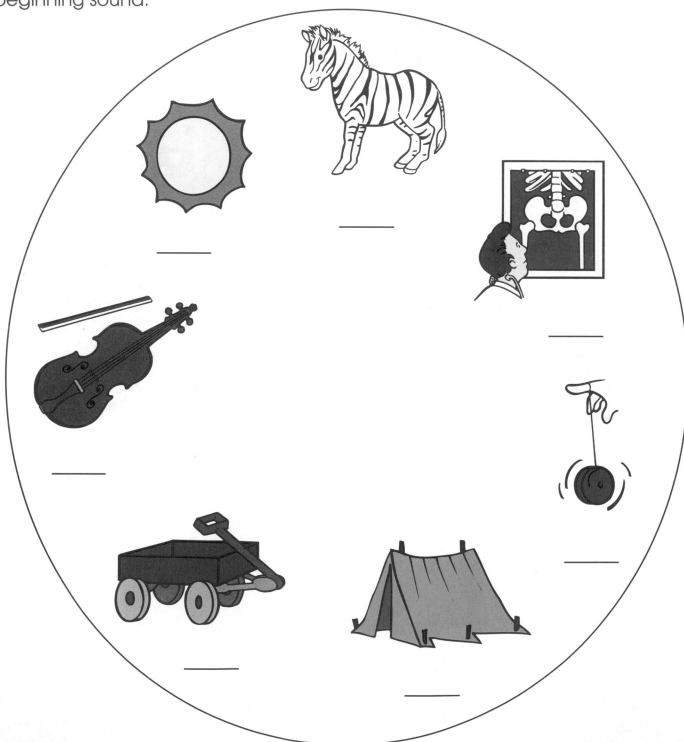

Beginning Consonants: *s, t, v, w, x, y, z*

Directions: Fill in the beginning consonant for each word.

Example: __s__ ock

___ipper

___able

___ray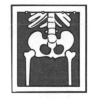

___ase

___olk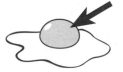

___and

NAME _____

Ending Consonants: *b, d, f, g*

Directions: Fill in the ending consonant for each word.

ma___

cu___

roo___

do___

be___

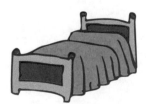

bi___

Ending Consonants: *k, l, m, n, p, r*

Directions: Fill in the ending consonant for each word.

nai___

ca___

gu___

ca___

truc___

ca___

pai___

NAME _____

Ending Consonants: *s, t, x*

Directions: Fill in the ending consonant for each word.

ca____

bo____

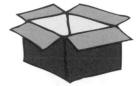

bu____

fo____

boa____

ma____

Consonant Blends

Consonant blends are two or three consonant letters in a word whose sounds combine, or blend. **Examples: br, fr, gr, pr, tr**

Directions: Look at each picture. Say its name. Write the blend you hear at the beginning of each word.

_____ _____ _____

_____ _____ _____

_____ _____ _____

_____ _____ _____

NAME _____

Blends: *fl, br, pl, sk, sn*

Blends are two consonants put together to form a single sound.

Directions: Look at the pictures and say their names. Write the letters for the beginning sound in each word.

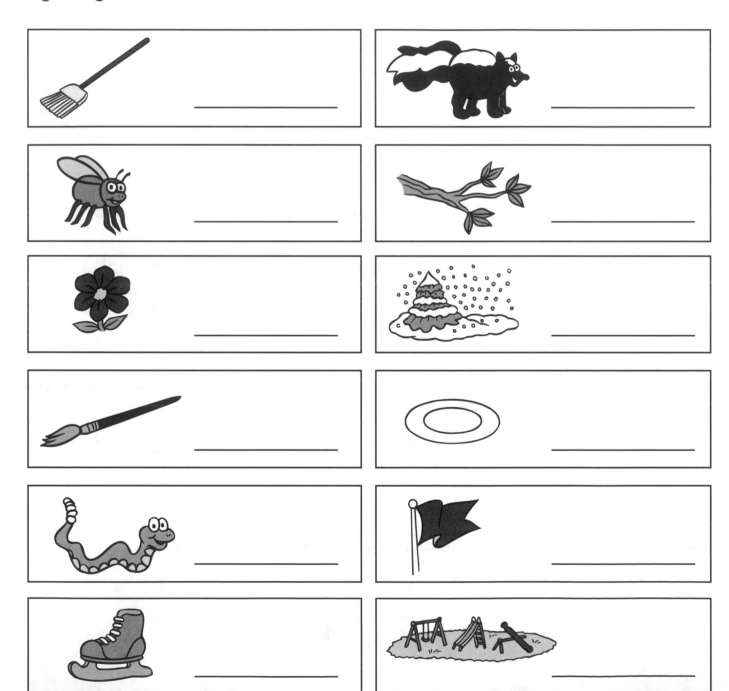

Blends: *bl, sl, cr, cl*

Directions: Look at the pictures and say their names. Write the letters for the beginning sound in each word.

____own

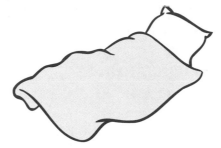

____anket

____ayon

____ock

____ide

____oud

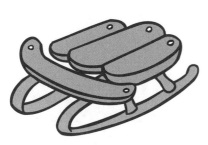

____ed

____ab

____ocodile

NAME _____

Consonant Blends

Directions: Write a word from the word box to answer each riddle.

clock sleep	glass gloves	blow clap	climb blocks	slipper flashlight

1. You need me when the lights go out.
What am I?

_____

2. People use me to tell the time.
What am I?

_____

3. You put me on your hands in the winter
to keep them warm. **What am I?**

_____

4. Cinderella lost one like me at midnight.
What am I?

_____

5. This is what you do with your hands when
you are pleased. **What is it?**

_____

6. You can do this with a whistle or with
bubble gum. **What is it?**

_____

7. These are what you might use to build a
castle when you are playing.
What are they?

_____

8. You do this to get to the top of a hill.
What is it?

_____

9. This is what you use to drink water or milk.
What is it?

_____

10. You do this at night with your eyes closed.
What is it?

_____

NAME _____

Nothing but Net

Directions: Write the missing consonant blends

| scr | mp | dr | lp | nk | ss | st | sk | nd | gr | sn | nt | fr | sl |

1. "My ___ ___ eakers he ___ ___ me run very fa ___ ___ !" exclaimed Jim Shooz.

2. "I really like to ___ ___ ibble the ball," announced Dub L. Dribble.

3. Team captain ___ ___ y-High Hook can easily ___ ___ am du ___ ___ the basketball into the net.

4. Will Kenny Dooit make an extra poi ___ ___ with his ___ ___ ee throw?

5. Harry Leggs can ju ___ ___ at lea ___ ___ 4 feet off the ___ ___ ound.

6. Wow! Willie Makeit finally caught the ball on the rebou ___ ___ !

7. "Watch me pa ___ ___ the ball!" yelled Holden Firm.

8. He ju ___ ___   ___ ___ opped the ball, and now they all will

    ___ ___ ___ amble to get it.

9. "I cannot tell which team will win at the e ___ ___ of the game," decided Ed G. Nerves.

10. "You silly boy! Of course, the team with the mo ___ ___

    poi ___ ___ s will win!" explained Kay G. Fann.

NAME _____

Consonant Digraph *th*

Some consonants work together to stand for a new sound. They are called **consonant digraphs**. Listen for the sound of consonant digraph **th** in **think**.

think

Directions: Print **th** under the pictures whose names begin with the sound of **th**. Color the **th** pictures.

_____

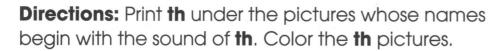

_____

_____

_____

_____

_____

_____

_____

Think About *th*

Directions: Say the name of each picture. Fill in the missing letter or letters.

_ _ ink   _ _ orn   _ _ orn

10 _ _ en   _ _ umb   30 _ _ irty

Directions: Find and circle these **th** words in the puzzle. The words may go **across** or **down**.

think	thorn	thumb	thirty

```
T  T  H  I  R  T  Y
T  H  I  N  K  H  J
H  O  B  H  N  U  L
O  R  N  E  H  M  X
J  N  H  R  T  B  Y
```

NAME _____

Consonant Digraph *sh*

Listen for the sound of consonant digraph **sh** in **sheep**.

Directions: Color the pictures whose names begin with the sound of **sh**.

sheep

Change a Word

Directions: Make a new word by changing the beginning sound to **sh**. Write the new word on the line.

made - m
+ sh = shade

zip	sell	beep
tin	line	lift
red	cape	cave
top	bake	feet

NAME _____

Consonant Digraph *wh*

Directions: Write **wh**, **th**, or **sh** to complete each word.

 _ _ eel

 _ _ ale

 _ _ eep

 _ _ ink

 _ _ eat

 _ _ orn

 _ _ ip

30 _ _ irty

 _ _ ite

Wheel of Fortune

Listen for the sound of consonant digraph **wh** in **whale**.

whale

Directions: Color the pictures whose names begin with consonant digraph **wh**.

NAME _____

Consonant Digraph *ch*

Listen for the sound of consonant digraph **ch** in **cherry**.

cherry

Directions: Trace the cherry if the name of the picture begins with the **ch** sound. Use a red crayon.

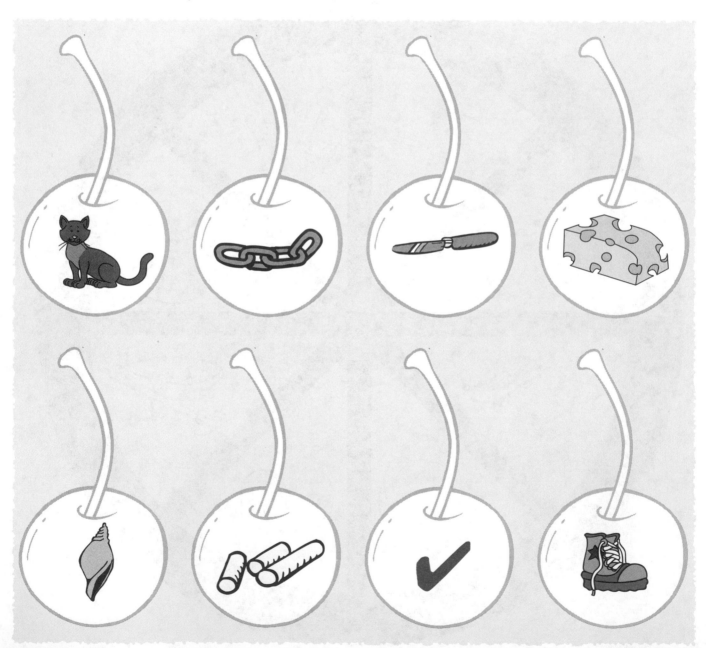

NAME _____

Read and Write Digraphs

Directions: Write a word from the box to label each picture.

chest	check	sheep
chimp	cherry	thirty
chain	cheese	wheel

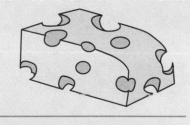

NAME _____

Consonant Digraph *kn*

Listen for the sound of consonant digraph **kn** in **knot**.
The **k** is silent.

knot

Directions: Color the pictures whose names begin with the **kn** sound.
Connect all the colored pictures from the knight to his horse.

Knocking Around in Knickers

A long time ago, golfers wore knickers when they played. **Knickers** are short, loose trousers gathered just below the knee. **Kn** at the beginning of a word makes the same sound as **n**.

Directions: Look at each picture and write **kn** or **k** at the beginning to complete the words.

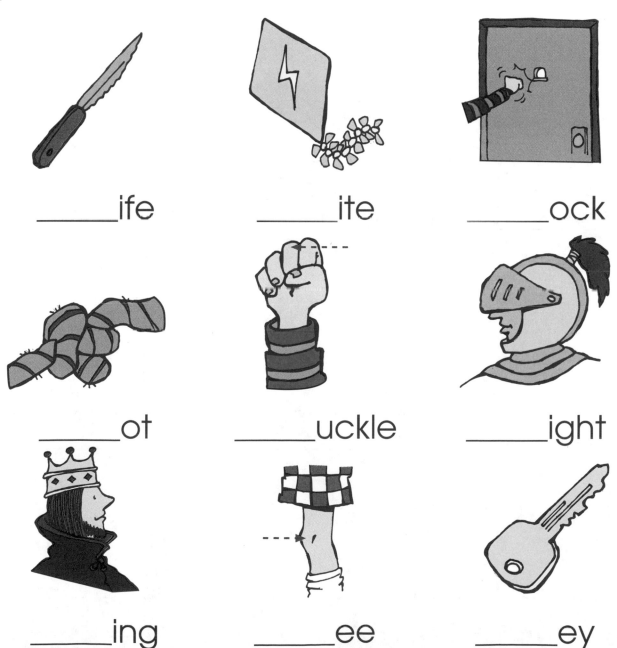

_____ife   _____ite   _____ock

_____ot   _____uckle   _____ight

_____ing   _____ee   _____ey

NAME _____

Consonant Digraph wr

Listen for the sound of consonant digraph **wr** in **wren**. The **w** is silent.

wren

Directions: Write a word from the box to label each picture.
Color the pictures whose names begin with **wr**.

web	wrist	wring	wrap	
worm	write	wreath	wink	wrench

Ending Digraphs

Some words end with consonant digraphs. Listen for the ending digraphs in **duck**, **moth**, **dish**, and **branch**.

du**ck**   mo**th**    di**sh**    bran**ch**

Directions: Say the name of each picture. Circle the letters that stand for the ending sound.

ck
th
sh
ch

ck
th
sh
wh

ck
th
sh
ch

ck
th
sh
ch

ck
th
sh
ch

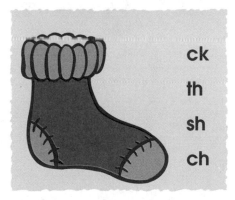
ck
th
sh
ch

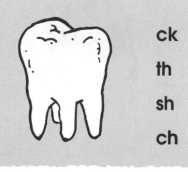
ck
th
sh
ch

ck
th
sh
ch

ck
th
sh
ch

NAME _____

Hear and Write Digraphs

Directions: The name of each picture below ends with **ck**, **th**, **sh**, or **ch**. Write each word on the lines below.

_____

- - - - - - - - -

_____

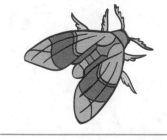

_____

- - - - - - - - -

_____

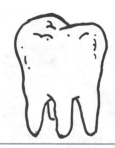

_____

- - - - - - - - -

_____

NAME _____

Missing Digraphs

Directions: Fill in the circle beside the missing digraph in each word.

___ale	pea___	___ife
○ wh ○ wr ○ ch	○ ck ○ th ○ ch	○ kn ○ ch ○ wr
___imp	___ell	clo___
○ ck ○ kn ○ ch	○ ch ○ sh ○ ck	○ ck ○ ch ○ kn
___ite	fi___	___orn
○ kn ○ wr ○ th	○ ch ○ sh ○ th	○ th ○ wr ○ ch

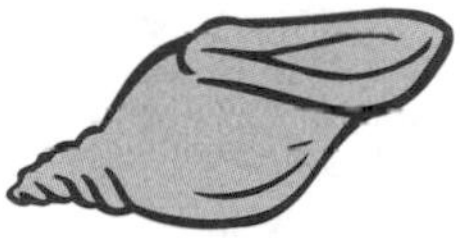

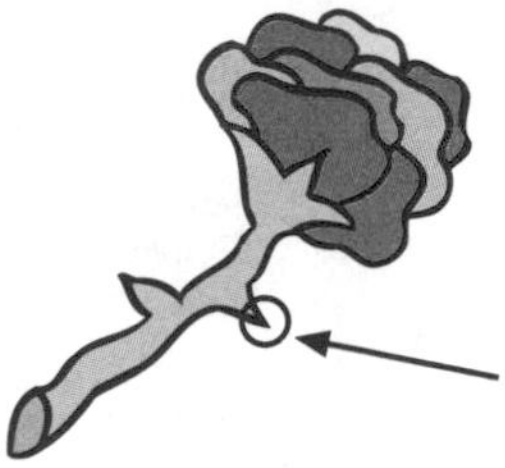

NAME _____

At the Pool

Directions: Write the correct letters from the word box to complete the word for each picture.

Word Box

wh

bl

sw

cl

st

ch

_____istle

_____ipboard

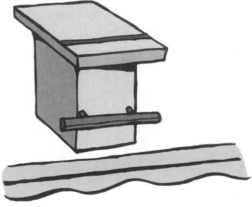

starting _____ock

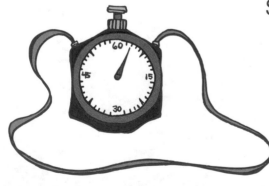

_____opwat_____

_____im cap

Silent Letters

Some words have letters you cannot hear at all, such as the **gh** in **night**, the **w** in **wrong**, the **l** in **walk**, the **k** in **knee**, the **b** in **climb**, and the **t** in **listen**.

Directions: Look at the words in the word box. Write the word under its picture. Underline the silent letters.

knife	light	calf	wrench	lamb	eight
wrist	whistle	comb	thumb	knob	knee

_____ _____ _____ _____

_____ _____ _____ _____

_____ _____ _____ _____

NAME _____

A Flying Saucer?

A **discus** is a flat circle made mostly of wood with a metal center and edge that looks a bit like a plate. A men's discus is about 9 inches across and weighs a little over 4 pounds. A women's discus is about 2 inches smaller and about 2 pounds lighter. The men's world record throw is 243 feet, but the women's world record is even greater—252 feet!

Directions: Read the word in each discus. Write its silent consonant in the center.

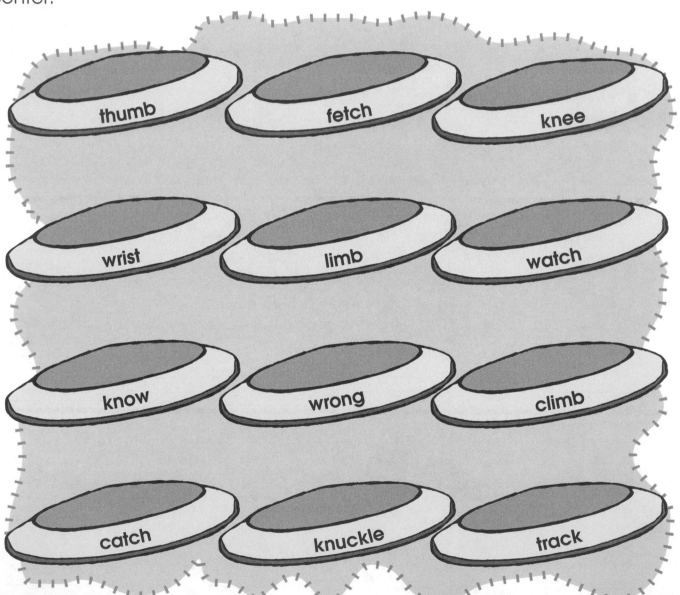

thumb   fetch   knee

wrist   limb   watch

know   wrong   climb

catch   knuckle   track

Hard and Soft *c* and *g*

Directions: Circle as many words in each word search as you can find. List them in the correct column. **Hint:** The words going up and down have the hard sound, and the words going across and backwards have the soft sound.

g

Hard ⬇

_____

_____

_____

_____

_____

```
t  s  g  e  m  n  r
e  l  t  n  e  g  p
g  n  s  g  e  r  m
i  t  o  a  h  o  f
r  i  h  p  r  a  o
l  e  g  i  a  n  t
```

Soft ➡

_____

_____

_____

_____

_____

Two words in the **c** word search go diagonally. They have both a hard and a soft **c** sound.

c

Hard ⬇

_____

_____

_____

_____

_____

```
c  e  n  t  e  r  c
a  i  c  r  a  i  a
s  x  r  a  r  g  r
t  n  e  c  l  f  p
p  y  u  a  l  n  e
a  s  r  n  s  e  t
c  i  t  y  o  m  u
```

Soft ➡

_____

_____

_____

_____

Both Hard and Soft

_____   _____

NAME _____

Sounds of *c* and *g*

Consonants **c** and **g** each have two sounds. Listen for the soft **c** sound in **pencil**. Listen for the hard **c** sound in **cup**.

Listen for the soft **g** sound in **giant**. Listen for the hard **g** sound in **goat**. **C** and **g** usually have the soft sound when they are followed by **e**, **i**, or **y**.

Directions: Say the name of each picture. Listen for the sound of **c** or **g**. Then, read the words in each list. Circle the words that have that sound of **c** or **g**.

Hard c	cup

car	race
city	rice
cone	can

Soft c	pencil

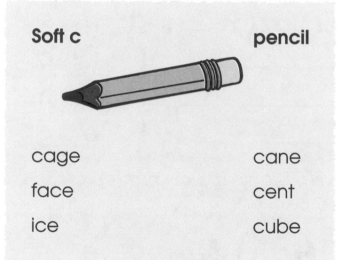

cage	cane
face	cent
ice	cube

Hard g	goat

good	magic
dragon	gum
stage	gentle

Soft g	giant

garden	gem
page	giraffe
gas	gorilla

NAME _____

Hard and Soft *c* and *g*

Directions: Underline the letter that follows the **c** or **g** in each word. Write **hard** if the word has the hard **c** or hard **g** sound. Write **soft** if the word has the soft **c** or soft **g** sound.

car

pencil

giant

gum

wagon

gym

gem

cymbals

cup

cot

celery

goat

NAME _____

Kick It In!

Directions: Write a vowel to complete each word below.

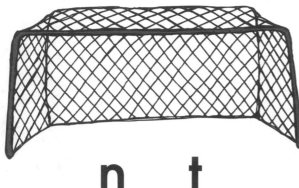

n___t

p___ss

s___cks

r___n

k___ck

NAME _____

Short a Picture Match

Directions: Cut out the cards. Read the words. Match the words and the pictures.

hat	van	bat	ham
bag	man	map	fan

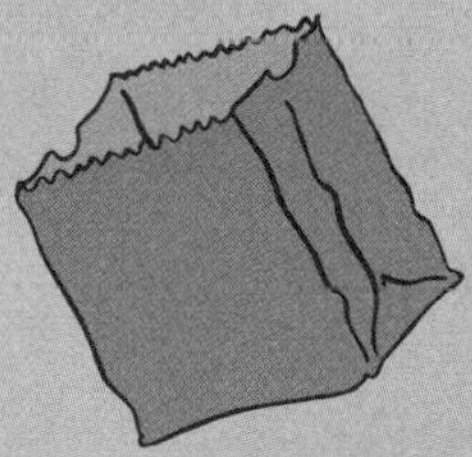

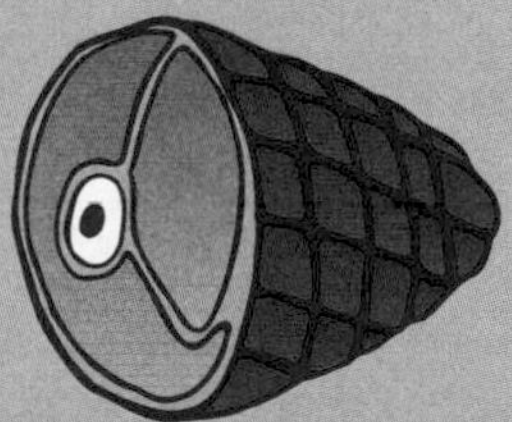

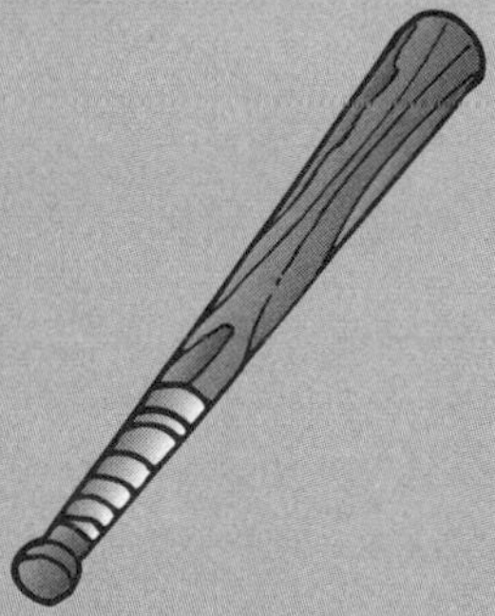

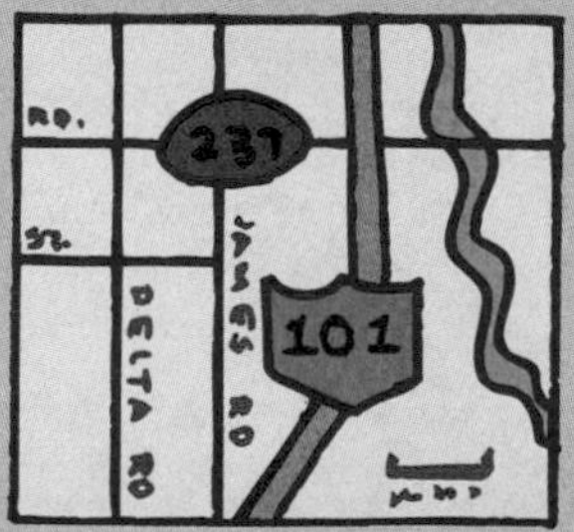

Page is blank for cutting exercise
on previous page.

The Donkey's Tail

Directions: Find the donkey tails with pictures whose names have the short **i** sound. Cut them out. Glue those tails onto the donkeys.

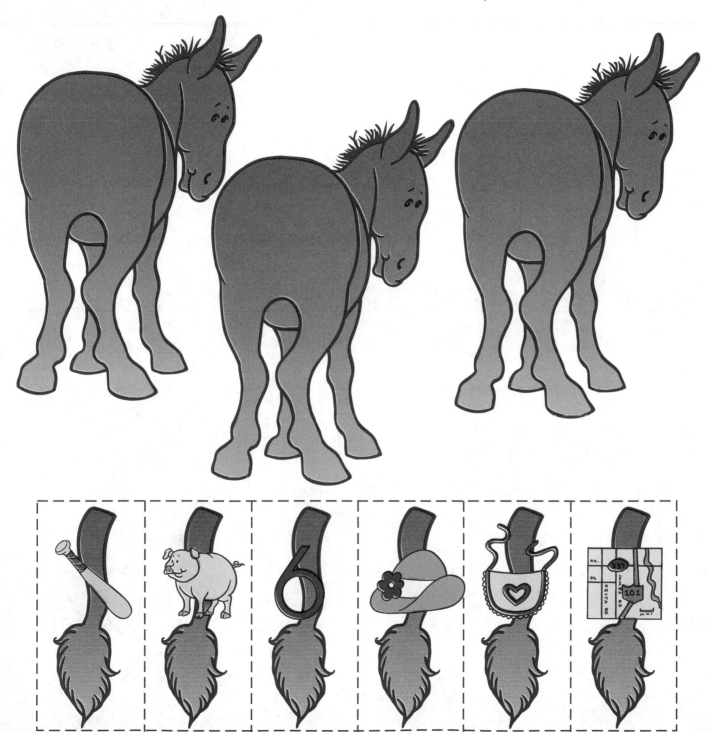

Page is blank for cutting exercise
on previous page.

NAME _____

Feed the Pup

Directions: Cut out the picture cards. Say the name of each picture. If the name has the sound of short **u**, glue the card in the pup's bowl.

**Page is blank for cutting exercise
on previous page.**

NAME _____

Short *o* Puzzles

Directions: Cut out the puzzle pieces. Match each picture with its name.

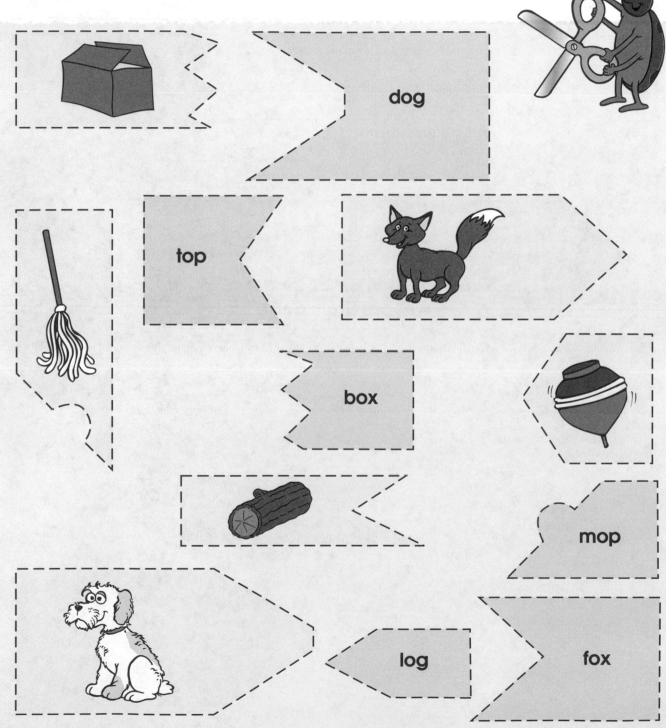

Page is blank for cutting exercise on previous page.

Super Silent e

Long vowel sounds have the same sound as their names. When a **Super Silent e** appears at the end of a word, you cannot hear it, but it makes the other vowel have a long sound. For example: **tub** has a **short** vowel sound, and **tube** has a **long** vowel sound.

Directions: Look at the following pictures. Decide if the word has a short or long vowel sound. Circle the correct word. Watch for the **Super Silent e**!

	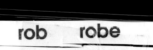		
can cane	tub tube	rob robe	rat rate

pin   pine   cap   cape   not   note   pan pane

slid   slide   dim   dime   tap   tape   cub   cube

NAME _____

Long Vowels

Long vowel sounds have the same sound as their names. When a **Super Silent e** comes at the end of a word, you cannot hear it, but it changes the short vowel sound to a long vowel sound.

Examples: rope, skate, line, cute

Directions: Say the name of the pictures. Listen for the long vowel sounds. Write the missing long vowel sound under each picture.

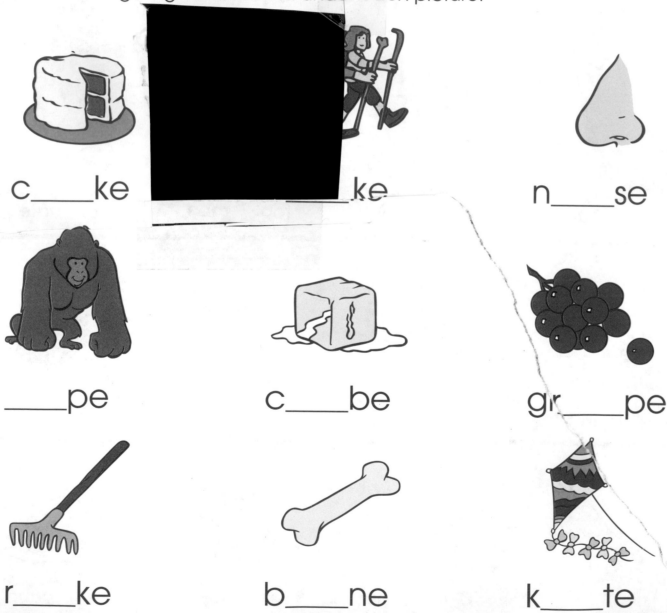

c____ke

____ke

n____se

____pe

c____be

gr____pe

r____ke

b____ne

k____te

Review

Directions: Read the words in each box. Cross out the word that does **not** belong.

long vowels	short vowels
cube	man
cup	pet
rake	fix
me	ice

long vowels	short vowels
soap	cat
seed	pin
read	rain
mat	frog

Directions: Write **short** or **long** to label the words in each box.

_____ vowels	_____ vowels
hose	frog
take	hot
bead	sled
cube	lap
eat	block
see	sit

NAME _____

Tricky *ar*

When **r** follows a vowel, it changes the vowel's sound. Listen for the **ar** sound in **star**.

Directions: Color the pictures whose names have the **ar** sound.

st**ar**

 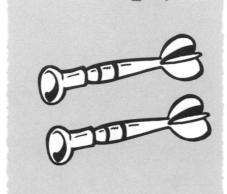 

 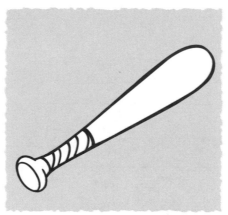 

NAME _____

Write **ar** or **or**

Listen for the **or** sound in **horn**.

h**or**n

Directions: Write **ar** or **or** to complete each word.

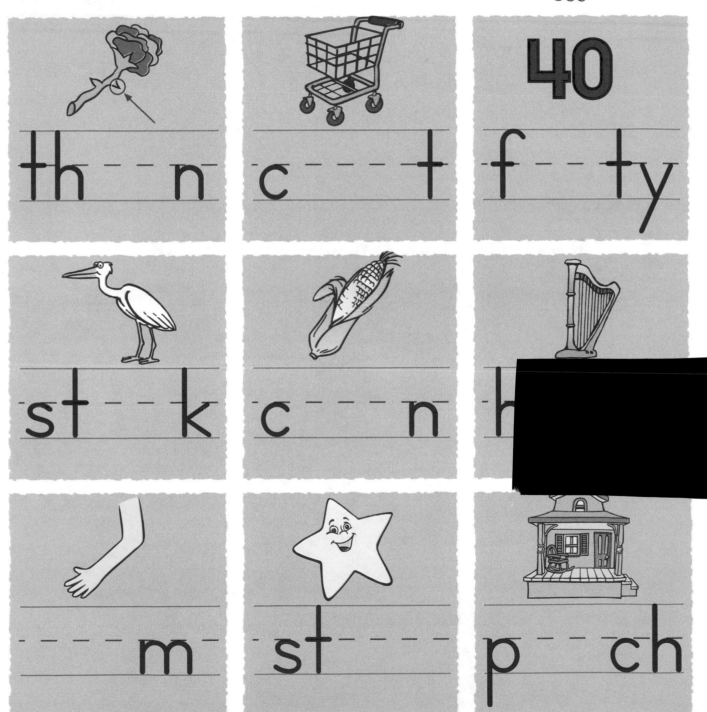

th __ n

c __ t

f __ ty

st __ k

c __ n

h __

__ m

st __

p __ ch

NAME _____

Mix and Match

The letters **ur**, **er**, and **ir** all have the same sound. Listen for the vowel sound in **surf**, **fern**, and **girl**.

s**ur**f    f**er**n    g**ir**l

Directions: Draw a line from each word in the circle to the picture it names.

herd

turkey

clerk

thirty

purse

bird

Write *ur*, *er*, and *ir*

Directions: Find a word from the box to name each picture. Write it on the line below the picture.

| turkey | clerk | dirt | fern | |
| girl | herd | purple | surf | thirty |

_____
- - - - - - - -
_____

_____
- - - - - - - -
_____

_____
- - - - - - - -
_____

_____
- - - - - - - -
_____

_____
- - - - - - - -
_____

_____
- - - - - - - -
_____

_____
- - - - - - - -
_____

_____
- - - - - - - -
_____

_____
- - - - - - - -
_____

NAME _____

Vowel Pairs *ai* and *ay*

You know that the letters **a__e** usually stand for the long **a** sound. The vowel pairs **ai** and **ay** can stand for the long **a** sound, too. Listen for the long **a** sound in **train** and **hay**.

Directions: Say the name of each picture below. Look at the vowel pair that stands for the long **a** sound. Under each picture, write the words from the box that have the same long **a** vowel pair.

cage	chain	gate	gray
mail	pay	snail	skate
play	snake	stay	tail

c**a**ke   tr**ai**n    h**ay**

NAME _____

Vowel Pairs *oa* and *ow*

You know that the letters **o__e** and **oe** usually stand for the long **o** sound. The vowel pairs **oa** and **ow** can stand for the long **o** sound, too. Listen for the long **o** sound in **road** and **snow**.

Directions: Find and circle eight long **o** words. The words may go **across** or **down**. Beside each picture, write the words that use the same long **o** vowel pair.

```
Z  L  I  A  C  R
B  O  C  R  O  W
S  W  R  J  A  G
O  G  O  A  L  R
A  L  A  G  X  O
P  Y  K  N  O  W
```

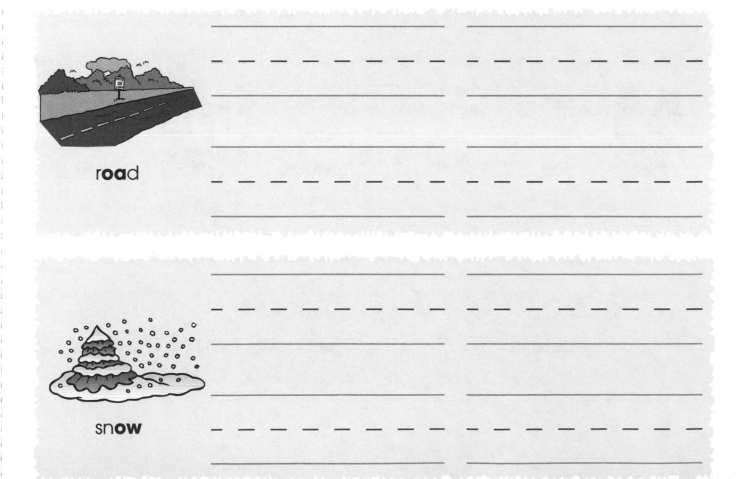

r**oa**d

sn**ow**

NAME _____

Vowel Pair *ui*

You know that the letters **u__e** and **ue** usually stand for the long **u** sound. The vowel pair **ui** can stand for the long **u** sound, too. Listen for the long **u** sound in **cruise**.

Directions: Circle the name of the picture. Then, write the name on the line.

cr**ui**se

mall
male
mule

_____

sun
Sue
say

_____

fruit
flat
frame

_____

sun
sit
suit

_____

cubes
cubs
caves

_____

Jake
juice
just

_____

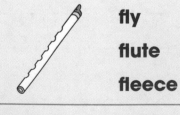

fly
flute
fleece

_____

globe
gull
glue

_____

blue
black
ball

_____

Vowel Pair *ie*

You know that the letters **i__e** usually stand for the long **i** sound. The vowel pair **ie** can stand for the long **i** sound, too. Listen for the long **i** sound in **butterflies**.

Directions: Write **i__e** or **ie** to complete each word. Draw a picture for one **i__e** word and one **ie** word.

butterfl**ie**s

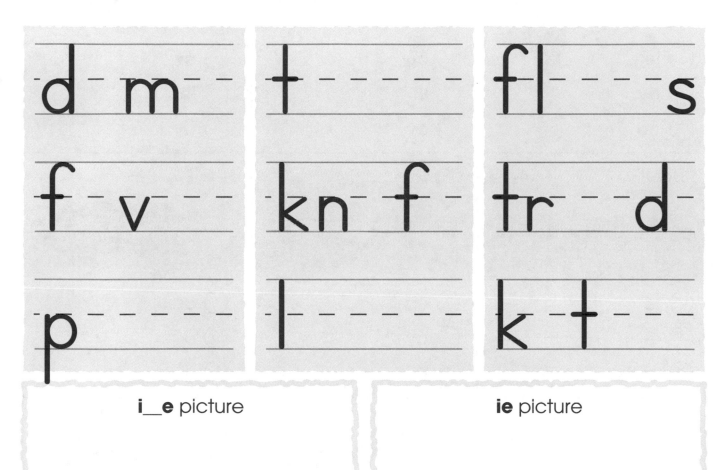

i__e picture

ie picture

NAME _____

Missing Vowel Pairs

Directions: Fill in the circle beside the missing vowel pair in each word.

t___	tr___	sn___
○ ie	○ ow	○ ow
○ ay	○ ui	○ ie
○ oa	○ ay	○ ay

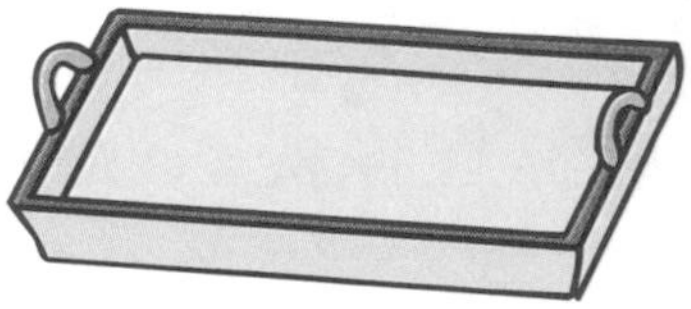

ch___n	gr___	r___d
○ ie	○ oa	○ oa
○ ui	○ ay	○ ay
○ ai	○ ie	○ ui

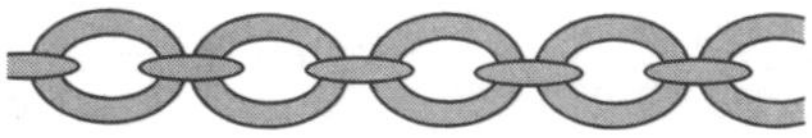

b___	fl___s	s___t
○ ai	○ ai	○ ui
○ ow	○ oa	○ ay
○ ui	○ ie	○ ie

NAME _____

Vowel Pair *ea*

Some vowel pairs can stand for more than one sound. The vowel pair **ea** has the sound of long **e** in **team** and short **e** in **head**.

t**ea**m    h**ea**d

Directions: Say the name of each picture. Listen for the sound that **ea** stands for. Circle **Long e** or **Short e**. Then, color the pictures whose names have the short **e** sound.

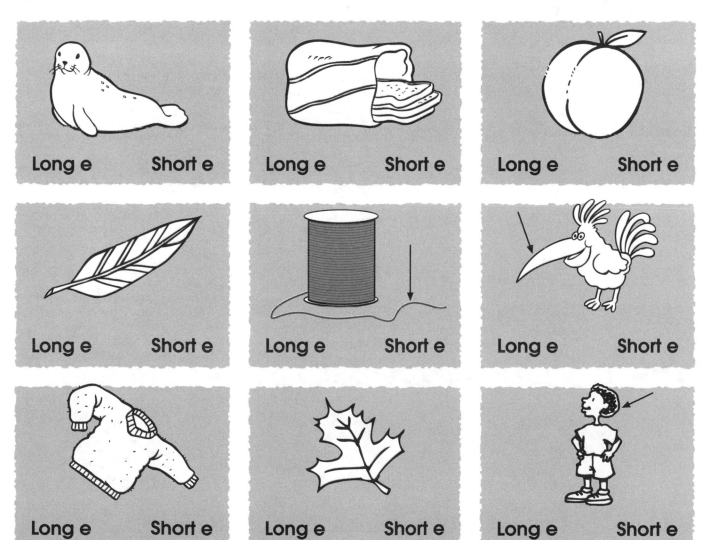

Long e Short e	Long e Short e	Long e Short e
Long e Short e	Long e Short e	Long e Short e
Long e Short e	Long e Short e	Long e Short e

NAME

Vowel Pair *oo*

Listen for the difference between the sound of the vowel pair **oo** in **moon** and its sound in **book**.

m**oo**n b**oo**k

Directions: Say the name of the picture. Circle the picture of the moon or the book to show the sound of vowel pair **oo**.

Y as a Vowel

Y as a vowel can make two sounds. **Y** can make the long sound of **e** or the long sound of **i**.

Directions: Color the spaces:
purple – **y** sounds like **i**.
yellow – **y** sounds like **e**.

What is the picture? _____

jelly fuzzy funny
kitty sky cry
try sleepy many
fry
my by penny
lazy candy
happy
baby
fly sunny
lucky sly rocky
windy shy

NAME _____

A Fork in the Road

Directions: Write the words below on the correct "road."

sky	jelly	try	kitty	fly	my
fry	cry	funny	dry	penny	
candy	by	sleepy	happy	lazy	baby
sly	fuzzy	shy	many	why	

_____   _____

_____   _____

_____   _____

_____   _____

_____   _____

_____   _____

_____   _____

_____   _____

_____   _____

Y sounds like **long e**.   **Y** sounds like **long i**.

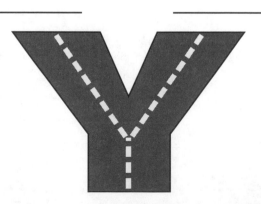

Short and Long *a e i o u*

Directions: Color the correct pictures in each box.

˘ means short vowel sound   ¯ means long vowel sound

ă **blue** ā **orange**	
ĕ **red** ē **yellow**	
ĭ **green** ī **purple**	
ŏ **yellow** ō **blue**	
ŭ **green** ū **orange**	

NAME _____

Review

Directions: Read the story. Fill in the blanks with words from the word box.

cookies	Joe	bowl	tooth	flour	eight
spoon	eats	enjoys	round	boy	either

Do you like to cook? I know a _____ named

_____ who loves to cook. When Joe has a sweet

_____, he makes _____. He puts

_____ and sugar in a _____ and

stirs it with a _____. Then, he adds the butter and eggs.

He makes cookies that are _____ or other shapes. He

likes them _____ way. Now is the part he

_____ the most: Joe _____ the cookies.

He might eat seven or _____ at a time!

NAME _____

Compound Your Effort

A **compound word** is made from two shorter words. An example of a compound word is **sandbox**, made from **sand** and **box**.

Directions: Find one word in the word box that goes with each of the words below to make a compound word. Write the compound words on the lines. Cross out each word that you use.

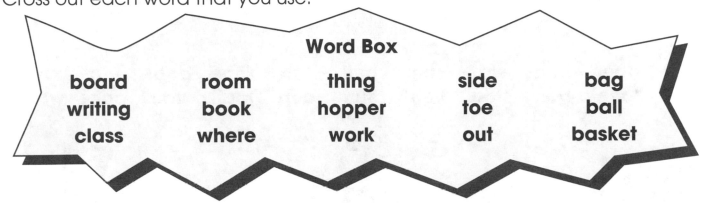

Word Box

board	room	thing	side	bag
writing	book	hopper	toe	ball
class	where	work	out	basket

1. coat _____

2. snow _____

3. home _____

4. waste _____

5. tip _____

6. chalk _____

7. note _____

8. grass _____

9. school _____

10. with _____

Look at the words in the word box that you did **not** use. Use those words to make your own compound words.

1. _____

2. _____

3. _____

4. _____

5. _____

NAME _____

Word Magic

Maggie Magician announced, "One plus one equals one!" The audience giggled. So, Maggie put two words into a hat and waved her magic wand. When she reached into the hat, Maggie pulled out one word and a picture. "See," said Maggie, "I was right!"

Directions: Use the word box to help you write a compound word for each picture below.

ball	door	rain	star	shirt	bell	fish	shoe	book	foot	basket
bow	lace	box	stool	light	sun	cup	mail	tail	cake	worm

_____   _____   _____

_____   _____   _____

_____   _____

Mixing a Compound

sometimes   downtown   girlfriend
everybody   maybe   myself   lunchbox
baseball   outside   today

Directions: Write the correct compound word on the line. Then, use the numbered letters to solve the code.

1. Opposite of inside   __ __ __ __ __ __ __
                  1

2. Another word for me   __ __ __ __ __ __
                2   3

3. A girl who is a friend   __ __ __ __ __ __ __ __ __ __
          4   5

4. Not yesterday or tomorrow, but . . .   __ __ __ __ __
                6

5. All of the people   __ __ __ __ __ __ __ __ __
            7   8

6. A sport   __ __ __ __ __ __ __ __
                      9

7. The main part of a town   __ __ __ __ __ __ __ __
          10   11

8. Not always, just . . .   __ __ __ __ __ __ __ __ __
     12   13

9. A box for carrying your lunch   __ __ __ __ __ __ __ __
             14

10. Perhaps or might   __ __ __ __ __
                15

__ __ __ __ __ __ __ __ __ ! __ __ __
10 8 11 6 15 7 3 1 9   2 8 1

__ __ __ __ __ __ __ __
3 8 1 11 6   13 14 15

__ __ __ __ __ __ __ __ __ __ __ __ !
7 5 4 14 13   12 8 9 1 13 5 8 11

NAME _____

Prefix *re*

A **prefix** is a word part. It is added to the beginning of a base word to change the base word's meaning. The prefix **re** means "again."

Example:    **Refill** means "to fill again."

Directions: Look at the pictures. Read the base words. Add the prefix re to the base word to show that the action is being done again. Write your new word on the line.

read

paint

build

write

use

pay

NAME _____

Prefixes *un* and *dis*

The prefixes **un** and **dis** mean "not" or "the opposite of."

Unlocked means "not locked."

Dismount is the opposite of "mount."

Directions: Look at the pictures. Circle the word that tells about the picture. Then, write the word on the line.

 tied

untied

_____

- - - - - - - - - - - - - - - -

_____

 like

dislike

_____

- - - - - - - - - - - - - - - -

_____

 happy

unhappy

_____

- - - - - - - - - - - - - - - -

_____

 obey

disobey

_____

- - - - - - - - - - - - - - - -

_____

 safe

unsafe

_____

- - - - - - - - - - - - - - - -

_____

 honest

dishonest

_____

- - - - - - - - - - - - - - - -

_____

NAME _____

Suffixes *ful, less, ness, ly*

A **suffix** is a word part that is added at the end of a base word to change the base word's meaning. Look at the suffixes below.

The suffix **ful** means "full of." **Cheerful** means "full of cheer."

The suffix **less** means "without." **Cloudless** means "without clouds."

The suffix **ness** means "a state of being." **Darkness** means "being dark."

The suffix **ly** means "in this way." **Slowly** means "in a slow way."

Directions: Add the suffixes to the base words to make new words.

care + ful = _____

pain + less = _____

brave + ly = _____

sad + ly = _____

sick + ness = _____

Suffixes and Meanings

Remember: The suffix **ful** means "full of."

The suffix **less** means "without."

The suffix **ness** means "a state of being."

The suffix **ly** means "in this way."

The sun shines **brightly**.

Directions: Write the word that matches the meaning.

without pain

_____

— — — — — — — —

_____

in a quick way

_____

— — — — — — — —

_____

in a neat way

_____

— — — — — — — —

_____

without fear

_____

— — — — — — — —

_____

full of grace

_____

— — — — — — — —

_____

the state of being soft

_____

— — — — — — — —

_____

the state of being sick

_____

— — — — — — — —

_____

in a glad way

_____

— — — — — — — —

_____

NAME _____

Suffixes *er* and *est*

Suffixes **er** and **est** can be used to compare. Use **er** when you compare two things. Use **est** when you compare more than two things.

Example: The puppy is small**er** than its mom.
This puppy is the small**est** puppy in the litter.

Directions: Add the suffixes to the base words to make words that compare.

Base Word	+ er	+ est
1. loud	louder	loudest
2. old		
3. neat		
4. fast		
5. kind		
6. tall		

NAME _____

Scale the Synonym Slope

Synonyms are words that have almost the same meaning. **Tired** and **sleepy** are synonyms. **Talk** and **speak** are synonyms.

Directions: Read the word. Find its synonym on the hill. Write the synonym on the line.

1. glad _____

2. little _____

3. begin _____

4. above _____

5. damp _____

6. large _____

wet

big

happy

over

small

start

NAME _____

Synonym Match

Directions: Look at the pictures. Read the words in the box. Write two synonyms you could use to tell about each picture.

| rocks | start | road | begin | street | stones | sad | unhappy |

Almost the Same!

Directions: Write a word that has almost the same meaning as the **boldfaced** word. Use the word list for clues.

Hey, you're *large*!

And you're *big*!

Word List		
itchy	fortress	phantom
instructor	job	difficult

10.4 x 1.2=

1. My **teacher** is very smart! _____

2. I don't like that sweater. It is too **scratchy**. _____

3. My teacher gave a very **hard** test in math. _____

4. The prince lived in a **castle**. _____

5. Everyone has a **task** to do in my house. _____

6. The **ghost** at the fun house was so scary! _____

NAME _____

We Go Together!

Directions: Circle the two words in each line that have almost the same meaning.

1. gooey   sticky   hard

2. slow   hurry   rush

3. slope   hill   sled

4. stop   red   end

5. treat   pledge   promise

6. piece   bit   pie

7. excuse   easy   simple

8. complete   whole   pile

Amazing Antonyms

Antonyms are words that have opposite meanings. **Old** and **new** are antonyms. **Laugh** and **cry** are antonyms, too.

Directions: Below each word, write its antonym. Use words from the word box.

down
go
left
sad
dry

stop

_____

- - - - - - - - -

_____

happy

_____

- - - - - - - - -

_____

right

_____

- - - - - - - - -

_____

up

_____

- - - - - - - - -

_____

wet

_____

- - - - - - - - -

_____

NAME

Who's Afraid?

Help Frog and Toad escape from the snake.

Directions: Read the two words in each space. If the words are antonyms, color the space green. Do not color the other spaces.

go
stop

large
small

wide
narrow

dinner
supper

scared
afraid

brave
afraid

shut
close

happy
sad

dark
light

fall
rise

outside
inside

higher
lower

leap
jump

none
all

tremble
shake

fast
quick

happy
glad

look
see

top
bottom

covers
blankets

friend
pal

stones
rocks

down
up

shout
whisper

loud
soft

under
over

Toad's
House

NAME _____

Trading Places

Directions: In each sentence below, circle the incorrect word. Then, rewrite the sentence replacing the circled word with its **antonym** from the word list. The first one has been done for you.

Word List	
happy	tall
full	tie
loud	lock
dangerous	

Swimming in the dark was (safe)

Swimming in the dark was dangerous.

The gorilla's scream sounded very quiet.

_____

The packed room was empty.

_____

My 6-foot brother is very short.

_____

George, the funny clown, makes me very unhappy.

_____

In an unsafe place, you should always unlock the door.

_____

You need to untie your shoes before you run.

_____

NAME _____

Antonym or Synonym?

Directions: Use yellow to color the spaces that have word pairs that are **antonyms**. Use blue to color the spaces that have word pairs that are **synonyms**.

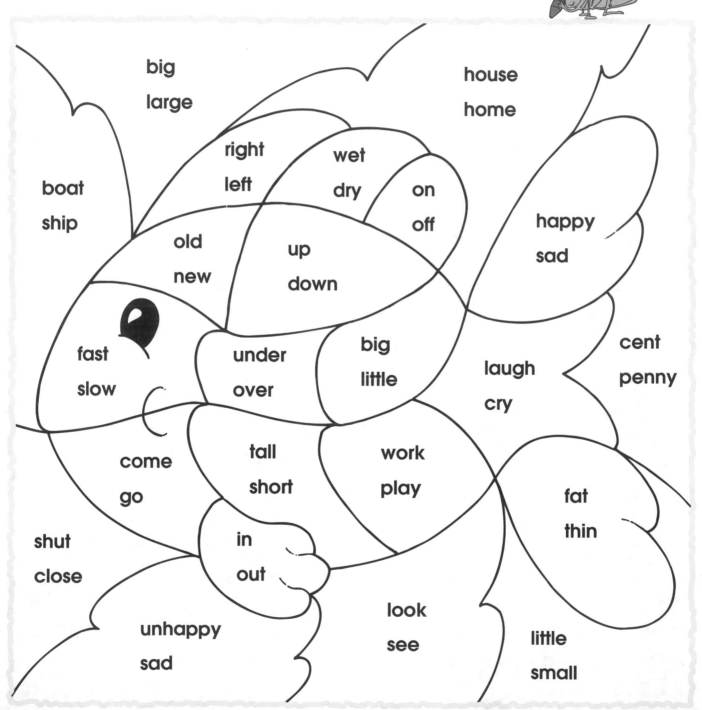

Contractions

A **contraction** is a word made up of two words joined together with one or more letters left out. An **apostrophe** is used in place of the missing letters.

Examples: I am—**I'm**
do not—**don't**
that is—**that's**

Directions: Draw a line to match each contraction to the words from which it was made. The first one is done for you.

1. he's	we are	**6.** they'll	are not
2. we're	cannot	**7.** aren't	they will
3. can't	he is	**8.** I've	you have
4. I'll	she is	**9.** you've	will not
5. she's	I will	**10.** won't	I have

Directions: Write the contraction for each pair of words.

1. you are _____   **5.** she is _____

2. does not _____   **6.** we have _____

3. do not _____   **7.** has not _____

4. would not _____   **8.** did not _____

NAME _____

Something Is Missing!

doesn't	it's	she's	
don't	aren't	who's	he's
didn't	that's	isn't	

Directions: Write the correct contraction for each set of words. Then, circle the letter that was left out when the contraction was made.

1. he is _____

2. are not _____

3. do not _____

4. who is _____

5. is not _____

6. did not _____

7. it is _____

8. she is _____

9. does not _____

10. that is _____

Directions: Write the missing contraction on the line.

1. _____ on her way to school.

2. There _____ enough time to finish the story.

3. Do you think _____ too long?

4. We _____ going to the party.

5. Donna _____ like the movie.

6. _____ going to try for a part in the play?

7. Bob said _____ going to run in the big race.

8. They _____ know how to bake a cake.

9. Tom _____ want to go skating on Saturday.

10. Look, _____ where they found the lost watch.

Tooth Tales!

Directions: Read the following information about your teeth. Then, complete page 266.

Did you know that your teeth are made of enamel? Enamel is the hardest material in your entire body. It makes your teeth strong.

There are four different types of teeth in your mouth. Your front four teeth on the top and front four teeth on the bottom are called *incisors*. Ouch! They are sharp teeth used for biting (for biting food that is, not for biting your brother!).

You have two very pointy teeth on the top and two on the bottom called *canines*. They are used for foods that are hard to chew.

In the very back of your mouth, you have 12 wide teeth called *molars*. They are used for grinding food. (These are worth a lot to the Tooth Fairy!)

Finally, you have eight teeth called *bicuspids* for crushing food.

Adults have 32 permanent teeth! That's a lot of teeth, so keep smiling!

NAME _____

Tooth Tales, cont.

Directions: Answer the questions from the story about your teeth.

What are your teeth made of? _____
Highlight where you found the answer.

What is the hardest material in your body? _____
Highlight where you found the answer.

How many different types of teeth are in your mouth? _____
Highlight where you found the answer.

What are your two very pointy teeth called? _____
Highlight where you found the answer.

What teeth are used for grinding food? _____
(Hint: The Tooth Fairy likes this type of tooth!)
Highlight where you found the answer.

How many teeth do adults have? _____
Highlight where you found the answer.

What teeth are used for biting? _____
Highlight where you found the answer.

How many molars do people have? _____
Highlight where you found the answer.

NAME _____

Clue Caper!

Directions: Read the clues below. Write each child's name under the correct picture. Color the hats using the following clues.

- Anna is tall and wearing a green top hat. There is a red baseball cap on top of her top hat!

- Sara is short and wearing a blue polka dotted hat.

- Talia has long hair and is standing between Anna and Sara. Talia is wearing a pretty ribbon in her hair with a flower on it.

- Kessia is standing next to Sara. She is wearing a white baker's hat with a purple veil!

How many hats do you count on the page? _____

NAME _____

Something's Fruity!

Directions: Find and circle **thirteen** things that are wrong with this picture.

Game Story

Directions: Put the basketball story in order.
Write the numbers **1–5** on the blanks to show
when each event happened.

_____ At the end of the regulation game, the score was tied.

_____ The teams warmed up before the game.

_____ The score at the half was Cougars 25, Lions 22.

_____ Kim made the first basket of the game.

_____ When the overtime ended, the Lions had won the game 50–49.

NAME _____

Story Sequence

Look at picture number 4. What do you think happened before Donna went to the beach? What might happen when she is at the beach?

Directions: You get to decide how the story will go from beginning to end. Write a number in the empty square in each of the other pictures. Choose any number from 1 through 7 (except 4). Number 1 will be what happened first. Number 7 will be what you think happened last.

Same/Different: Shell Homes

Read the story about shells.

Shells are the homes of some animals. Snails live in shells on the land. Clams live in shells in the water. Clam shells open. Snail shells stay closed. Both shells keep the animals safe.

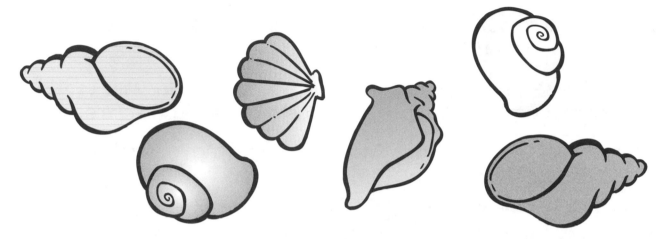

Directions: Answer the questions. For numbers 1 and 2, circle the correct answer.

1. Snails live in shells on the

      water.   land.

2. Clam shells are different from snail shells because

      they open.   they stay closed.

3. Write one way all shells are the same. _____

_____

NAME _____

Same/Different: Venn Diagram

A **Venn diagram** is a diagram that shows how two things are the same and different.

Directions: Choose two outdoor sports. Then, follow the instructions to complete the Venn diagram.

1. Write the first sport name under the first circle. Write some words that describe the sport. Write them in the first circle.

2. Write the second sport name under the second circle. Write some words that describe the sport. Write them in the second circle.

3. Where the 2 circles overlap, write some words that describe both sports.

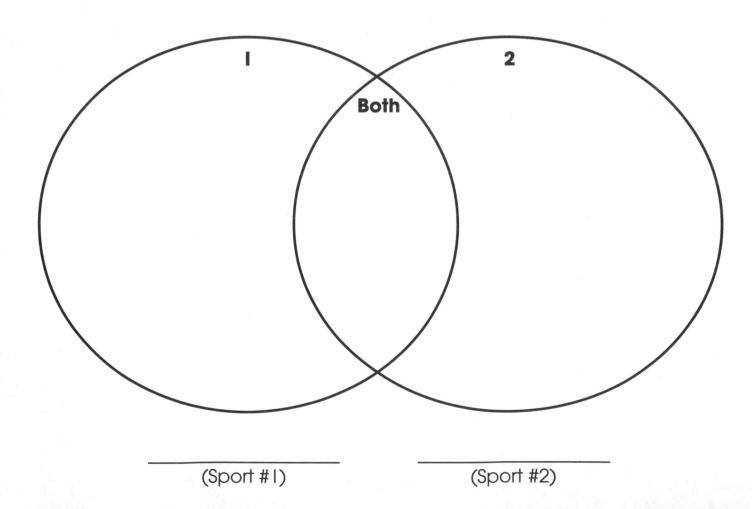

(Sport #1)   (Sport #2)

NAME _____

Same/Different: Dina and Dina

Directions: Read the story. Then, complete the Venn diagram, telling how Dina, the duck, is the same or different than Dina, the girl.

One day in the library, Dina found a story about a duck named Dina!

My name is Dina. I am a duck, and I like to swim. When I am not swimming, I walk on land or fly. I have two feet and two eyes. My feathers keep me warm. Ducks can be different colors. I am gray, brown, and black. I really like being a duck. It is fun.

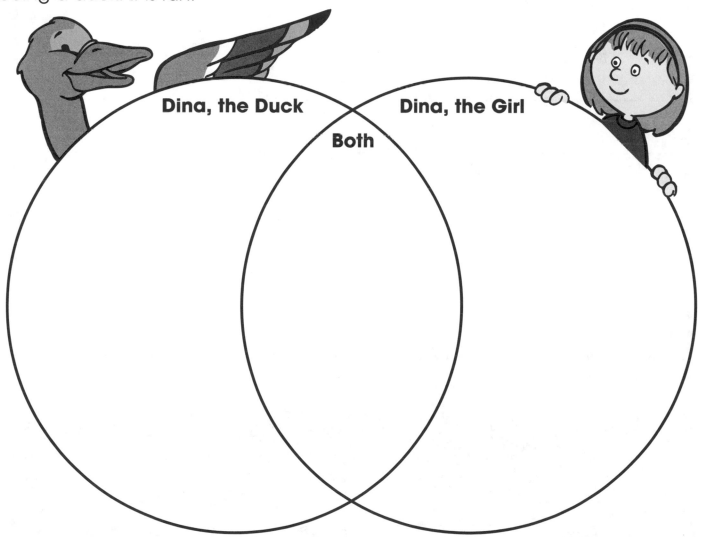

Dina, the Duck   **Both**   **Dina, the Girl**

Running! Jumping! Throwing!

To be a strong athlete in track and field events, you must be good at running, jumping, and throwing. Many track and field words are listed below.

Directions: Write the words under the correct track and field event.

Running	Jumping	Throwing
_____	_____	_____
_____	_____	_____
_____	_____	_____
_____	_____	_____
_____	_____	_____
_____	_____	_____
_____	_____	_____

lap   javelin   high jump   baton   relay   long jump

discus   cross country   broad jump   shot put

track   pole vault   hurdles   triple jump   hammer

NAME _____

Classifying

Sometimes, you want to put things in groups. One way to put things in groups is to sort them by how they are alike. When you put things together that are alike in some way, you classify them.

You can classify the things in your room. In one group, you can put toys and fun things. In the other group, you can put things that you wear.

Directions: Look at the words on the bedroom door. Put the toys and playthings in the toy box. Put the things you wear in the dresser drawers.

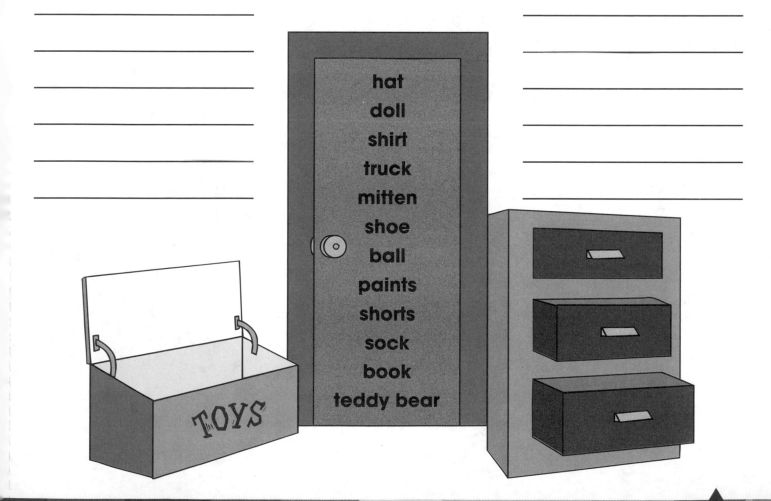

hat
doll
shirt
truck
mitten
shoe
ball
paints
shorts
sock
book
teddy bear

TOYS

NAME _____

Shrews

A shrew (*shroo*) is a small animal. It looks like a mouse with a sharp, pointed nose. This animal is sometimes mistaken for a mouse. It has tiny eyes and ears. Its body is covered with short, dark hair. A shrew moves very fast. A shrew eats all day. The shrew's long, pointed nose can fit into tiny holes to find the insects and worms it eats.

The shrew lives in fields, woodlands, gardens, and marshes. Shrews are harmless to humans. They are helpful in gardens because they eat grubs and other insects. The smallest shrew weighs as little as a penny.

Directions: After reading about the shrew, put an **X** on one word that does **not** belong in each group.

1. small	large	tiny
2. bugs	corn	insects
3. move	run	sleep
4. bird	mouse	dish
5. fast	quick	water
6. sharp	pointed	hair
7. nickel	penny	rain
8. garden	fields	sun

NAME _____

Birds

There are <u>many</u> kinds of birds. The cardinal is a <u>red</u> bird. The cardinal lays <u>three</u> or <u>four</u> eggs. The brown-headed cowbird is <u>black</u> with a <u>brown</u> head. The hummingbird is a very <u>small</u> bird. It lays <u>two</u> eggs. The bald eagle is a <u>large</u> bird. It is brown with a <u>white</u> head. The bald eagle lays from <u>one</u> to <u>four</u> eggs. Bluebirds are <u>blue</u> with <u>orange</u> or light <u>blue</u> breasts. The bluebird lays up to <u>six</u> eggs.

Directions: In the story above, the underlined words are called **adjectives**. Put these describing words in the nests where they belong.

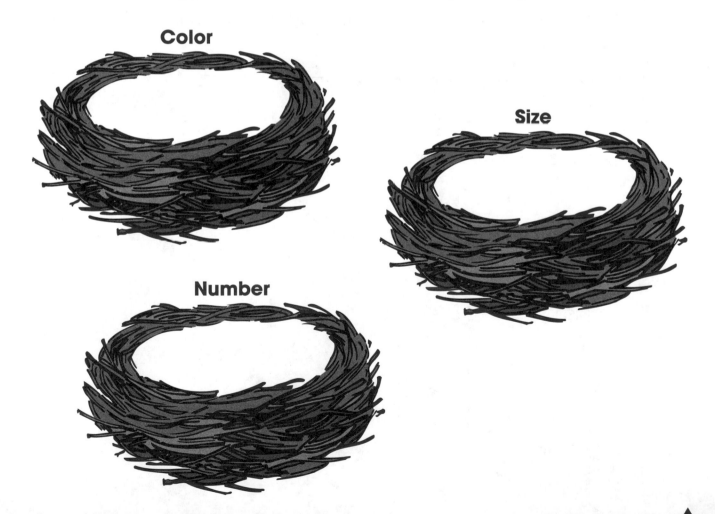

Color

Size

Number

NAME _____

All Animals

There are many kinds of animals. Three kinds of animals are mammals, birds, and reptiles.

Mammals have fur or hair. Baby mammals drink milk from their mothers' bodies. A whale is a mammal.

Birds are the only animals that have feathers. A robin is a bird.

Reptiles have scaly skin. Most reptiles lay eggs on the land. An alligator is a reptile.

Directions: Read the sentences below. Is the animal in the sentence a mammal, bird, or reptile? Put an **M** on the line if it is a mammal, a **B** if it is a bird, or an **R** if it is a reptile.

_____ **1.** Maggie brushes her horse's coat.

_____ **2.** The turtle lays its eggs in the sand.

_____ **3.** Adam cleans the feathers from his pet's cage.

_____ **4.** The baby penguin hides in its father's feathers to stay warm.

_____ **5.** The piglets drink their mother's milk.

_____ **6.** The scaly skin on the snake is dry.

_____ **7.** A blue jay has blue feathers.

_____ **8.** The bunny pulls fur from her body to build a nest.

NAME _____

Winter's Sleepers

Directions: Read about hibernation. Then, complete page 280.

As days grow shorter and it gets colder, some animals get ready for their winter's sleep. This winter's sleep is called hibernation. Scientists do not know all the secrets of hibernating animals. They do know enough to put hibernating animals into two groups. One group is called "true hibernators." The other group is called "light sleepers."

True hibernators go into a very deep sleep. To get ready for this long winter's sleep, true hibernators will eat and eat so they become fat. As these animals sleep, their body temperature drops below normal. If the animal gets too cold, it will shiver to warm itself. The breathing of true hibernators slows so much that they hardly seem to breathe at all.

True hibernators are animals such as woodchucks, some ground squirrels, the

jumping mouse, brown bat, frogs, and snapping turtles.

Light sleepers include skunks, raccoons, the eastern chipmunk, and the grizzly bear.

Some light sleepers will store up food to have during winter while others will eat and become fat. A big difference between light sleepers and true hibernators is that the light sleeper's body temperature drops only a little, and its breathing only slows. These animals are easy to wake and may even get up if the temperature warms. They then go back to sleep when it becomes colder again.

NAME _____

Winter Sleepers, cont.

Directions: Read all of the word groups. Then, place them under the correct hibernation type. Use the story on page 279.

will shiver to warm itself
body temperature drops a little
hardly breathes at all
seems more dead than alive
moves about and then goes back to sleep
breathing only slows
easily awakens
stores up food
body temperature drops far below normal
uses body fat while sleeping

True Hibernator

_____

_____

_____

_____

_____

Light Sleeper

_____

_____

_____

_____

Use the Clues

Context clues can help you figure out words you do not know. Read the words around the new word. Think of a word that makes sense.

Kate swam in a _____?_____.

Did Kate swim in a cake or a lake? The word **swim** is a context clue.

Directions: Kate wrote this letter from camp. Read the letter. Use context clues to write the missing words from the word box. What clues did you use?

| lake | six |
| pancakes | forest |

Dear Mom and Dad,

_____

I woke up at _____ o'clock and got

_____

dressed. My friends and I ate _____ for

_____

breakfast. We went hiking in the _____.

_____

Then, we went swimming in the _____.
Camp is fun!

Love,
Kate

NAME _____

Context Clues in Action

Directions: Read the story. Use context clues to figure out the meanings of the **boldfaced** words. Draw a line from the word to its meaning. The first one is done for you.

Jack has a plan. He wants to take his parents out to lunch to show that he **appreciates** all the nice things they do for him. His sister Jessica will go, too, so she won't feel left out. Jack is **thrifty**. He saves the **allowance** he earns for doing **chores** around the house. So far, Jack has saved 25 dollars. He needs only five dollars more. He is excited about paying the check himself. He will feel like an **adult**.

appreciates	jobs
allowance	grown-up
chores	is grateful for
thrifty	money earned for work
adult	careful about spending money

Cathy Uses Context Clues

When you read, it is important to know about context clues. **Context clues** can help you figure out the meaning of a word, or a missing word, just by looking at the **other words** in the sentence.

Directions: Read each sentence below. Circle the context clues, or other words in the sentence that give you hints.

Write the answer that fits in each blank. The first one is done for you.

1. The (joke) was so _____**funny**_____ I couldn't stop (laughing.)

   bad   long   nice   funny

   The correct answer is **funny** because of the context clues **joke** and **laughing**. They are hints that go best with the word **funny**. Now you try it.

2. We baked a sweet cinnamon apple pie. It smelled _____.

   sour   delicious   funny   odd

3. You have such a long walk home. Do you need a

   _____ home from school?

   letter   balloon   ride   scooter

4. My brother loves to _____. He has
   visited over fifty different countries!

   travel   shout   buy   play

NAME _____

Five Senses

Directions: Read this story about the senses. Then, do the activities on page 285.

As you use your eyes to read this, you are using one of your five senses. You are using your sight. Your sense of sight lets you see faces, places, shapes, letters, and words. Your sight helps you see beautiful things and helps keep you safe.

Bells ringing, children singing, and your mother calling you to dinner all use the sense of hearing. Your ears catch sound waves that travel through the air and you hear them.

Your sense of hearing warns you with a *beep-beep* that a truck is backing up. A phone rings and you hear it. Could it be a friend calling?

Your sense of smell lets you know that a pizza is cooking without you even seeing it.

Your nose smells the fresh sheets on your bed and lets you know that your dog has been playing in the rain or with a skunk.

You use your tongue for tasting. Foods can taste salty, sweet, sour, or bitter. Your sense of smell and taste work together so you can enjoy food. Dill pickles or tangy oranges are tasty treats. Cotton candy and popcorn are also tasty treats.

Your largest sense organ is your skin. Your sense of touch is found in your skin. You can feel smooth, soft, rough, sharp, hot, and cold. Velvet is a smooth touch. Sandpaper is rough. Snow is cold, and cotton balls are soft.

Your five senses help to keep you safe and help you enjoy life.

Five Senses, cont.

Directions: Draw a line to match the sense to the body part that works with it.

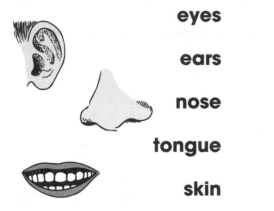

eyes

ears

nose

tongue

skin

taste

smell

sight

hearing

touch

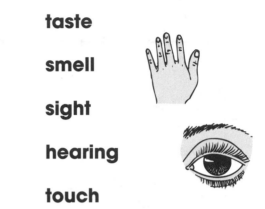

Directions: List three of your favorites under each sense. An example is given.

Taste pretzel
_____

_____

Smell baking cookies
_____

_____

Sight Mommy
_____

_____

Hearing barking dog
_____

_____

Touch cold snow
_____

_____

NAME _____

Comprehension: Singing Whales

Directions: Read about singing whales. Then, follow the instructions.

Some whales can sing! We cannot understand the words. But we can hear the tune of the humpback whale. Each season, humpback whales sing a different song.

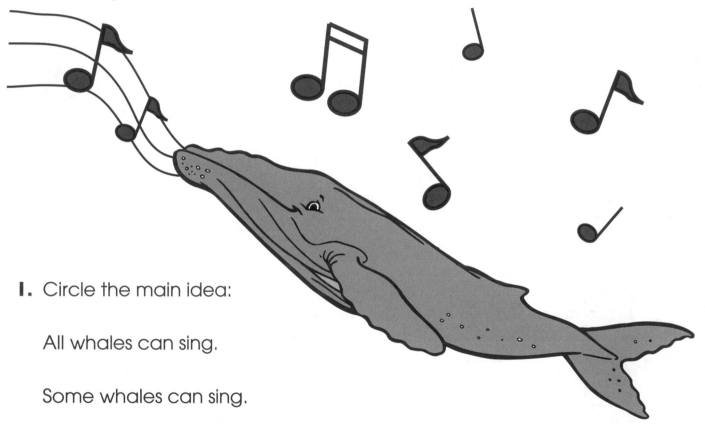

1. Circle the main idea:

All whales can sing.

Some whales can sing.

2. Name the kind of whale that sings.

_____

3. How many different songs does the humpback whale sing each year?

1   2   3   4

Hermit Crabs

The hermit crab lives in a shell in or near the ocean. It does not make its own shell. It moves into a shell left by another sea animal. As the hermit crab grows, it gets too big for its shell. It will hunt for a new shell. It will feel the new shell with its claw. If the shell feels just right, the crab will leave its old shell and move into the bigger one. It might even take a shell away from another hermit crab.

Directions: Read about hermit crabs. Use what you learn to finish the sentences.

1. This story is mostly about the _____.

2. The hermit crab lives _____.

3. When it gets too big for its shell, it will _____.

4. The crab will feel the shell with its _____.

5. It might take a shell away from _____.

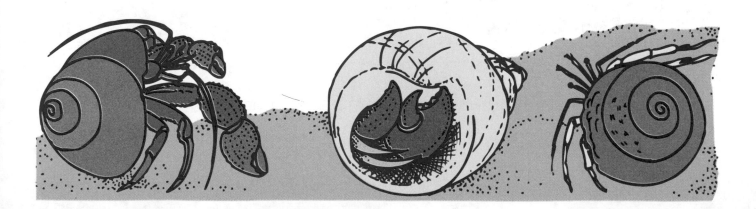

NAME _____

The Statue of Liberty

The Statue of Liberty is a symbol of the United States. It stands for freedom. It is the tallest statue in the United States.

The statue is of a woman wearing a robe. She is holding a torch in her right hand. She is holding a book in her left hand. She is wearing a crown. The Statue of Liberty was a gift from the country of France.

Each year, people come from all over the world to visit the statue. Not only do they look at it, they can also go inside the statue. At one time, visitors could go all the way up into the arm. In 1916, the arm was closed to visitors because it was too dangerous. The Statue of Liberty is located on an island in New York Harbor.

Directions: Read the facts above. Then, read each sentence below. If it is true, put a **T** on the line. If it is false, put an **F** on the line.

_____ **1.** The Statue of Liberty is a symbol of the United States.

_____ **2.** People cannot go inside the statue.

_____ **3.** The statue was a gift from Mexico.

_____ **4.** People used to be able to climb up into the statue's arm.

_____ **5.** It is a very short statue.

_____ **6.** The woman statue has a torch in her right hand.

_____ **7.** People come from all over to see the statue.

Venus Flytraps

Many insects eat plants. There is one kind of plant that eats insects. It is the Venus flytrap. The Venus flytrap works like a trap. Each leaf is shaped like a circle. The circle is in two parts. When the leaf closes, the two parts fold together. The leaf has little spikes all the way around it. Inside the leaf, there are little hairs. If an insect touches the little hairs, the two sides of the Venus flytrap leaf will clap together. The spikes will trap the insect inside. The Venus flytrap will then eat the insect.

Directions: Read about the Venus flytrap. Then, read each sentence below. If it is true, circle the sentence. If it is **not** true, draw an **X** on the sentence.

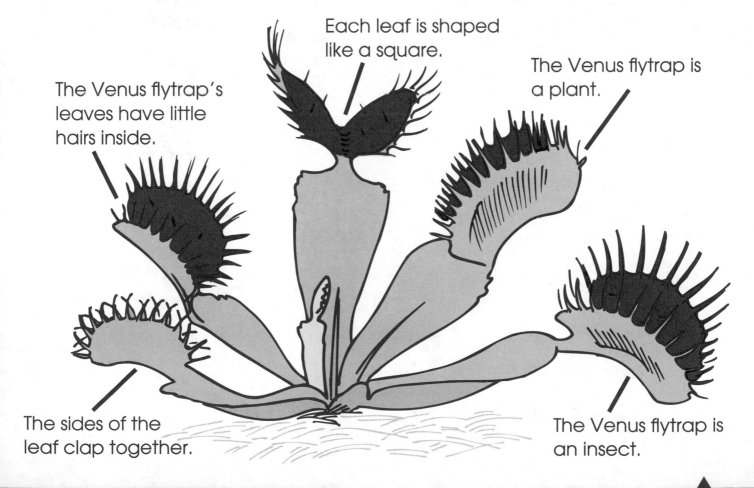

Each leaf is shaped like a square.

The Venus flytrap is a plant.

The Venus flytrap's leaves have little hairs inside.

The sides of the leaf clap together.

The Venus flytrap is an insect.

NAME _____

Main Idea

The **main idea** tells about the **whole picture**.

Directions: Which sentence tells the main idea of the picture? Fill in the circle next to the correct answer.

○ The dog is happy.

○ The dog is hot.

○ The garden was in bloom.

○ The garden was messy.

○ I have a new sister.

○ I want to be a babysitter.

○ I met my new teacher.

○ This is the last day of school.

○ The juggler needed practice.

○ The juggler likes scrambled eggs.

NAME _____

What's the Main Idea?

The **main idea** tells about the **whole story**.

Directions: Read the story below.

Visiting the city zoo with my class was a lot of fun. Everyone in my class got to pet the llamas. Next, we were given a bag of peanuts to feed the elephants. Finally, we were allowed to take pictures in front of the monkeys' cage. Then, my teacher made a joke. She said she had never seen so much monkeying around!

Read each sentence below and decide whether it tells the main idea. Write **yes** or **no**.

Finally, we were allowed to take pictures in front of the monkeys' cage.

_____

Then, my teacher made a joke.

_____

Next, we were given a bag of peanuts to feed the elephants.

_____

Visiting the city zoo with my class was a lot of fun.

_____

Write the one sentence that tells the main idea:

_____

_____

NAME _____

Main Idea

The **main idea** tells about the **whole story**.

Directions: Read the story carefully. Then, write a sentence that tells the main idea.

My brother, Scott, loves to fly planes. He flies planes every chance he gets. His favorite type of plane is a Cessna 182. He also likes to go scuba diving. He likes to go scuba diving in the Gulf of Mexico best. Sometimes, he goes flying in the morning and scuba diving in the afternoon. Scott is very adventurous!

_____

_____

_____

My dad is a very talented musician. He taught himself how to play the piano and now he is an excellent piano player. When people hear him play, they can't believe he has never taken any lessons! People say he has "natural talent," and it's true!

_____

_____

_____

Marco Polo!

Marco Polo is a fun summertime game. The game Marco Polo was named after a famous Italian explorer.

This game of tag is played in a swimming pool. One person chooses to be Marco. This person swims around the pool trying to tag someone else—except that she or he must keep his or her eyes closed! To find someone to tag, Marco calls out, "Marco!" Everybody else in the pool answers, "Polo!" Soon, Marco tags someone, and the game is over.

Directions: What is the main idea of this story? Fill in the circle next to the correct answer.

○ Marco Polo was a famous explorer.

○ Marco Polo is from Italy.

○ Marco Polo is a fun summertime game.

What is one important rule of the game Marco Polo?

_____

_____

_____

NAME _____

Read All About It

Directions: Read each part of the paper. Fill in the circle beside the sentence that tells the main idea.

Hundreds Enjoy Town Carnival

○ Many people had fun at the carnival.

○ The carnival was not a success.

Bank Robbers Caught

○ Five bank robbers got away.

○ Two bank robbers were caught.

○ Someone wants to buy kittens and puppies.

○ Someone wants to sell kittens and puppies.

CLASSIFIEDS

For Sale

3 black kittens
2 brown puppies

Call 555-4109

Garden Club to Meet
Wednesday and Thursday This Week

○ The Garden Club will not meet this week.

○ The Garden Club will meet two times this week.

NAME _____

Ouch!

Directions: Read the story below. Then, complete the activity at the bottom of the page.

Marsha and I went for a bike ride on Sunday morning. The streets weren't crowded so we rode down Main Street. A delivery truck in front of us had just gone over a huge bump. Suddenly, a box labeled NAILS flew off the truck and into the air...

Tell what happens next:

_____

_____

_____

_____

_____

_____

_____

_____

_____

NAME _____

What Happens Next?

Directions: Read each paragraph. Predict what will happen next by placing an **X** in front of the best answer.

1. Robin went hiking with her friend. It was very hot outside. In the distance, they saw a blue glimmering lake.

   _____ They turned around and went home.

   _____ They yelled for help.

   _____ They waded into the cool water.

2. Jack and Tina are brother and sister. They love to watch basketball games. They also like to practice basketball in their driveway. Their grandma wants to get them the best birthday present ever. What should she get them?

   _____ Four pairs of shoes.

   _____ Season tickets to see a professional basketball team.

   _____ A new video game.

NAME _____

How Will It End?

Directions: Read each story. Fill in the circle beside the sentence that tells what will happen next.

It is a snowy winter night. The lights flicker once, twice, and then they go out. It is cold and dark. Dad finds the flashlight and matches. He brings logs in from outside. What will Dad do?

○ Dad will make a fire.

○ Dad will cook dinner.

○ Dad will clean the fireplace.

Maggie has a garden. She likes fresh, homegrown vegetables. She says they make salads taste better. Maggie is going to make a salad for a picnic. What will Maggie do?

○ Maggie will buy the salad at the store.

○ Maggie will buy the vegetables at the store.

○ Maggie will use vegetables from her garden.

The big white goose wakes up. It stands and stretches its wings. It looks all around. It feels very hungry. What will the goose do?

○ The goose will go swimming.

○ The goose will look for food.

○ The goose will go back to sleep.

NAME _____

Boa Constrictors

Boa constrictors are very big. They may grow up to 14 feet long. A boa kills its prey by squeezing it. Then, the prey is swallowed.

Boas do not eat cows or other large animals. They do eat animals that are larger than their own heads. The bones in their jaws stretch so they can swallow small animals such as rodents and birds.

Boa constrictors hunt while hanging from trees. They watch for their prey. Then, they attack. After eating, they may sleep for a week. Boas do not need to eat often. They can live without food for many months.

Boas are not poisonous. They defend themselves by striking and biting with their sharp teeth.

Boa constrictors give birth to live baby snakes. They do not lay eggs. They may have up to 50 baby snakes at one time.

Directions: Use facts from the story to help predict what will happen. Fill in the circle next to the correct answer.

1. A boa is hanging from a tree. Suddenly, a bird hops under it. The boa will _____.
   - ○ strike and bite it
   - ○ squeeze it, then swallow it
   - ○ poison it, then eat it
   - ○ sleep for one week

2. The boa is hungry and hunting for food. Which type of prey will the snake most likely eat?
   - ○ cow   ○ panther   ○ horse   ○ mouse

3. A boa constrictor is slithering through the grass. Out of the grass comes a hunter walking toward it. The boa will probably _____.
   - ○ strike the hunter
   - ○ slither up a tree to sleep
   - ○ squeeze and kill the hunter
   - ○ poison the hunter

Fact or Opinion?

In sports, there are many facts and opinions. A **fact** is something that is true. An **opinion** is a belief someone has about something.

Directions: Read the sports sentences below. Next to each sentence, write **F** if it is a fact and **O** if it is an opinion.

1. _____ In bowling, a poodle is a ball that rolls down the gutter.

2. _____ I think poodles are cute.

3. _____ Julio is my favorite football player.

4. _____ A football player is a person who plays in a football game.

5. _____ A catcher's mask protects the catcher's face.

6. _____ My catcher's mask is too tight.

7. _____ I had a great putt!

8. _____ A putt is when a golfer hits the ball into the hole on a green.

9. _____ A referee is a person who enforces the rules in a game.

10. _____ Josh thought the referee did a good job.

11. _____ This silly javelin is really hard to throw!

12. _____ A metal spear that is thrown for a distance is called a javelin.

13. _____ Jake said, "The defense tried its best to block the ball."

NAME _____

Fact and Opinion: Recycling

Directions: Read about recycling. Then, follow the instructions.

What do you throw away every day? What could you do with these things? You could change an old greeting card into a new card. You could make a puppet with an old paper bag. Old buttons make great refrigerator magnets. You can plant seeds in plastic cups. Cardboard tubes make perfect rockets. So, use your imagination!

1. Write **F** next to each fact and **O** next to each opinion.

_____ Cardboard tubes are ugly.

_____ Buttons can be made into refrigerator magnets.

_____ An old greeting card can be changed into a new card.

_____ Paper-bag puppets are cute.

_____ Seeds can be planted in plastic cups.

_____ Rockets can be made from cardboard tubes.

2. What could you do with a cardboard tube? _____

_____

Strings Attached!

Directions: Draw a line to connect each string of words on the left with a string of words on the right to make a complete sentence. Make sure that each sentence you form makes sense.

Hint: There are several ways to connect the groups of words. Try out different combinations to find the ones you like best.

MATCHING

A
B
C
D

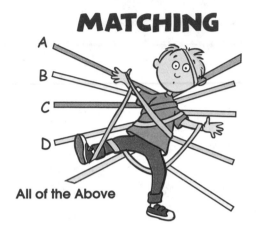

All of the Above

The tired mom

the stinky garbage.

We picked apples

had a shaky voice.

I threw out

smelled bad.

The nervous man

and made a pie!

I love to eat

rocked her baby.

The wet cat

vanilla ice cream.

NAME _____

Best Guess!

Directions: Read each sentence below. Using the information in the first sentence, decide which answer best completes each question. Fill in the circle next to your answer choice.

"Is it cold in here?" asked my grandma as she shivered.

What do you think your grandma would like you to do?

○ Open a window.

○ Turn on the heat.

○ Give her a hug.

James' stomach growled really loudly in class today!

What would help James?

○ medicine

○ a new toy

○ food

Who Will Help Me?

Directions: Write the best choice from the word list to answer each question.

Word List			
captain	dentist	fireman	doctor
plumber	police	teacher	baker

I think I have a cavity in my tooth.
Who can help me?

_____

My mom needs to order a wedding cake
for my uncle. Who can help her?

_____

I hurt my ankle during gym class.
Who can help me?

_____

My pipes are leaking.
Who can help me?

_____

Making Inferences

Not every story tells you all the facts. Sometimes, you need to put together details to understand what is happening in a story. When you put details together, you **make inferences**.

Directions: Read each story. Fill in the circle beside the inference you can make from the details you have.

Everyone on the Pine School baseball team wears a blue shirt on Mondays. It is Monday, and Brenda is wearing a blue shirt.

○ Brenda always wears blue clothes.

○ Brenda cannot find her red shirt.

○ Brenda is on the baseball team.

My cat has brown and white stripes. It meows when it wants to be fed. My cat is meowing now.

○ The cat wants to go outside.

○ The cat is hungry.

○ The cat doesn't like brown and white stripes.

Every afternoon the children run outside when they hear a bell ring. At 2:00, Mr. Chocovan drives by in his ice-cream truck. The children hear a bell ringing. They run outside.

○ It is time for ice cream.

○ It is time for the children to go home.

○ It is time for a fire drill.

Mind-Reading Tricks

Samantha thought of a good joke. She bragged that she could read Maria's mind. She put her hand on Maria's head, closed her eyes, and said, "You had red punch with your lunch!"

"Wow! You're right!" replied Maria, not realizing that she had a little red ring around her lips.

"That was easy. But I bet you can't tell me what I just ate," said Thomas.

"That's a bunch of baloney," answered Samantha.

"How did you know?" gasped Thomas.

"It's my little secret," said Samantha, with a sigh of relief.

"Here comes your mom," said Maria. "Can you read her mind, too?"

Samantha looked down at her watch. She should have been home half an hour ago. As she ran to meet her mother, she yelled back, "Yes, I know exactly what she's thinking!"

Directions: Make inferences about Samantha's mind-reading tricks. Fill in the circle beside the correct inference.

1. Was Samantha sure that Thomas had eaten bologna for lunch?

○ No, she was just lucky.

○ Yes, she saw him eat his bologna sandwich.

2. What was Samantha's mother probably thinking?

○ Samantha was a great mind reader.

○ Samantha was late.

NAME _____

What Is It?

When you don't get the whole picture, you may need to **draw conclusions** for yourself. To draw a conclusion, think about what you see or read. Think about what you already know. Then, make a good guess.

Directions: Look at each picture. Use what you know and what you see to draw a conclusion. Draw a line to the sentence that tells about each picture.

It must be a clown.

It must be a cowhand.

It must be a baby.

It must be a ballet dancer.

It must be a football player.

Who Said It?

Directions: Use what you see, what you read, and what you know to draw conclusions. Draw a line from the animal to what it might say.

"I save lots of bones and bury them in the yard."

"I live in the ocean and have sharp teeth."

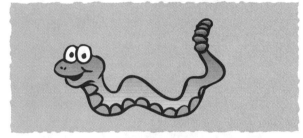

"I love to walk in the snow and slide on the ice."

"I hop on lily pads in a pond with my webbed feet."

"I slither on the ground because I have no arms or legs."

NAME _____

What Happened?

Directions: Look at the pictures. Fill in the circle beside the sentence that tells what happened in the missing picture. Draw a picture that shows what happened.

What happened?

○ The boy dropped the string.   ○ The boy took his kite home.

What happened?

○ The angry baby played in its bed.   ○ The hungry baby drank the milk.

I Conclude!

Directions: Read each story. Fill in the circle beside the answer that completes the last sentence.

    The little house is in the backyard. Inside is a bowl of water. Next to the bowl is a big bone. This house belongs to . . .

○ some birds.   ○ a family of elves.   ○ a puppy.

    The yellow cat is fluffy. The black cat is thin. The tan and white cat acts friendly. The little gray cat is shy. Cats are all . . .

○ different.   ○ angry.   ○ silly.

    Lois keeps her pet in an aquarium. Her pet can hop. It eats flies and is green. Her pet is . . .

○ a bunny.   ○ a frog.   ○ very tall.

    We played a game. We ran away from Sofia. When she tapped Raymond, he was It. We were playing . . .

○ soccer.   ○ basketball.   ○ tag.

NAME _____

Cause and Effect

Cause: An action or act that makes something happen.

Effect: Something that happens because of an action or cause.

Look at the following example of cause and effect.

 We forgot to put the lid on the trash can.

 The raccoons ate the trash.

Directions: Now, draw a line connecting each cause on the left side of the page to its effect on the right side of the page.

How Did It Happen?

Directions: Read the stories below. Then, write the missing cause or effect.

Audrey left her bike outside in the rain for weeks. When she finally put it back inside the garage, it had rusted.

Cause: Audrey left her bike outside in the rain.

What was the **effect**? _____

I dropped a heavy box on my foot by accident. Yoweeeee! That hurt! My mom took me to the doctor.

Cause: _____

Effect: _____

Noah Webster loved words so much that he decided to write a dictionary!

Cause: _____

Effect: _____

NAME _____

Do You Know Why?

Directions: Write the cause from the answer box for each sentence.

Answer Box

The bathtub overflowed.

I studied all the spelling words.

Gill tried to grab the cat.

I didn't water my plants.

A tornado hit our town.

---

1. _____

   The cat ran away.

2. _____

   The floor got wet.

3. _____

   There was a lot of damage.

4. _____

   My plants died.

5. _____

   I won the school spelling bee!

NAME _____

Tricky Cause and Effect

Things that happen can make other things happen. The event that happens is the **effect**. Why the event happens is the **cause**.

Example: Marcie tripped on the step and fell down.
      Cause: Marcie tripped on the step.
      Effect: Marcie fell down.

Directions: Read the story.

Marcie knows a magic trick. She can make a ring seem to go up and down by itself on a pencil. Marcie has to get ready ahead of time. She ties a piece of skinny thread under the pencil's eraser. Then, she ties the thread to a button on her blouse. In front of her audience, Marcie puts a ring on the pencil. When Marcie leans forward, the thread goes loose, so the ring goes down. Then, Marcie leans back. The thread tightens and makes the ring go up the pencil.

Directions: Write the cause to complete each sentence.

1. The audience cannot see the thread because

_____

_____

_____

_____

2. _____

makes the ring go down.

NAME _____

A Cause-and-Effect Fable

Directions: Read the story.

Four animals caught a talking fish. "If you let me go, I will grant each of you one wish," announced the fish.

"Make my trunk smaller!" demanded the vain elephant. "I wish to be the most beautiful elephant that ever lived."

"Make my legs longer!" commanded the alligator. "I want to be taller than all my alligator friends."

"Make my neck shorter!" ordered the giraffe. "I am tired of always staring at the tops of trees."

"Dear Fish, please make me be satisfied with who-o-o-o-o I am," whispered the wise old owl.

Poof! Kazaam! Their wishes were granted. However, soon after, only one of these animals was happy. Can you guess who-o-o-o-o?

Directions: Draw a line to match a cause to an effect.

Because of its short trunk,	the giraffe could no longer eat leaves from treetops.
Because of its long legs,	the elephant could no longer spray water on its back.
Because of its short neck,	the owl was happy about his wish.
Because he could still do all the things he needed,	the alligator could no longer hide in shallow water.

NAME _____

Fiction or Nonfiction?

Some stories are made up and some are true. **Fiction** stories are made up, and **nonfiction** stories are true.

Directions: Read the passages below. Then, write if they are **fiction** or **nonfiction**.

Following a balanced diet is important for good health. Your body needs many kinds of vitamins and minerals found in different types of food. For example, oranges provide vitamin C, and bananas are a good source of the mineral potassium.

_____

We call my dog the alphabet dog. Why? Because my dog can sing the alphabet! That's right! My dog, Smarty Pants, is a dog genius! Smarty Pants can sing the entire alphabet! "S.P.," as we sometimes call her, is also starting her own dog academy to teach other dogs how to sing the alphabet. You should sign up your dog for classes with Smarty Pants today!

_____

NAME _____

Nonfiction: Tornado Tips

Directions: Read about tornadoes. Then, follow the instructions.

A tornado begins over land with strong winds and thunderstorms. The spinning air becomes a funnel. It can cause damage. If you are inside, go to the lowest floor of the building. A basement is a safe place. A bathroom or closet in the middle of a building can be a safe place, too. If you are outside, lie in a ditch. Remember, tornadoes are dangerous.

Write five facts about tornadoes.

1. _____

_____

2. _____

_____

3. _____

_____

4. _____

_____

5. _____

_____

Fiction: Hercules

The **setting** is where a story takes place. The **characters** are the people in a story or play.

Directions: Read about Hercules. Then, answer the questions.

Hercules was born in the warm Atlantic Ocean. He was a very small and weak baby. He wanted to be the strongest hurricane in the world. But he had one problem. He couldn't blow 75-mile-per-hour winds. Hercules blew and blew in the ocean, until one day, his sister, Hola, told him it would be more fun to be a breeze than a hurricane. Hercules agreed. It was a breeze to be a breeze!

I. What is the setting of the story? _____

2. Who are the characters? _____

3. What is the problem? _____

_____

4. How does Hercules solve his problem? _____

_____

NAME _____

Fiction/Nonfiction: The Fourth of July

Directions: Read each story. Then, write whether it is fiction or nonfiction.

One sunny day in July, a dog named Stan ran away from home. He went up one street and down the other looking for fun, but all the yards were empty. Where was everybody? Stan kept walking until he heard the sound of band music and happy people. Stan walked faster until he got to Central

 Street. There he saw men, women, children, and dogs getting ready to walk in a parade. It was the Fourth of July!

Fiction or nonfiction? _____

Americans celebrate the Fourth of July every year, because it is the birthday of the United States of America. On July 4, 1776, the United States got its independence from Great Britain. Today, Americans celebrate this holiday with parades, picnics, and fireworks as they proudly wave the red, white, and blue American flag.

Fiction or nonfiction? _____

Fiction and Nonfiction: Which Is It?

Directions: Read about fiction and nonfiction books. Then, follow the instructions.

There are many kinds of books. Some books have make-believe stories about princesses and dragons. Some books contain poetry and rhymes, like Mother Goose. These are fiction.

Some books contain facts about space and plants. And still other books have stories about famous people in history, like Abraham Lincoln. These are nonfiction.

Write **F** for **fiction** and **NF** for **nonfiction**.

_____ **1.** nursery rhyme

_____ **2.** fairy tale

_____ **3.** true life story of a famous athlete

_____ **4.** Aesop's fables

_____ **5.** dictionary entry about foxes

_____ **6.** weather report

_____ **7.** story about a talking tree

_____ **8.** text about how a tadpole becomes a frog

_____ **9.** text about animal habitats

_____ **10.** riddles and jokes

NAME _____

What Is a Character?

A **character** is the person, animal, or object that a story is about. You cannot have a story without a character.

Characters are usually people, but sometimes they can be animals, aliens, or even objects that come to life. You can have many characters in a story.

Directions: Read the story below, and then answer the questions about character on the next page.

Adventurous Alenna!

Alenna was seven years old and lived on a tropical island. She had long, blond hair and sea-green eyes. Alenna was very adventurous and was always exploring new things. She started an Adventure Club at her school and led her friends on long bike rides. She also was the youngest person in her family to learn to water-ski!

When her dad asked, "Who wants to go snorkeling to see some fish?"

Alenna answered, "I want to go snorkeling!" Alenna was very adventurous.

The End

Character, cont.

First, authors must decide who their main character is going to be. Next, they decide what their main character looks like. Then, they reveal the character's personality by:

what the character does

what the character says

Directions: Answer the questions about the story you just read.

Who is the main character in "Adventurous Alenna!"?

_____

What does Alenna look like? Describe her appearance on the line below:

_____

Give two examples of what Alenna **does** that shows that she is adventurous:

1. _____

2. _____

Give an example of what Alenna **says** that reveals she is adventurous.

_____

_____

NAME _____

Character Interview—Lights! Camera! Action!

An **interview** takes place between two people, usually a reporter and another person. The interviewer asks questions for the person to answer.

Directions: Pretend that you are a reporter. Choose a character from a book you read. If you could ask the character anything you wanted to, what would you ask?

Make a **list of questions** you would like to ask your character:

1. _____

2. _____

3. _____

4. _____

Now, pretend your character has come to life and could **answer your questions**. Write what you think he, she, or it would say:

1. _____

2. _____

3. _____

4. _____

Setting—Place

Every story has a **setting**. The setting is the **place** where the story happens. Think of a place that you know well. It could be your room, your kitchen, your backyard, your classroom, or an imaginary place.

Directions: Brainstorm some words and ideas about that place. Think about what you see, hear, smell, taste, or feel in that place.

Brainstorm your ideas for a setting below:

see   hear   smell

taste   touch

_____

_____

_____

_____

_____

_____

_____

_____

_____

_____

_____

Where are we? _____

NAME _____

Setting—Place

Directions: Read the story below and answer the questions about the setting.

The Amazing Amazon

The Amazon jungle is a huge rain forest in South America. It is full of gigantic green trees, thick jungle vines, and many species of dangerous animals. It is very humid in the jungle.

What is the temperature like in the Amazon jungle?

_____

Where is the Amazon jungle located?

_____

Would it be easy to travel in the Amazon jungle? Why or why not?

_____

_____

_____

Does it rain a lot in the Amazon jungle?

_____

Setting—Time

The **setting** is the **place** where the story happens. The setting is also the **time** in which the story happens. A reader needs to know **when** the story is happening. Does it take place at night? On a sunny day? In the future? During the winter?

Time can be:

| time of day | a holiday | a season of the year | a time in the future | a time in history |

Directions: Read the following story. Then, answer the questions below.

Knock, Knock!

One windy fall night there was a knock at the door. "Who is it?" I asked.

"It's your dog, Max. Please let me in," Max said.

"Oh, good. I was getting worried about you!" I said. Then, I let Max inside.

I thought to myself how glad I was that scientists had invented voice boxes for dogs. How did people in the olden days ever know when to let their dogs inside if their dogs couldn't talk? The Doggie Voice Box is such a wonderful invention. I'm so happy that I live in the year 2090!

What time of day is it? _____

What season is it? _____

What year does this story take place? _____

NAME _____

Make a Map!

In a story or book you read, the character or characters may have taken a journey or simply walked around their town. Where did the main events in the story take place?

"I can't wait to tell you about my story!"

Directions: Create a detailed map showing the place where the characters lived. You may wish to ask an adult for help.

1. Draw the outline of your map on a sheet of paper.

2. Be sure to write the title and the author of the book at the top of the map.

3. Think about what places you want to include on your map and draw them.

4. Label the important places, adding a short sentence about what happened there.

5. Add color and details.

6. Share your map with friends, and tell them about the story you read.

Postcard

Have you ever received or written a postcard? Usually, people send postcards when they are on vacation. A postcard usually shows a **picture** of the place someone is visiting and provides room for a **short message** about the trip.

Directions: Create a postcard about a book you have just read.

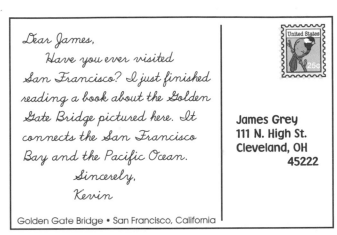

Dear James,
   Have you ever visited San Francisco? I just finished reading a book about the Golden Gate Bridge pictured here. It connects the San Francisco Bay and the Pacific Ocean.
   Sincerely,
   Kevin

Golden Gate Bridge • San Francisco, California

James Grey
111 N. High St.
Cleveland, OH
            45222

1. Brainstorm a list of parts of the book that you liked best.

2. On scrap paper, sketch a picture that illustrates your favorite part.

3. Copy your picture onto the blank side of a large index card.

4. Write a message on the lined side of the index card. Tell about the book you read, your favorite part, and the picture that goes with it.

5. Address the card to someone you know or to a character from the book.

6. Show your postcard to your friends and tell them about your book.

NAME _____

Extra! Extra! Read All About It!

Newspaper reporters have very important jobs. They have to catch a reader's attention and, at the same time, **tell the facts**.

Newspaper reporters write their stories by answering **who**, **what**, **where**, **when**, **why**, and **how**.

Directions: Think about a book you just read and answer the questions below.

Who: **Who** is the story about?

_____

What: **What** happened to the main character?

_____

Where: **Where** does the story take place?

_____

When: **When** does the story take place?

_____

Why: **Why** do these story events happen?

_____

How: **How** do these events happen?

_____

NAME _____

Extra! Extra! Read All About It!

Directions: Use your answers on page 328 to write a newspaper article about the book you read.

BIG CITY TIMES

Title

_____

(Write a catchy title for your article.)

_____

_____

_____

_____

_____

_____

_____

_____

NAME _____

Common Nouns

A **common noun** names a person, place, or thing.

Example: The **boy** had several **chores** to do.

Directions: Fill in the circle below each common noun.

1. First, the boy had to feed his puppy.
   ○   ○   ○   ○

2. He got fresh water for his pet.
           ○   ○   ○ ○

3. Next, the boy poured some dry food into a bowl.
           ○   ○   ○   ○

4. He set the dish on the floor in the kitchen.
        ○   ○   ○   ○

5. Then, he called his dog to come to dinner
          ○   ○   ○

6. The boy and his dad worked in the garden.
        ○   ○   ○   ○

7. The father turned the dirt with a shovel.
          ○   ○   ○   ○

8. The boy carefully dropped seeds into little holes.
        ○   ○   ○   ○

9. Soon, tiny plants would sprout from the soil.
              ○   ○   ○   ○

10. Sunshine and showers would help the radishes grow.
        ○   ○   ○   ○

NAME _____

Proper Nouns

A **proper noun** names a specific or certain person, place, or thing. A proper noun always begins with a capital letter.

Example: Becky flew to **St. Louis** in a **Boeing 747**.

Directions: Put a ✔ in front of each proper noun.

_____ **1.** uncle

_____ **2.** Aunt Retta

_____ **3.** Forest Park

_____ **4.** Gateway Arch

_____ **5.** Missouri

_____ **6.** school

_____ **7.** Miss Hunter

_____ **8.** Northwest Plaza

_____ **9.** New York Science Center

_____ **10.** Ms. Small

_____ **11.** Doctor Chang

_____ **12.** Union Station

_____ **13.** Henry Shaw

_____ **14.** museum

_____ **15.** librarian

_____ **16.** shopping mall

Directions: Underline the proper nouns.

1. Becky went to visit Uncle Harry.

2. He took her to see the Cardinals play baseball.

3. The game was at Busch Stadium.

4. The St. Louis Cardinals played the Chicago Cubs.

5. Aledmys Diaz hit a home run.

NAME _____

Singular Nouns

A **singular noun** names one person, place, or thing.

Example: My **mother** unlocked the old **trunk** in the **attic**.

Directions: If the noun is singular, draw a line from it to the trunk. If the noun is **not** singular, draw an **X** on the word.

teddy bear	**hammer**	**picture**	**sweater**
bonnet	**letters**	**seashells**	**fiddle**
kite	**ring**	**feather**	**books**
postcard	**crayon**	**doll**	**dishes**
blocks	**hats**	**bicycle**	**blanket**

Plural Nouns

A **plural noun** names more than one person, place, or thing.

Example: Some **dinosaurs** ate **plants** in **swamps**.

Directions: Underline each plural noun.

1. Large animals lived millions of years ago.

2. Dinosaurs roamed many parts of the Earth.

3. Scientists look for fossils.

4. The bones can tell a scientist many things.

5. These bones help tell what the creatures were like.

6. Some had curved claws and whip-like tails.

7. Others had beaks and plates of armor.

8. Some dinosaurs lived on the plains, and others lived in forests.

9. You can see the skeletons of dinosaurs at some museums.

10. We often read about these animals in books.

NAME _____

Action Verbs

A **verb** is a word that can show action.

Example: I **jump**.   He **kicks**.   He **walked**.

Directions: Underline the verb in each sentence. Write it on the line.

1. Our school plays games on Field Day. _____

2. Juan runs 50 yards. _____

3. Carmen hops in a sack race. _____

4. Paula tosses a ball through a hoop. _____

5. One girl carries a jellybean on a spoon. _____

6. Lola bounces the ball. _____

7. Some boys chase after balloons. _____

8. Mark chooses me for his team. _____

9. The children cheer for the winners. _____

10. Everyone enjoys Field Day. _____

NAME

Ready for Action!

Directions: Draw a line to match each action word to the picture that shows it.

kick

catch

slide

run

jump

NAME _____

Irregular Verbs

Verbs that do not add **ed** to show what happened in the past are called **irregular verbs**.

Example: Present   Past
    run, runs   ran
    fall, falls   fell

Jim **ran** past our house yesterday.
He **fell** over a wagon on the sidewalk.

Directions: Fill in the verbs that tell what happened in the past in the chart. The first one is done for you.

Present	Past
hear, hears	heard
draw, draws	
do, does	
give, gives	
sell, sells	
come, comes	
fly, flies	
build, builds	
know, knows	
bring, brings	

Linking Verbs

A **linking verb** does not show action. Instead, it links the subject with a word in the predicate. **Am, is, are, was,** and **were** are **linking verbs**.

Example: Many people **are** collectors.
    (**Are** connects **people** and **collectors**.)
    The collection **was** large.
    (**Was** connects **collection** and **large**.)

Directions: Underline the linking verb in each sentence.

1. I am happy.

2. Toy collecting is a nice hobby.

3. Mom and Dad are helpful.

4. The rabbit is beautiful.

5. Itsy and Bitsy are stuffed mice.

6. Monday was special.

7. I was excited.

8. The class was impressed.

9. The elephants were gray.

10. My friends were a good audience.

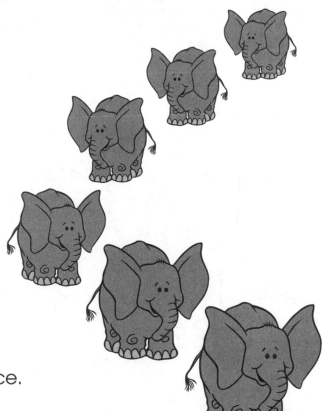

NAME _____

Adjectives

An **adjective** is a word that describes a noun.

It tells **how many**, **what kind**, or **which one**.

Example: Yolanda has a **tasty** lunch.

Directions: Color each space that has an adjective. Do not color the other spaces.

again

juicy

thick

big

tasty

with

orange

smooth

eat

sour

crunchy

red

long

hard

white

fresh

cold

drink

NAME _____

Add the Adjectives

Directions: Write a describing word on each line. Draw a picture to match each sentence.

high mountain

The _____ flag waved over the _____ building.

A _____ lion searched for food in the _____ jungle.

We saw _____ fish in the _____ aquarium.

Her _____ car was parked by the _____ van.

The _____ dog barked and chased the _____ truck.

The _____ building was filled with _____ packages.

NAME _____

Better Sentences

Directions: Describing words like adjectives can make a better sentence. Write a word on each line to make the sentences more interesting. Draw pictures of your sentences.

1. The skater won a medal.

The _____ skater won a _____ medal.

2. The jewels were in the safe.

The _____ jewels were in the _____ safe.

3. The airplane flew through the storm.

The _____ airplane flew through the _____ storm.

4. A fireman rushed into the house.

A _____ fireman rushed into the _____ house.

5. The detective hid behind the tree.

The _____ detective hid behind the _____ tree.

1.	2.

3.	4.	5.

Describing People

Directions: Choose two words from the box that describe each character. Then, complete each sentence to tell why you chose those words.

| understanding | spoiled | responsible | lazy | helpful | upset | happy |
| busy | caring | kind | mean | confused | unhappy | patient | nice |

The girl is _____ and _____

because she _____

_____

_____

_____

Mother is _____ and _____

because she _____

_____

_____

_____

Father is _____ and _____

because he _____

_____

_____

_____

NAME _____

Using Exact Adjectives

Use an **adjective** that best describes the noun or pronoun. Be specific.

Example: David had a nice birthday.
David had a **fun** birthday.

Directions: Rewrite each sentence, replacing **nice** or **good** with a better adjective from the box or one of your own.

sturdy   **new**   **great**   **chocolate**   **delicious**   **special**

1. David bought a nice pair of in-line skates.

_____

2. He received a nice helmet.

_____

3. He got nice knee pads.

_____

4. Father baked a good cake.

_____

5. David made a good wish.

_____

6. Mom served good ice cream.

_____

Subjects of Sentences

The **subject** of a sentence tells **who** or **what** does something.

Example: Some people eat foods that may seem strange to you.

Directions: Underline the subject of each sentence.

1. Some people like crocodile steak.

2. The meat tastes like fish.

3. Australians eat kangaroo meat.

4. Kangaroo meat tastes like beef.

5. People in the Southwest eat rattlesnake meat.

6. Snails make a delicious treat for some people.

7. Some Africans think roasted termites are tasty.

8. Bird's-nest soup is a famous Chinese dish.

9. People in Florida serve alligator meat.

10. Almost everyone treats themselves with ice cream.

NAME _____

Predicates of Sentences

The **predicate** of a sentence tells what the subject is or does. It is the verb part of the sentence.

Examples: Sally Ride **flew in a space shuttle**.

She **was an astronaut**.

Directions: Underline the predicate in each sentence.

1. She was the first American woman astronaut in space.

2. Sally worked hard for many years to become an astronaut.

3. She studied math and science in college.

4. Ms. Ride passed many tests.

5. She learned things quickly.

6. Sally trained to become a jet pilot.

7. This astronaut practiced using a robot arm.

8. Ms. Ride used the robot arm on two space missions.

9. She conducted experiments with it.

10. The robot arm is called a remote manipulator.

Compound Subjects

A **compound subject** has two or more subjects joined by the word **and**.

Example: Owls are predators. **Wolves** are predators.
Owls and wolves are predators. (compound subject)

Directions: If the sentence has a compound subject, write **CS**. If it does not, write **No**.

_____ 1. A predator is an animal that eats other animals.

_____ 2. Prey is eaten by predators.

_____ 3. Robins and bluejays are predators.

_____ 4. Some predators eat only meat.

_____ 5. Crocodiles and hawks eat meat only.

_____ 6. Raccoons and foxes eat both meat and plants.

Directions: Combine the subjects of the two sentences to make a compound subject. Write the new sentence on the line.

1. Snakes are predators. Spiders are predators.

_____

2. Frogs prey on insects. Chameleons prey on insects.

_____

NAME _____

Compound Predicates

A **compound predicate** has two or more predicates joined by the word **and**.

Example: Abe Lincoln was born in Kentucky. Abe Lincoln lived in a log cabin there.
Abe Lincoln **was born in Kentucky and lived in a log cabin there**.

Directions: If the sentence has a compound predicate, write **CP**. If it does not, write **No**.

_____ **1.** Abe Lincoln cut trees and chopped wood.

_____ **2.** Abe and his sister walked to a spring for water.

_____ **3.** Abe's family packed up and left Kentucky.

_____ **4.** They crossed the Ohio River to Indiana.

_____ **5.** Abe's father built a new home.

_____ **6.** Abe's mother became sick and died.

_____ **7.** Mr. Lincoln married again.

_____ **8.** Abe's new mother loved Abe and his sister and cared for them.

Complete Sentences

A **sentence** is a group of words that tells a whole idea. It has a subject and a predicate.

Examples: Some animals have stripes.
(sentence)
Help to protect.
(not a sentence)

Directions: Write **S** in front of each sentence. Write **No** if it is **not** a sentence.

_____ **1.** There are different kinds of chipmunks.

_____ **2.** They all have.

_____ **3.** They all have stripes to help protect them.

_____ **4.** The stripes make them hard to see in the forest.

_____ **5.** Zebras have stripes, too.

_____ **6.** Some caterpillars also.

_____ **7.** Other animals have spots.

_____ **8.** Some dogs have spots.

_____ **9.** Beautiful, little fawns.

_____ **10.** Their spots help to hide them in the woods.

NAME _____

Summer Camp

A **statement** is a telling sentence. It begins with a capital letter and ends with a period.

Directions: Write each statement correctly on the lines.

1. everyone goes to breakfast at 6:30 each morning

   _____

2. only three people can ride in one canoe

   _____

3. each person must help clean the cabins

   _____

4. older campers should help younger campers

   _____

5. all lights are out by 9:00 each night

   _____

6. everyone should write home at least once a week

   _____

Questions

A **question** is an asking sentence. It begins with a capital letter and ends with a question mark.

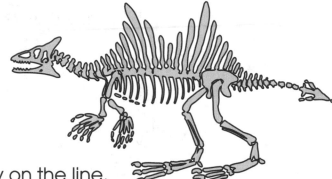

Directions: Write each question correctly on the line.

1. is our class going to the science museum

_____

2. will we get to spend the whole day there

_____

3. will a guide take us through the museum

_____

4. do you think we will see dinosaur bones

_____

5. is it true that the museum has a mummy

_____

6. can we take lots of pictures at the museum

_____

7. will you spend the whole day at the museum

_____

NAME _____

Kinds of Sentences

A **statement** ends with a period. **.** A **question** ends with a question mark. **?**

Directions: Write the correct mark in each box.

1. Would you like to help me make an aquarium ☐

2. We can use my brother's big fish tank ☐

3. Will you put this colored sand in the bottom ☐

4. I have three shells to put on the sand ☐

5. Can we use your little toy boat, too ☐

6. Let's go buy some fish for our aquarium ☐

7. Will 12 fish be enough ☐

8. Look, they seem to like their new home ☐

9. How often do we give them fish food ☐

10. Let's tell our friends about our new aquarium ☐

NAME _____

Writing Sentences

Every sentence begins with a capital letter.

Directions: Write three statements about the picture.

_____

_____

_____

Directions: Write three questions about the picture.

_____

_____

_____

NAME _____

Four Kinds of Sentences

A **statement** tells something. A **question** asks something. An **exclamation** shows surprise or strong feeling. A **command** tells someone to do something.

Example: The shuttle is ready for takeoff. (statement)
Are all systems go? (question)
What a sight! (exclamation)
Take a picture of this. (command)

Directions: Use the code to color the spaces.

> **Code**
> statement—**yellow**
> question—**red**
> exclamation—**blue**
> command—**gray**

That's incredible!

There it goes!

How exciting!

This is a thrill!

How high does it fly?

Will they land soon?

Are there any animals on board?

There are five astronauts.

Can the astronauts see the Moon?

Way to go!

How brave they are!

The shuttle goes fast.

They do experiments.

One uses the robot arm.

What a view!

What a sight!

Stay out of the way.

It orbits the Earth.

Take the picture now.

Look up there.

Watch the liftoff.

Review of Sentences

Directions: Underline the sentence that is written correctly in each group.

1. Do Penguins live in antarctica?

do penguins live in Antarctica.

Do penguins live in Antarctica?

2. penguins cannot fly?

Penguins cannot fly.

penguins cannot fly.

Directions: Write **S** for **statement**, **Q** for **question**, **E** for **exclamation**, or **C** for **command** on the line.

_____ **1.** Two different kinds of penguins live in Antarctica.

_____ **2.** Do emperor penguins have black and white bodies?

_____ **3.** Look at their webbed feet.

_____ **4.** They're amazing!

Directions: Underline the **subject** of the sentence with **one** line. Underline the **predicate** with **two** lines.

1. Penguins eat fish, squid, and shrimp.

2. Leopard seals and killer whales hunt penguins.

3. A female penguin lays one egg.

NAME _____

My Bag's Ready!

The first letter of a word is used to put words in alphabetical (ABC) order.

Directions: Write the golf words below in ABC order. If two or more words begin with the same letter, go to the next letter to put them in ABC order.

| club | tee | bag | ball | scorecard | cart | towel |

1. _____

2. _____

3. _____

4. _____

5. _____

6. _____

7. _____

Slam Dunk!

Directions: Put the words in the box in ABC order

coach	points	team	hoop
player	game	score	dunk

1. _____

2. _____

3. _____

4. _____

5. _____

6. _____

7. _____

8. _____

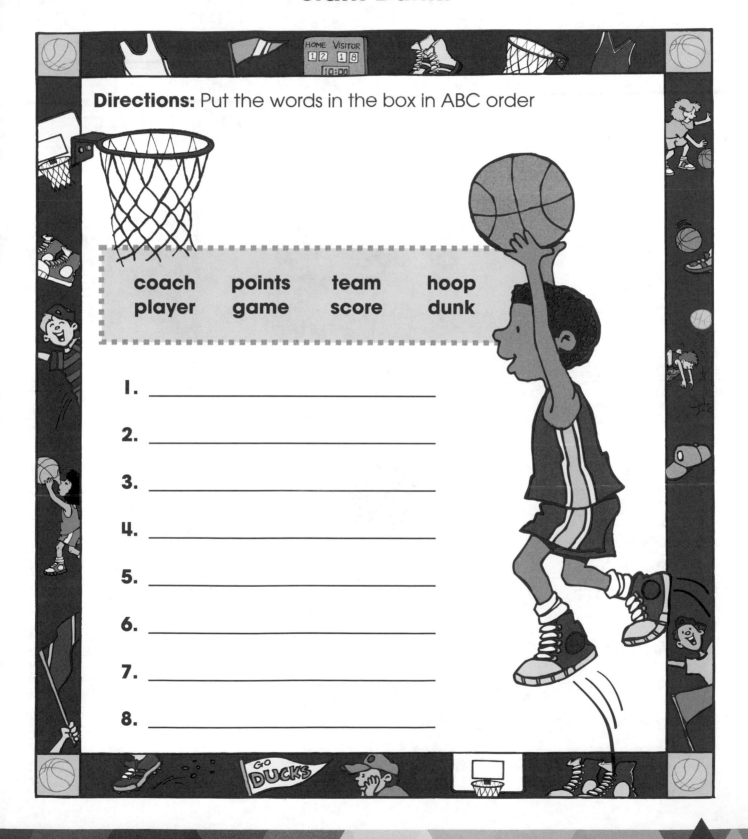

NAME _____

Learning Dictionary Skills

A dictionary is a book that gives the meaning of words. It also tells how words sound. Words in a dictionary are in ABC order. That makes them easier to find. A picture dictionary lists a word, a picture of the word, and its meaning.

Directions: Look at this page from a picture dictionary. Then, answer the questions.

baby

A very young child.

band

A group of people who play music.

bank

A place where money is kept.

bark

The sound a dog makes.

berry

A small, juicy fruit.

board

A flat piece of wood.

1. What is a small, juicy fruit? _____

2. What is a group of people who play music? _____

3. What is the name for a very young child? _____

4. What is a flat piece of wood called? _____

NAME _____

Learning Dictionary Skills

Directions: Look at this page from a picture dictionary. Then, answer the questions.

safe

A metal box.

sea

A body of water.

seed

The beginning of a plant.

sheep

An animal that has wool.

skate

A shoe with wheels or a blade on it.

snowstorm

A time when much snow falls.

squirrel

A small animal with a bushy tail.

stone

A small rock.

store

A place where items are sold.

1. What kind of animal has wool? _____

2. What do you call a shoe with wheels on it? _____

3. When a lot of snow falls, what is it called? _____

4. What is a small animal with a bushy tail? _____

5. What is a place where items are sold? _____

6. When a plant starts, what is it called? _____

NAME _____

Learning Dictionary Skills

The **guide words** at the top of a page in a dictionary tell you what the first and last words on the page will be. Only words that come in ABC order between those two words will be on that page. Guide words help you find the page you need to look up a word.

Directions: Write each word from the box in ABC order between each pair of guide words.

| faint | fence | farmer | feet | family |
| far | feed | fan | farm | face |

face   **fence**

_____   _____

_____   _____

_____   _____

_____   _____

Page 6

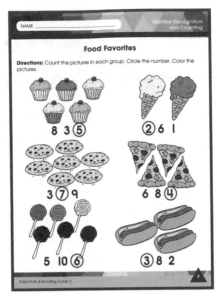

Page 7

Page 8

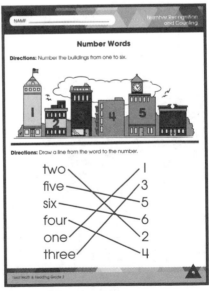

Page 9

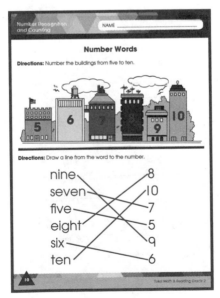

Page 10

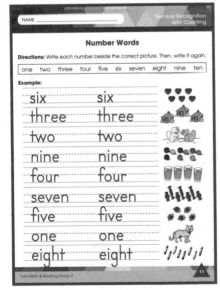

Page 11

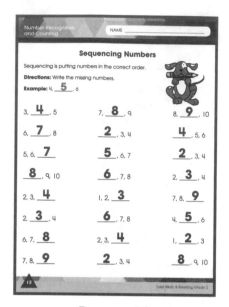

Page 12

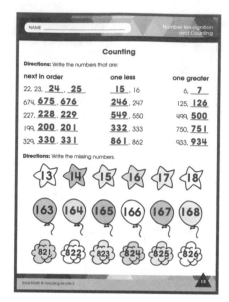

Page 13

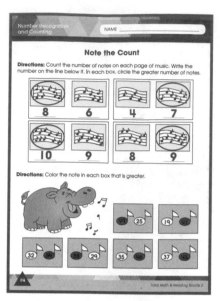

Page 14

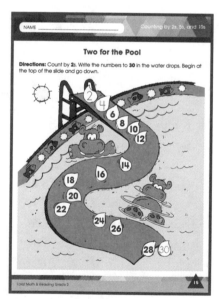

Page 15

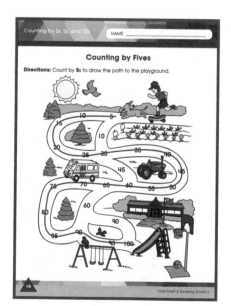

Page 16

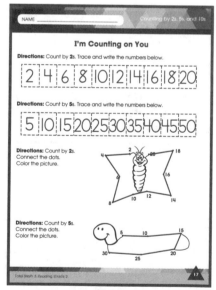

Page 17

Page 18

Page 19

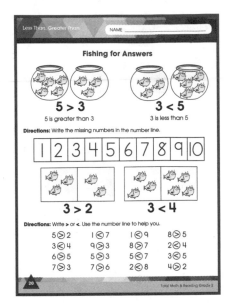

Page 20

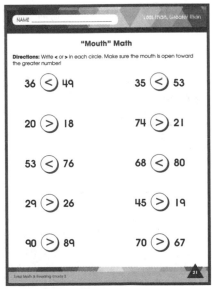

Page 21

Page 22

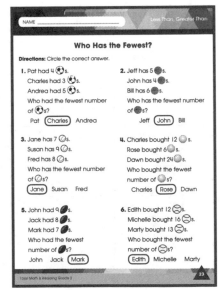

Page 23

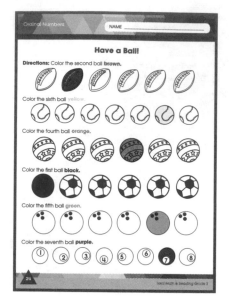

Page 24

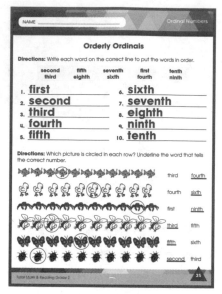

Page 25

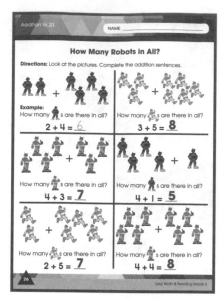

Page 26

Page 27

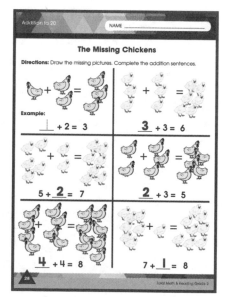

Page 28

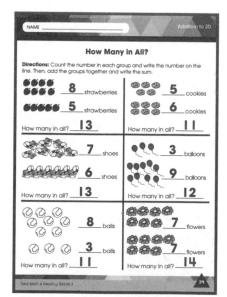

Page 29

Page 30

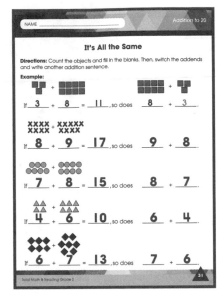

Page 31

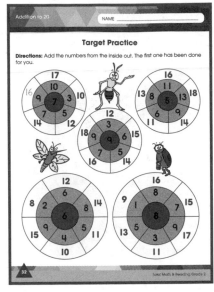

Page 32

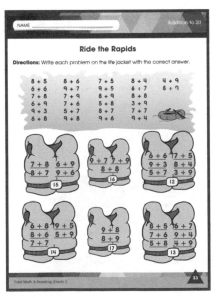

Page 33

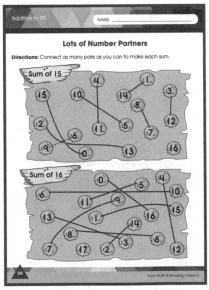

Page 34

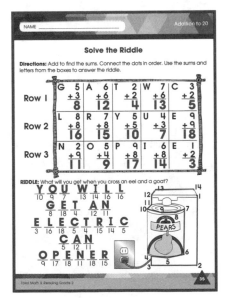

Page 35

Answer Key

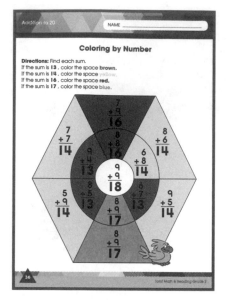

Page 36

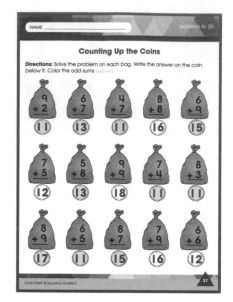

Page 37

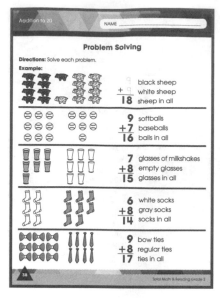

Page 38

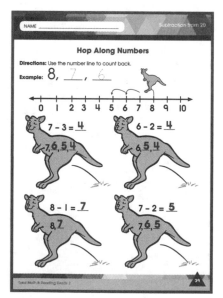

Page 39

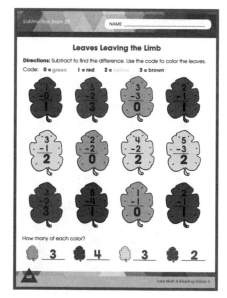

Page 40

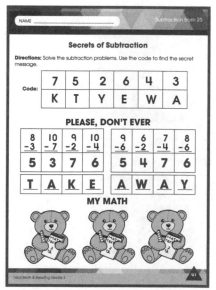

Page 41

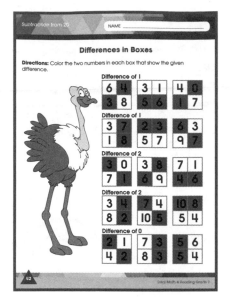

Page 42

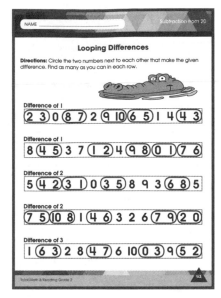

Page 43

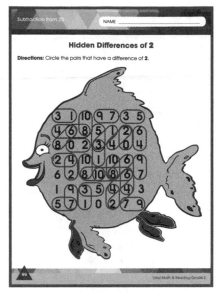

Page 44

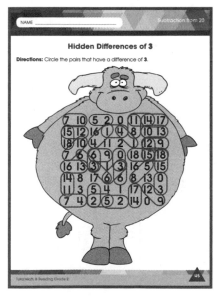

Page 45

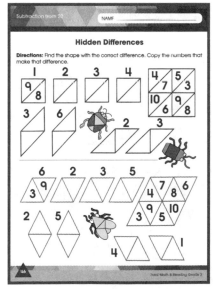

Page 46

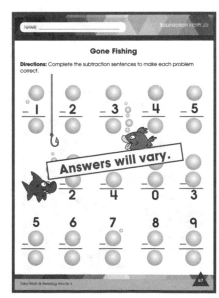

Page 47

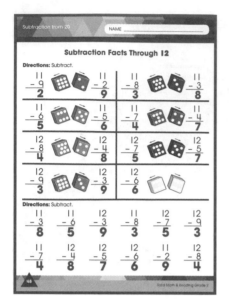

Page 48

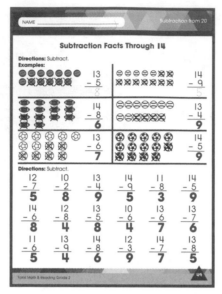

Page 49

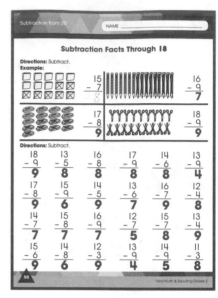

Page 50

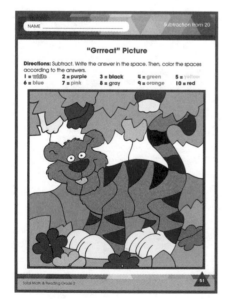

Page 51

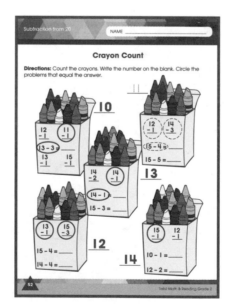

Page 52

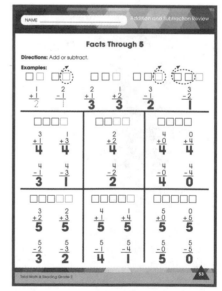

Page 53

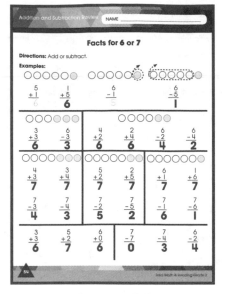

Page 54

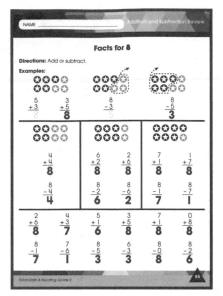

Page 55

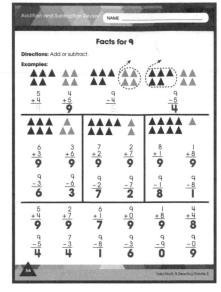

Page 56

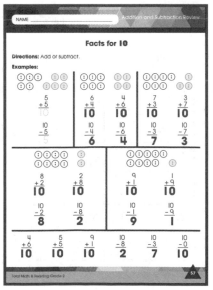

Page 57

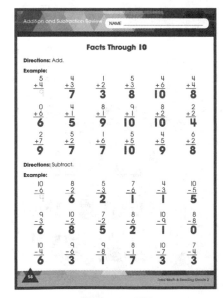

Page 58

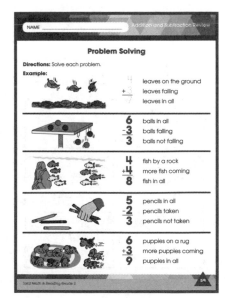

Page 59

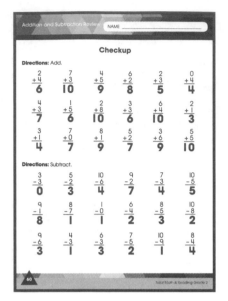

Page 60

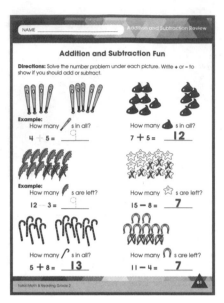

Page 61

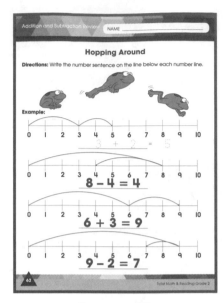

Page 62

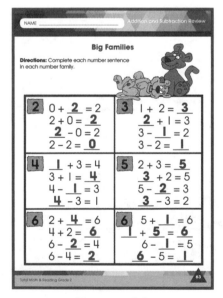

Page 63

Page 64

Page 65

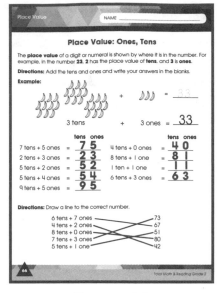

Page 66

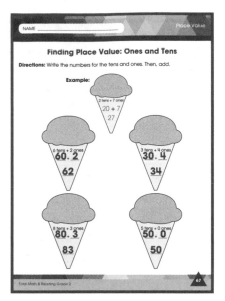

Page 67

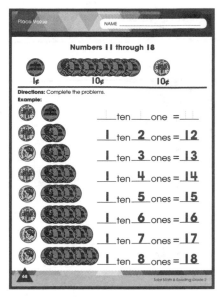

Page 68

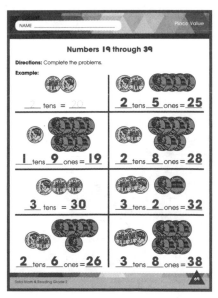

Page 69

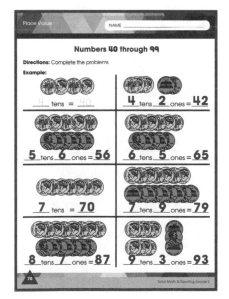

Page 70

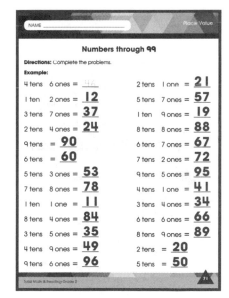

Page 71

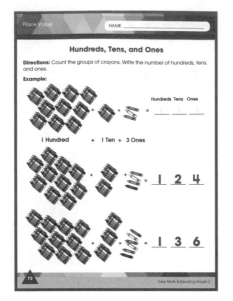

Page 72

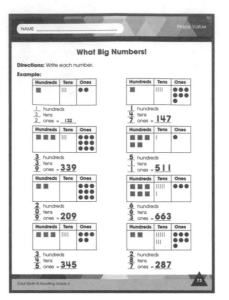

Page 73

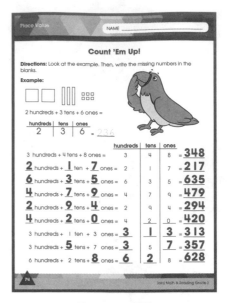

Page 74

Page 75

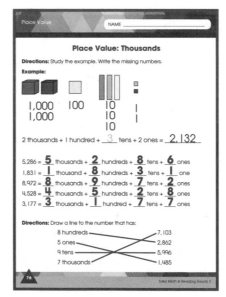

Page 76

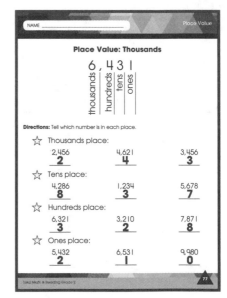

Page 77

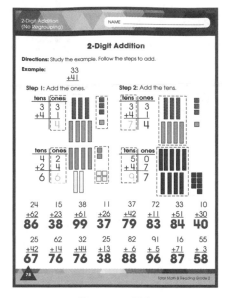

Page 78

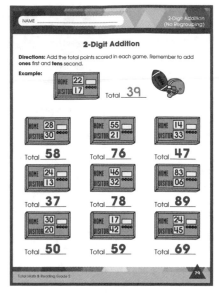

Page 79

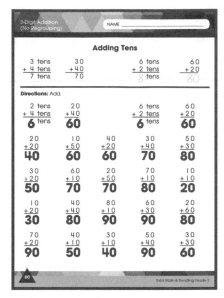

Page 80

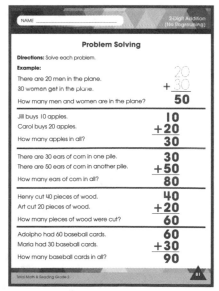

Page 81

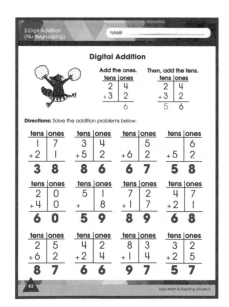

Page 82

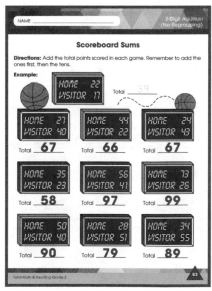

Page 83

Answer Key

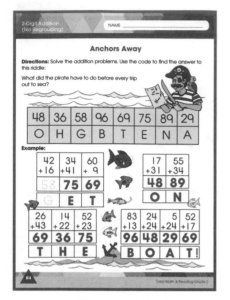

Page 84

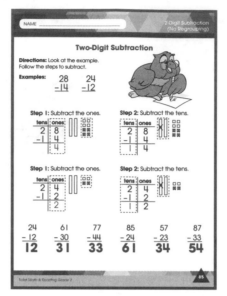

Page 85

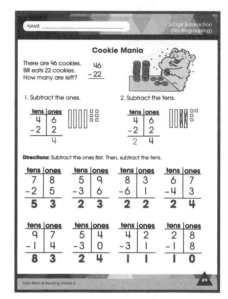

Page 86

Page 87

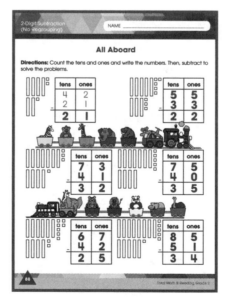

Page 88

Page 89

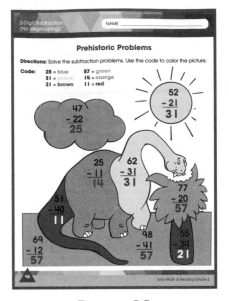

Page 90

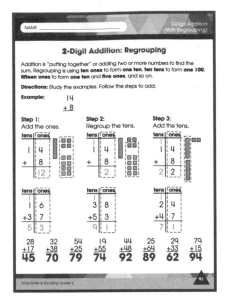

Page 91

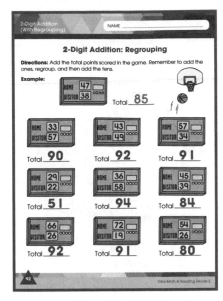

Page 92

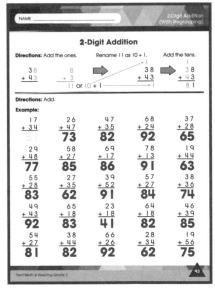

Page 93

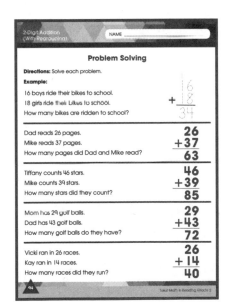

Page 94

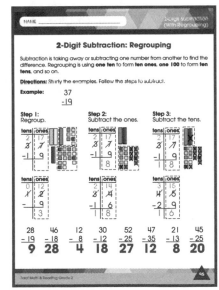

Page 95

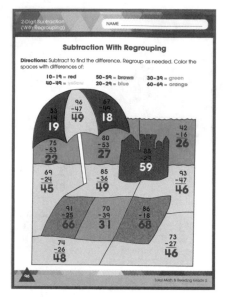

Page 96

Page 97

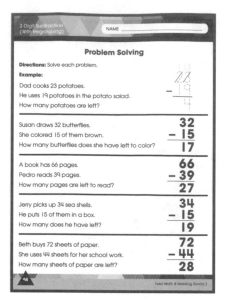

Page 98

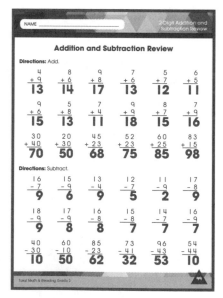

Page 99

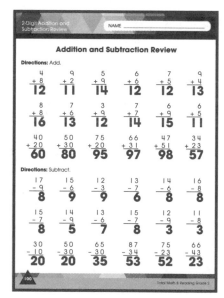

Page 100

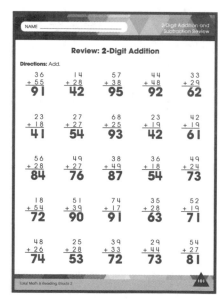

Page 101

Page 102

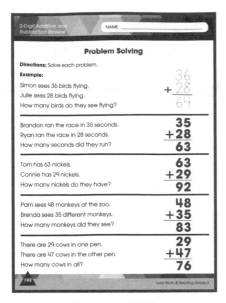

2-Digit Addition and Subtraction Review

NAME _____

Problem Solving

Directions: Solve each problem.

Example:

Simon sees 36 birds flying.
Julie sees 28 birds flying.
How many birds do they see flying?

$$\begin{array}{r} 36 \\ +28 \\ \hline 64 \end{array}$$

Brandon ran the race in 35 seconds.
Ryan ran the race in 28 seconds.
How many seconds did they run?

$$\begin{array}{r} 35 \\ +28 \\ \hline 63 \end{array}$$

Tom has 63 nickels.
Connie has 29 nickels.
How many nickels do they have?

$$\begin{array}{r} 63 \\ +29 \\ \hline 92 \end{array}$$

Pam sees 48 monkeys at the zoo.
Brenda sees 35 different monkeys.
How many monkeys did they see?

$$\begin{array}{r} 48 \\ +35 \\ \hline 83 \end{array}$$

There are 29 cows in one pen.
There are 47 cows in the other pen.
How many cows in all?

$$\begin{array}{r} 29 \\ +47 \\ \hline 76 \end{array}$$

102

Page 103

NAME _____

2-Digit Addition and Subtraction Review

Shoot for the Stars

Directions: Add the total points scored in the game. Remember to add the ones first and regroup. Then, add the tens.

Example:

HOME 53
VISITOR 27   Total 80

HOME 29
VISITOR 45   Total 74

HOME 57
VISITOR 39   Total 96

HOME 63
VISITOR 19   Total 82

HOME 66
VISITOR 28   Total 94

HOME 47
VISITOR 49   Total 96

HOME 36
VISITOR 45   Total 81

HOME 27
VISITOR 38   Total 65

HOME 54
VISITOR 39   Total 93

HOME 37
VISITOR 59   Total 96

103

Page 104

2-Digit Addition and Subtraction Review

NAME _____

Review: 2-Digit Subtraction

Directions: Subtract.

85 − 16 = **69**	93 − 48 = **45**	72 − 35 = **37**	63 − 27 = **36**	43 − 38 = **5**
56 − 29 = **27**	75 − 49 = **26**	84 − 38 = **46**	91 − 65 = **26**	37 − 18 = **19**
21 − 14 = **7**	35 − 18 = **17**	42 − 29 = **13**	72 − 47 = **25**	81 − 54 = **27**
64 − 38 = **26**	53 − 28 = **25**	94 − 57 = **37**	48 − 39 = **9**	23 − 18 = **5**
74 − 58 = **16**	83 − 36 = **47**	62 − 26 = **36**	54 − 28 = **26**	32 − 17 = **15**

104

Page 105

NAME _____

2-Digit Addition and Subtraction Review

Go "Fore" It!

Directions: Add or subtract using regrouping.

$$\begin{array}{c} \text{tens} \mid \text{ones} \\ 2 \mid 15 \\ \cancel{3} \mid \cancel{5} \\ -2 \mid 7 \\ \hline 8 \end{array}$$

$$\begin{array}{r} 40 \\ -16 \\ \hline 24 \end{array}$$

$$\begin{array}{r} 35 \\ +27 \\ \hline 62 \end{array}$$

$$\begin{array}{r} 56 \\ -27 \\ \hline 29 \end{array}$$

$$\begin{array}{r} 93 \\ -39 \\ \hline 54 \end{array}$$

$$\begin{array}{r} 42 \\ -14 \\ \hline 28 \end{array}$$

$$\begin{array}{r} 44 \\ +28 \\ \hline 72 \end{array}$$

$$\begin{array}{r} 33 \\ +18 \\ \hline 51 \end{array}$$

$$\begin{array}{r} 97 \\ -48 \\ \hline 49 \end{array}$$

$$\begin{array}{r} 73 \\ -24 \\ \hline 49 \end{array}$$

$$\begin{array}{r} 56 \\ -17 \\ \hline 39 \end{array}$$

$$\begin{array}{r} 68 \\ -49 \\ \hline 19 \end{array}$$

$$\begin{array}{r} 49 \\ +32 \\ \hline 81 \end{array}$$

$$\begin{array}{r} 77 \\ -68 \\ \hline 9 \end{array}$$

$$\begin{array}{r} 27 \\ +19 \\ \hline 46 \end{array}$$

105

Page 106

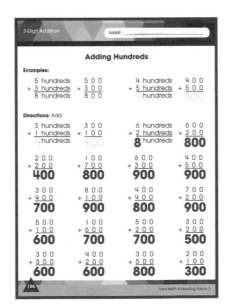

3-Digit Addition

NAME _____

Adding Hundreds

Examples:

5 hundreds + 3 hundreds = 8 hundreds	500 + 300 = 800	4 hundreds + 5 hundreds = 9 hundreds	400 + 500 = 900

Directions: Add.

3 hundreds + 1 hundreds = 4 hundreds	300 + 100 = 400	6 hundreds + 2 hundreds = 8 hundreds	600 + 200 = 800
200 + 200 = **400**	100 + 700 = **800**	600 + 300 = **900**	400 + 500 = **900**
300 + 400 = **700**	800 + 100 = **900**	400 + 400 = **800**	700 + 200 = **900**
500 + 100 = **600**	100 + 600 = **700**	500 + 200 = **700**	300 + 200 = **500**
300 + 300 = **600**	400 + 200 = **600**	300 + 500 = **800**	200 + 100 = **300**

106

Page 107

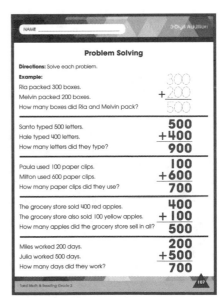

NAME _____

3-Digit Addition

Problem Solving

Directions: Solve each problem.

Example:

Ria packed 300 boxes.
Melvin packed 200 boxes.
How many boxes did Ria and Melvin pack?

$$\begin{array}{r} 300 \\ +200 \\ \hline 500 \end{array}$$

Santo typed 500 letters.
Hale typed 400 letters.
How many letters did they type?

$$\begin{array}{r} 500 \\ +400 \\ \hline 900 \end{array}$$

Paula used 100 paper clips.
Milton used 600 paper clips.
How many paper clips did they use?

$$\begin{array}{r} 100 \\ +600 \\ \hline 700 \end{array}$$

The grocery store sold 400 red apples.
The grocery store also sold 100 yellow apples.
How many apples did the grocery store sell in all?

$$\begin{array}{r} 400 \\ +100 \\ \hline 500 \end{array}$$

Miles worked 200 days.
Julia worked 500 days.
How many days did they work?

$$\begin{array}{r} 200 \\ +500 \\ \hline 700 \end{array}$$

107

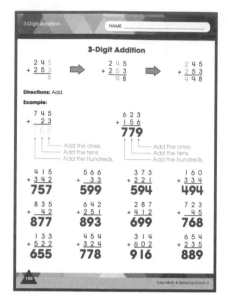

Page 108

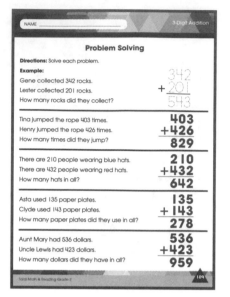

Page 109

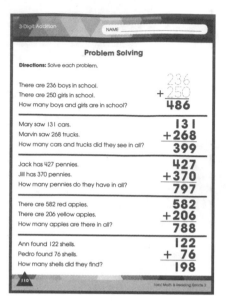

Page 110

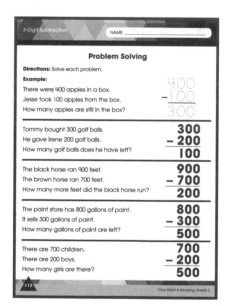

Page 111

Page 112

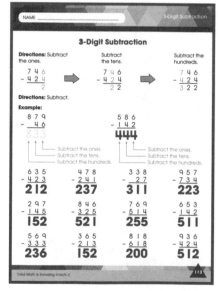

Page 113

Page 114

3-Digit Subtraction

NAME _____

Problem Solving

Directions: Solve each problem.

Example:

The grocery store buys 568 cans of beans.
It sells 345 cans of beans.
How many cans of beans are left?

$$\begin{array}{r} 568 \\ -345 \\ \hline 223 \end{array}$$

The cooler holds 732 gallons of milk.
It has 412 gallons of milk in it.
How many more gallons of milk
will it take to fill the cooler?

$$\begin{array}{r} 732 \\ -412 \\ \hline 320 \end{array}$$

Ann does 635 push-ups.
Carl does 421 push-ups.
How many more push-ups does Ann do?

$$\begin{array}{r} 635 \\ -421 \\ \hline 214 \end{array}$$

Kurt has 386 pennies.
Neal has 32 pennies.
How many more pennies does Kurt have?

$$\begin{array}{r} 386 \\ -\ 32 \\ \hline 354 \end{array}$$

It takes 874 nails to build a tree house.
Jillian has 532 nails.
How many more nails does she need?

$$\begin{array}{r} 874 \\ -532 \\ \hline 342 \end{array}$$

Page 115

NAME _____

3-Digit Addition and Subtraction Review

Review: Addition and Subtraction

Directions: Add.

$$\begin{array}{r} 124 \\ +323 \\ \hline 447 \end{array} \quad \begin{array}{r} 520 \\ +407 \\ \hline 927 \end{array} \quad \begin{array}{r} 739 \\ +150 \\ \hline 889 \end{array} \quad \begin{array}{r} 861 \\ +\ 6 \\ \hline 867 \end{array}$$

Directions: Subtract.

$$\begin{array}{r} 900 \\ -600 \\ \hline 300 \end{array} \quad \begin{array}{r} 800 \\ -200 \\ \hline 600 \end{array} \quad \begin{array}{r} 974 \\ -564 \\ \hline 410 \end{array} \quad \begin{array}{r} 508 \\ -\ 7 \\ \hline 501 \end{array}$$

$$\begin{array}{r} 728 \\ -326 \\ \hline 402 \end{array} \quad \begin{array}{r} 657 \\ -\ 45 \\ \hline 612 \end{array} \quad \begin{array}{r} 894 \\ -464 \\ \hline 430 \end{array} \quad \begin{array}{r} 596 \\ -352 \\ \hline 244 \end{array}$$

Directions: Solve each problem.

There are 275 nails in a box.
123 nails are taken out of the box.
How many nails are still in the box?

$$\begin{array}{r} 275 \\ -123 \\ \hline 152 \end{array}$$

Gerald peeled 212 apples.
Anna peeled 84 apples.
How many apples did they peel in all?

$$\begin{array}{r} 212 \\ +\ 84 \\ \hline 296 \end{array}$$

Page 116

3-Digit Addition and Subtraction Review

NAME _____

Review: 3-Digit Addition

Directions: Add.

Example:

$$\begin{array}{r} 340 \\ +225 \\ \hline 565 \end{array} \quad \begin{array}{r} 754 \\ +\ 32 \\ \hline 786 \end{array} \quad \begin{array}{r} 826 \\ +\ 3 \\ \hline 829 \end{array} \quad \begin{array}{r} 632 \\ +322 \\ \hline 954 \end{array}$$

$$\begin{array}{r} 198 \\ +200 \\ \hline 398 \end{array} \quad \begin{array}{r} 456 \\ +\ 31 \\ \hline 487 \end{array} \quad \begin{array}{r} 541 \\ +333 \\ \hline 874 \end{array} \quad \begin{array}{r} 273 \\ +415 \\ \hline 688 \end{array}$$

$$\begin{array}{r} 900 \\ +\ 34 \\ \hline 934 \end{array} \quad \begin{array}{r} 847 \\ +131 \\ \hline 978 \end{array} \quad \begin{array}{r} 721 \\ +176 \\ \hline 897 \end{array} \quad \begin{array}{r} 402 \\ +383 \\ \hline 785 \end{array}$$

$$\begin{array}{r} 156 \\ +423 \\ \hline 579 \end{array} \quad \begin{array}{r} 644 \\ +251 \\ \hline 895 \end{array} \quad \begin{array}{r} 215 \\ +542 \\ \hline 757 \end{array} \quad \begin{array}{r} 372 \\ +417 \\ \hline 789 \end{array}$$

$$\begin{array}{r} 518 \\ +351 \\ \hline 869 \end{array} \quad \begin{array}{r} 783 \\ +\ 5 \\ \hline 788 \end{array} \quad \begin{array}{r} 684 \\ +\ 14 \\ \hline 698 \end{array} \quad \begin{array}{r} 710 \\ +260 \\ \hline 970 \end{array}$$

Page 117

NAME _____

3-Digit Addition and Subtraction Review

Review: 3-Digit Subtraction

Directions: Subtract.

Example:

$$\begin{array}{r} 856 \\ -352 \\ \hline 504 \end{array} \quad \begin{array}{r} 432 \\ -\ 21 \\ \hline 411 \end{array} \quad \begin{array}{r} 598 \\ -416 \\ \hline 182 \end{array} \quad \begin{array}{r} 769 \\ -345 \\ \hline 424 \end{array}$$

$$\begin{array}{r} 319 \\ -\ 6 \\ \hline 313 \end{array} \quad \begin{array}{r} 954 \\ -731 \\ \hline 223 \end{array} \quad \begin{array}{r} 275 \\ -\ 3 \\ \hline 272 \end{array} \quad \begin{array}{r} 643 \\ -313 \\ \hline 330 \end{array}$$

$$\begin{array}{r} 775 \\ -261 \\ \hline 514 \end{array} \quad \begin{array}{r} 834 \\ -\ 12 \\ \hline 822 \end{array} \quad \begin{array}{r} 942 \\ -111 \\ \hline 831 \end{array} \quad \begin{array}{r} 478 \\ -324 \\ \hline 154 \end{array}$$

$$\begin{array}{r} 562 \\ -431 \\ \hline 131 \end{array} \quad \begin{array}{r} 444 \\ -212 \\ \hline 232 \end{array} \quad \begin{array}{r} 385 \\ -152 \\ \hline 233 \end{array} \quad \begin{array}{r} 754 \\ -\ 3 \\ \hline 751 \end{array}$$

$$\begin{array}{r} 868 \\ -234 \\ \hline 634 \end{array} \quad \begin{array}{r} 943 \\ -843 \\ \hline 100 \end{array} \quad \begin{array}{r} 689 \\ -417 \\ \hline 272 \end{array} \quad \begin{array}{r} 577 \\ -\ 37 \\ \hline 540 \end{array}$$

Page 118

Multiplication

NAME _____

Multiplication

Multiplication is a short way to find the sum of adding the same number a certain amount of times. For example, $7 \times 4 = 28$ instead of $7 + 7 + 7 + 7 = 28$.

Directions: Study the example. Solve the problems.

Example:

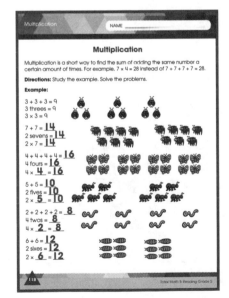

$3 + 3 + 3 = 9$
3 threes = 9
$3 \times 3 = 9$

$7 + 7 = 14$
2 sevens = 14
$2 \times 7 = 14$

$4 + 4 + 4 + 4 = 16$
4 fours = 16
$4 \times 4 = 16$

$5 + 5 = 10$
2 fives = 10
$2 \times 5 = 10$

$2 + 2 + 2 + 2 = 8$
4 twos = 8
$4 \times 2 = 8$

$6 + 6 = 12$
2 sixes = 12
$2 \times 6 = 12$

Page 119

NAME _____

Multiplication

Multiplication

Multiplication is repeated addition.

Directions: Draw a picture for each problem. Then, write the missing numbers.

Example:
Draw 2 groups of three apples.

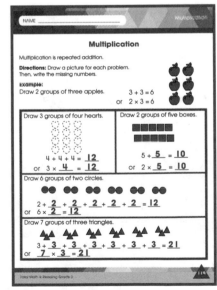

$3 + 3 = 6$
or $2 \times 3 = 6$

Draw 3 groups of four hearts.	Draw 2 groups of five boxes.
$4 + 4 + 4 = 12$ or $3 \times 4 = 12$	$5 + 5 = 10$ or $2 \times 5 = 10$

Draw 6 groups of two circles.

$2 + 2 + 2 + 2 + 2 + 2 = 12$
or $6 \times 2 = 12$

Draw 7 groups of three triangles.

$3 + 3 + 3 + 3 + 3 + 3 + 3 = 21$
or $7 \times 3 = 21$

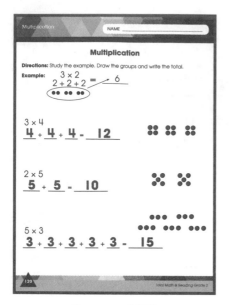

Page 120

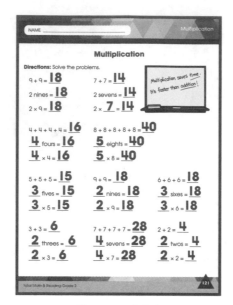

Page 121

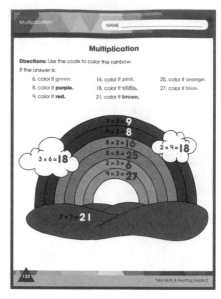

Page 122

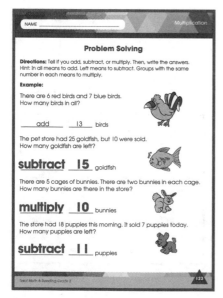

Page 123

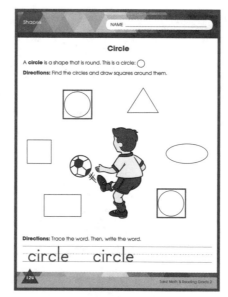

Page 124

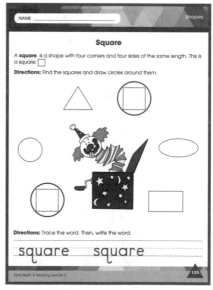

Page 125

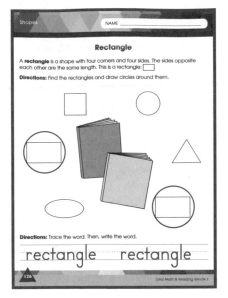

Page 126

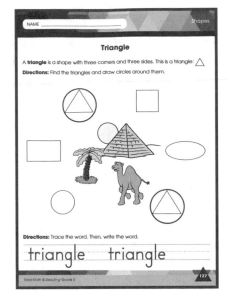

Page 127

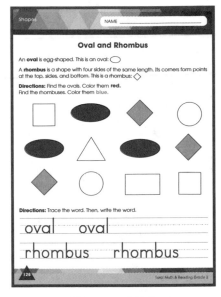

Page 128

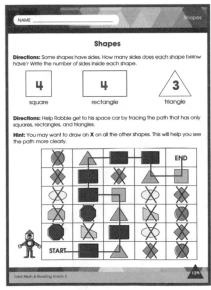

Page 129

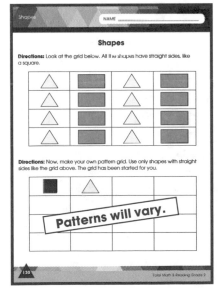

Page 130

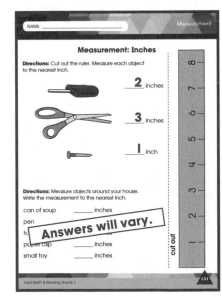

Page 131

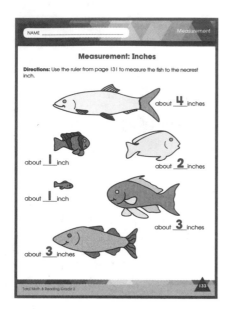

Page 133

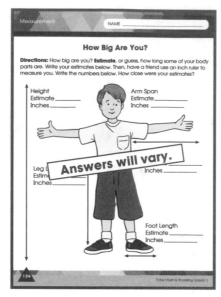

Page 134

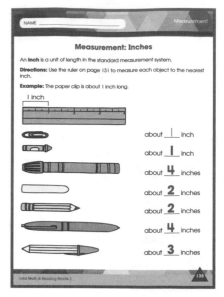

Page 135

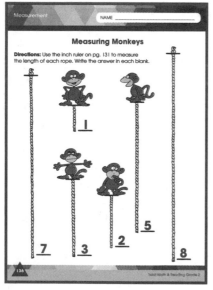

Page 136

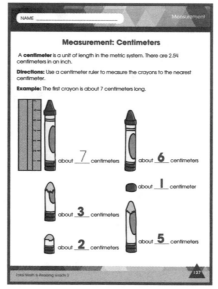

Page 137

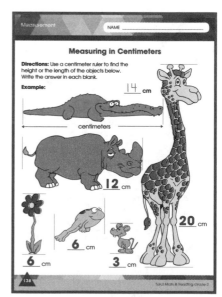

Page 138

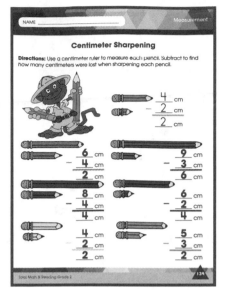

Page 139

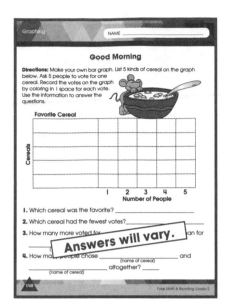

Page 140

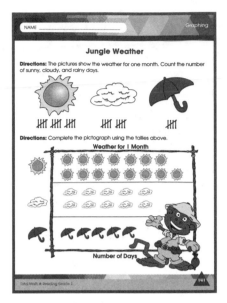

Page 141

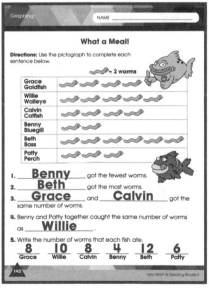

Page 142

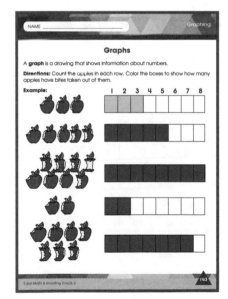

Page 143

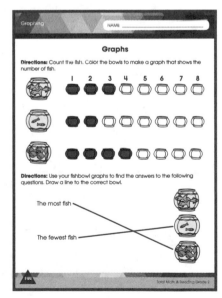

Page 144

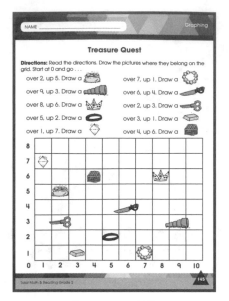

Page 145

Page 146

Page 147

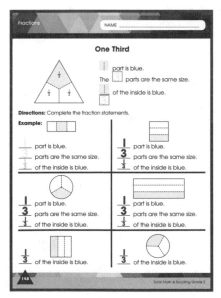

Page 148

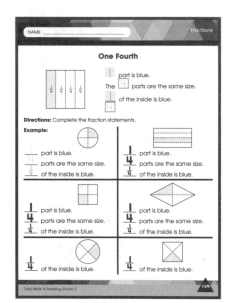

Page 149

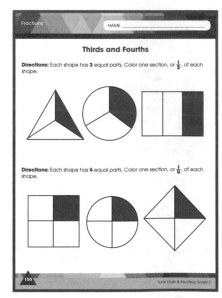

Page 150

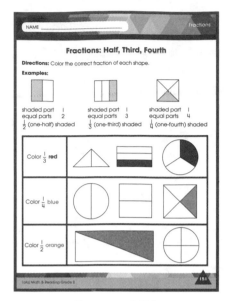

Page 151

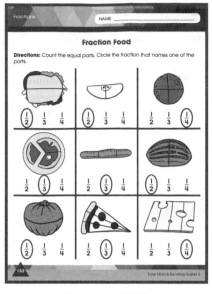

Page 152

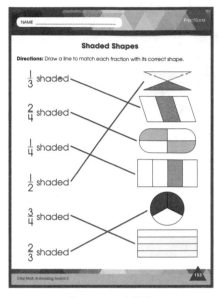

Page 153

Page 154

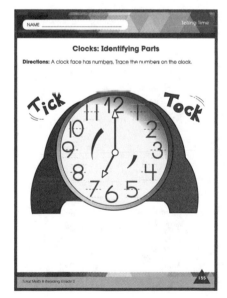

Page 155

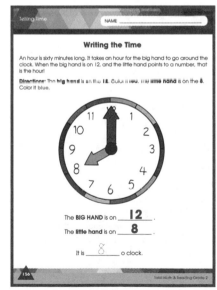

Page 156

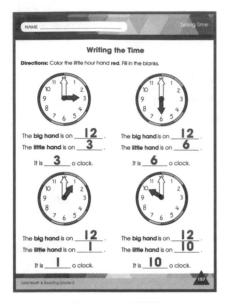

Page 157

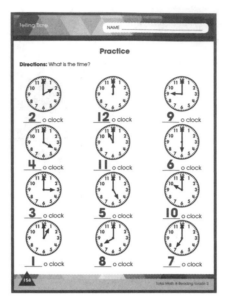

Page 158

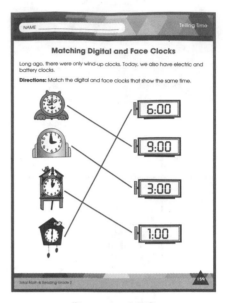

Page 159

Page 160

Page 161

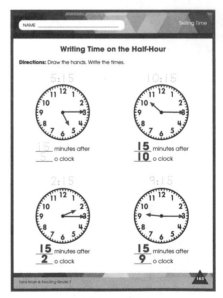

Page 163

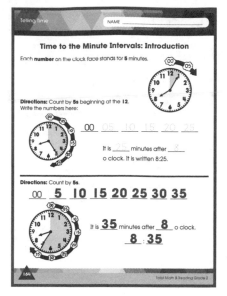

Page 164

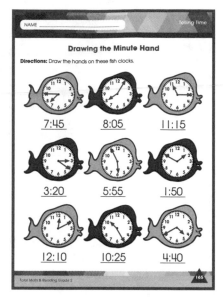

Page 165

Page 166

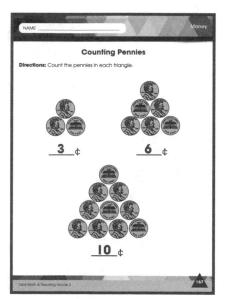

Page 167

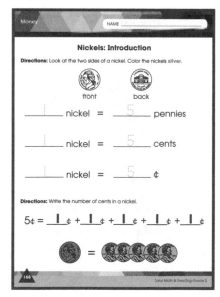

Page 168

Page 169

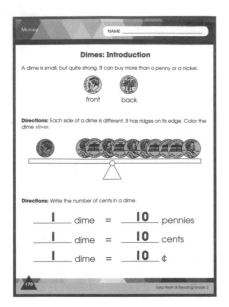

Page 170

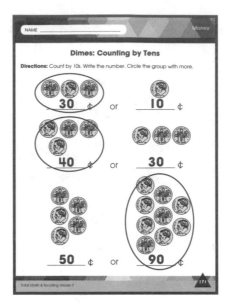

Page 171

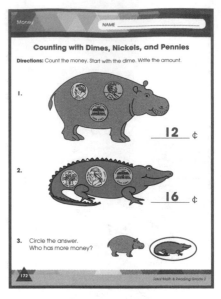

Page 172

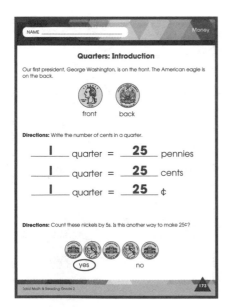

Page 173

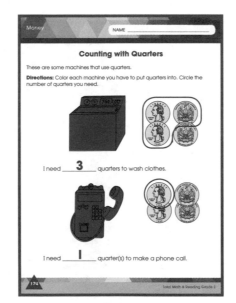

Page 174

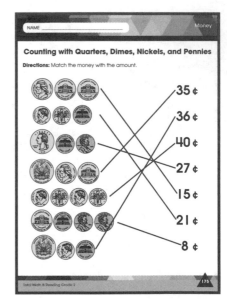

Page 175

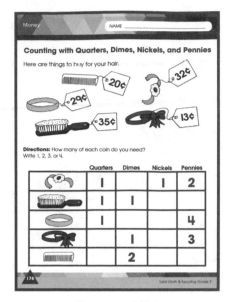

Page 176

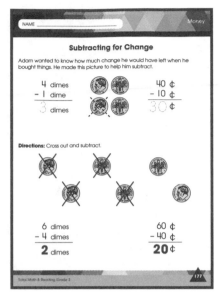

Page 177

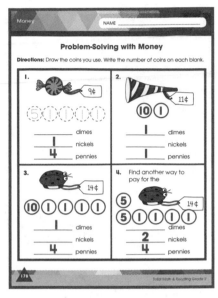

Page 178

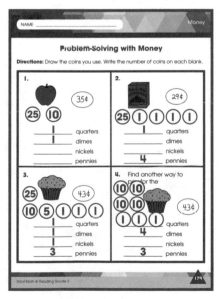

Page 179

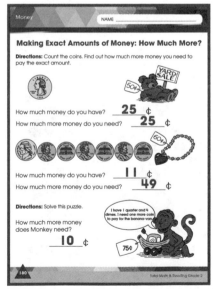

Page 180

Page 182

Answer Key

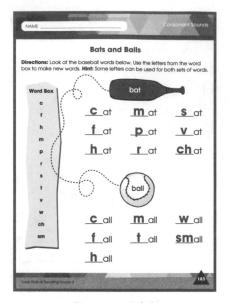

Page 183

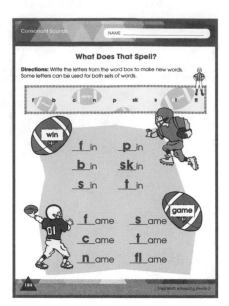

Page 184

Page 185

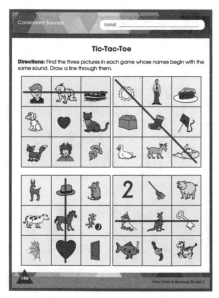

Page 186

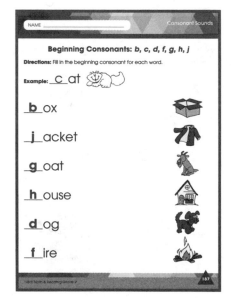

Page 187

Page 188

Page 189

NAME _____   Consonant Sounds

Beginning Consonants: k, l, m, n, p, q, r

Directions: Fill in the beginning consonant for each word.

Example: __r__ ose

__m__ oney

__q__ uilt

__l__ ion

__p__ an

__k__ ey

__n__ ose

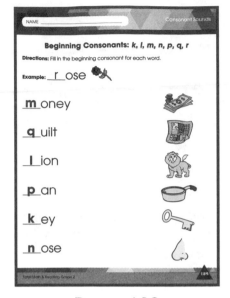

Page 189

Page 190

Consonant Sounds   NAME _____

Beginning Consonants: s, t, v, w, x, y, z

Directions: Write the letter under each picture that makes the beginning sound.

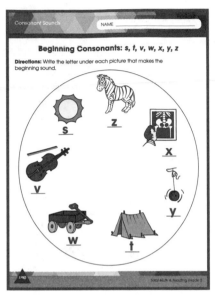

s   **z**   **x**   **v**   **y**   **w**   **t**

Page 190

Page 191

NAME _____   Consonant Sounds

Beginning Consonants: s, t, v, w, x, y, z

Directions: Fill in the beginning consonant for each word.

Example: __s__ ock

__z__ ipper

__t__ able

__x__ ray

__v__ ase

__y__ olk

__w__ and

Page 191

Page 192

Consonant Sounds   NAME _____

Ending Consonants: b, d, f, g

Directions: Fill in the ending consonant for each word.

ma __n__

cu __b__

roo __f__

do __g__

be __d__

bi __b__

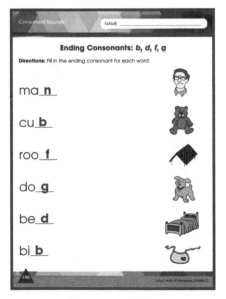

Page 192

Page 193

NAME _____   Consonant Sounds

Ending Consonants: k, l, m, n, p, r

Directions: Fill in the ending consonant for each word.

nai __l__

ca __n__

gu __m__

ca __r__

truc __k__

ca __p__

pai __l__

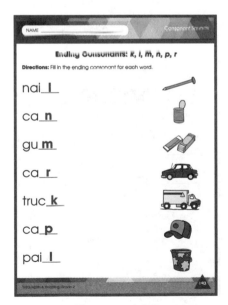

Page 193

Page 194

Consonant Sounds   NAME _____

Ending Consonants: s, t, x

Directions: Fill in the ending consonant for each word.

ca ___

bo ___

bu ___

fo ___

boa ___

ma ___

Page 194

Answer Key

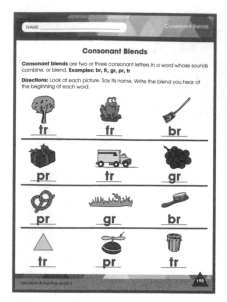

Page 195

Page 196

Page 197

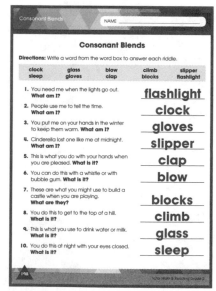

Page 198

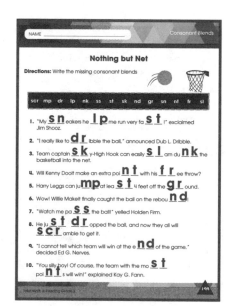

Page 199

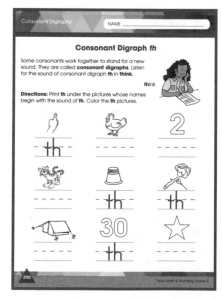

Page 200

Page 201

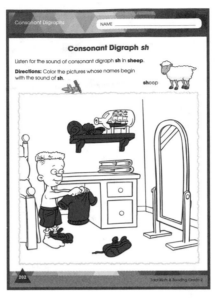

Page 202

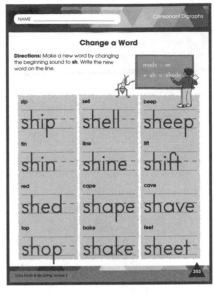

Page 203

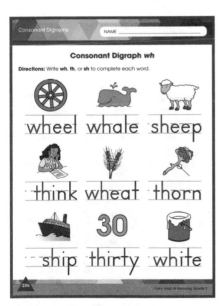

Page 204

Page 205

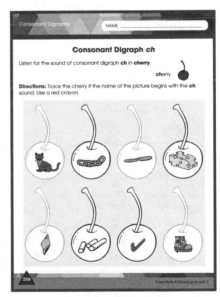

Page 206

Page 207

Page 208

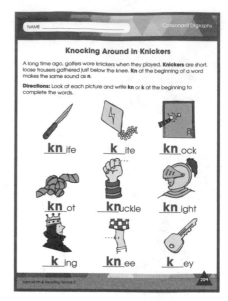

Page 209

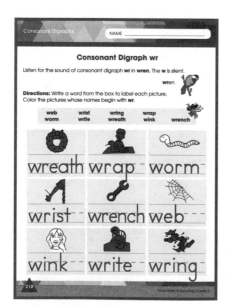

Page 210

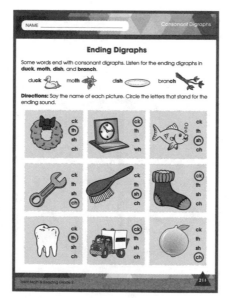

Page 211

Page 212

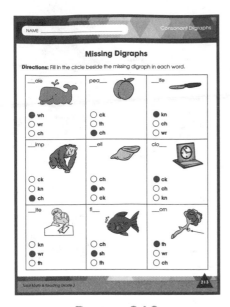

Page 213

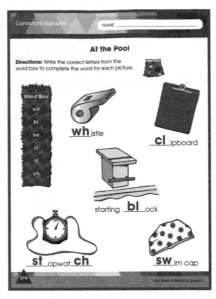

Page 214

Page 215

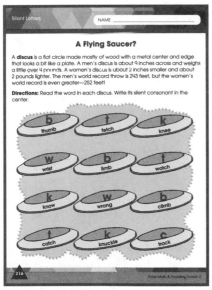

Page 216

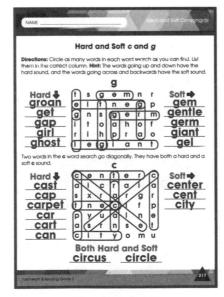

Page 217

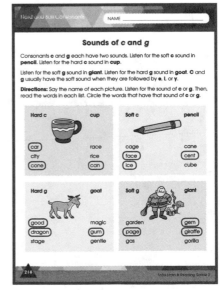

Page 218

Answer Key

Page 219

Page 220

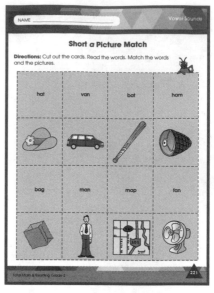

Page 221

Page 223

Page 225

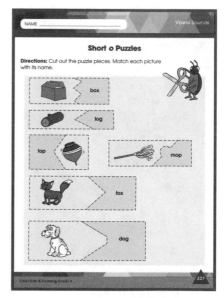

Page 227

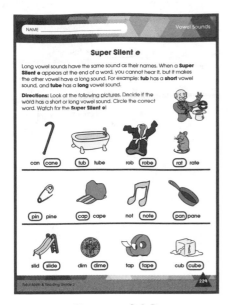

Page 229

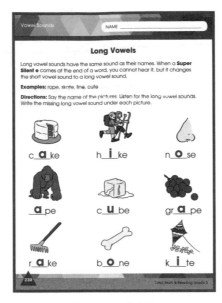

Page 230

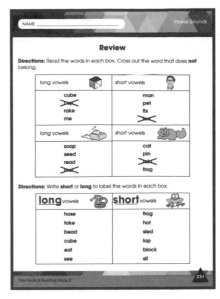

Page 231

Page 232

Page 233

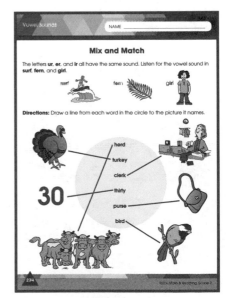

Page 234

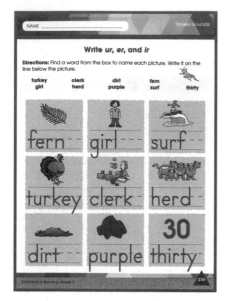

Page 235

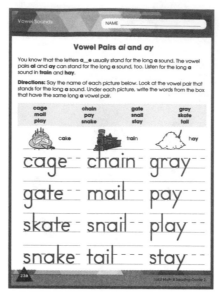

Page 236

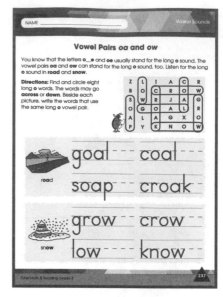

Page 237

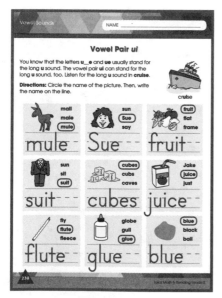

Page 238

Page 239

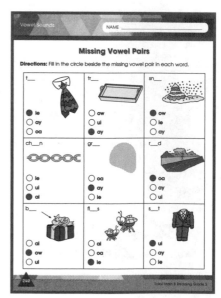

Page 240

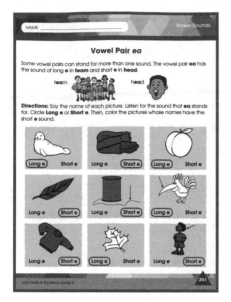

Page 241

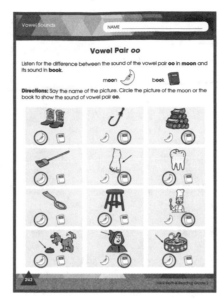

Page 242

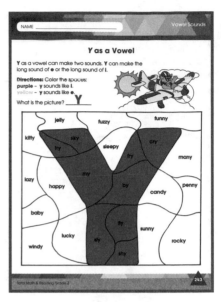

Page 243

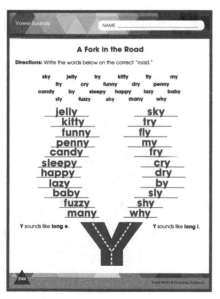

Page 244

Page 245

Page 246

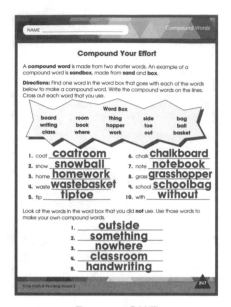

Page 247

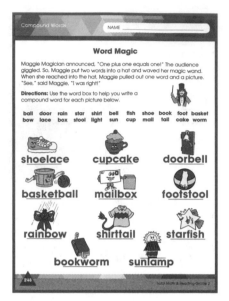

Page 248

Page 249

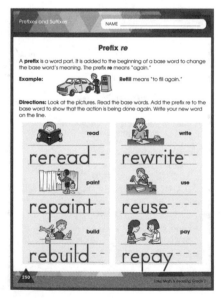

Page 250

Page 251

Page 252

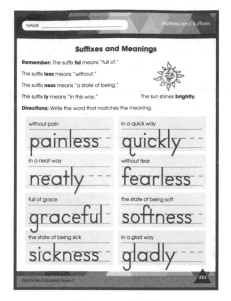

Page 253

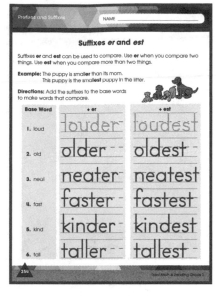

Page 254

Page 255

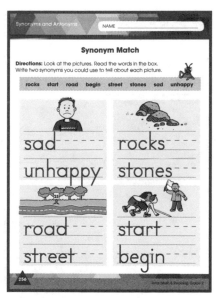

Page 256

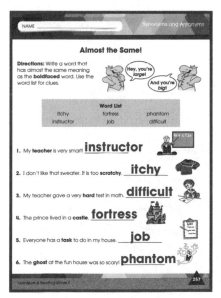

Page 257

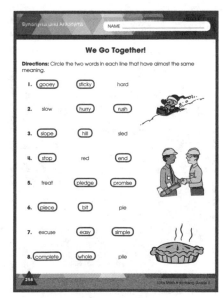

Page 258

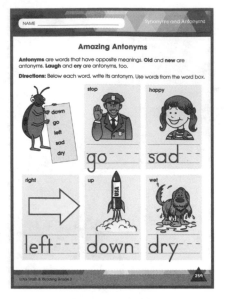

Page 259

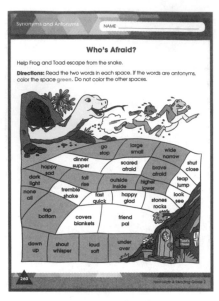

Page 260

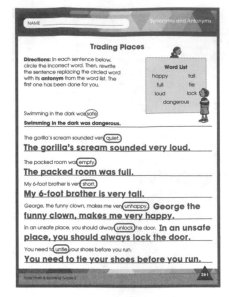

Page 261

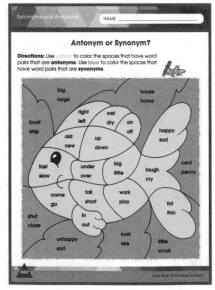

Page 262

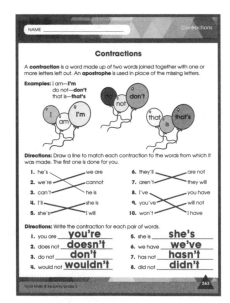

Page 263

Page 264

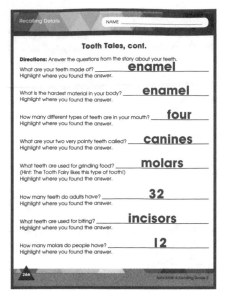

Page 266

Page 267

Page 268

Page 269

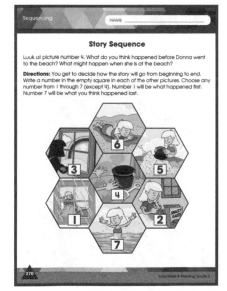

Page 270

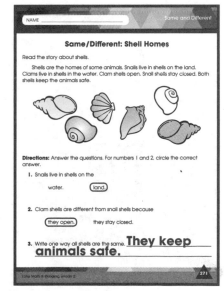

Page 271

Answer Key

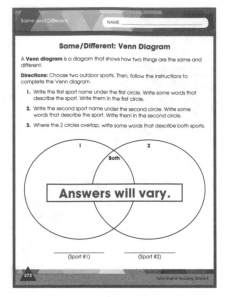

Page 272

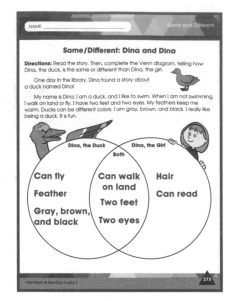

Page 273

Page 274

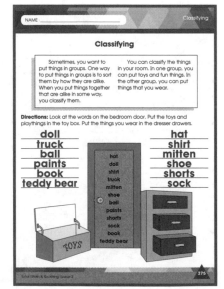

Page 275

Page 276

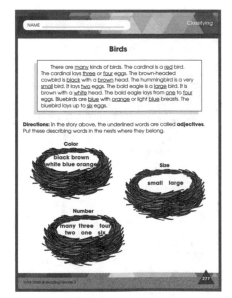

Page 277

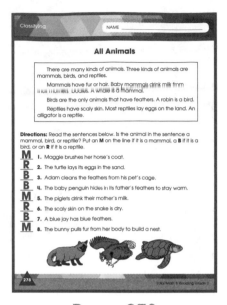

Page 278

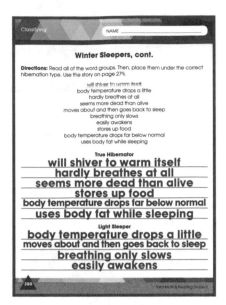

Page 280

Page 281

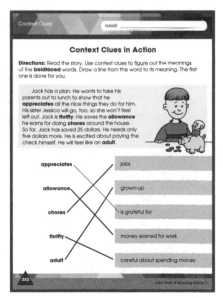

Page 282

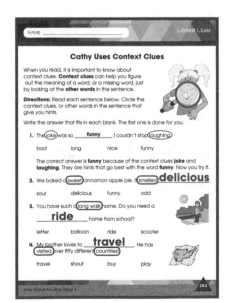

Page 283

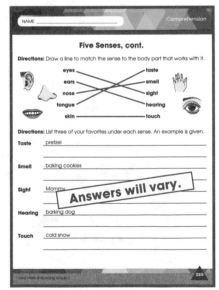

Page 285

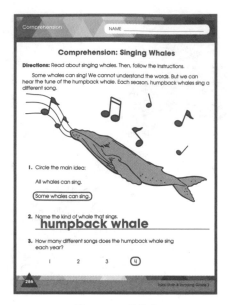

Page 286

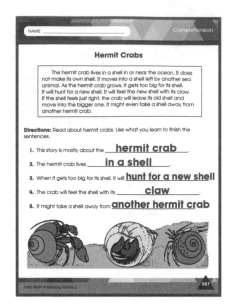

Page 287

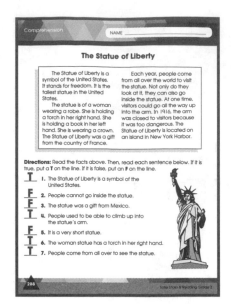

Page 288

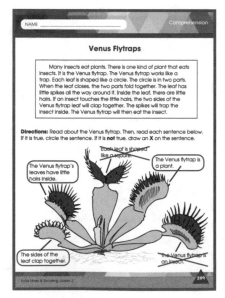

Page 289

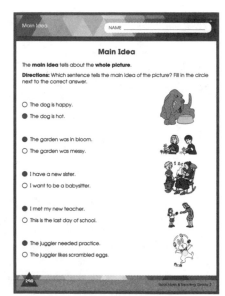

Page 290

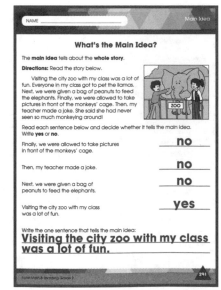

Page 291

Page 292

Main Idea

The **main idea** tells about the **whole story**.

Directions: Read the story carefully. Then, write a sentence that tells the main idea.

My brother, Scott, loves to fly planes. He flies planes every chance he gets. His favorite type of plane is a Cessna 182. He also likes to go scuba diving. He likes to go scuba diving in the Gulf of Mexico best. Sometimes, he goes flying in the morning and scuba diving in the afternoon. Scott is very adventurous!

Scott is very adventurous because he loves to fly planes and go scuba diving.

My dad is a very talented musician. He taught himself how to play the piano and now he is an excellent piano player. When people hear him play, they can't believe he has never taken any lessons! People say he has "natural talent," and it's true!

My dad has natural talent for music because he plays piano without having had lessons.

Page 293

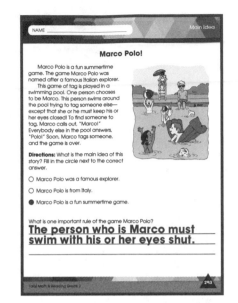

Marco Polo!

Marco Polo is a fun summertime game. The game Marco Polo was named after a famous Italian explorer.

This game of tag is played in a swimming pool. One person chooses to be Marco. This person swims around the pool trying to tag someone else—except that she or he must keep his or her eyes closed! To find someone to tag, Marco calls out, "Marco!" Everybody else in the pool answers, "Polo!" Soon, Marco tags someone, and the game is over.

Directions: What is the main idea of this story? Fill in the circle next to the correct answer.

○ Marco Polo was a famous explorer.

○ Marco Polo is from Italy.

● Marco Polo is a fun summertime game.

What is one important rule of the game Marco Polo?

The person who is Marco must swim with his or her eyes shut.

Page 294

Read All About It

Directions: Read each part of the paper. Fill in the circle beside the sentence that tells the main idea.

Hundreds Enjoy Town Carnival
● Many people had fun at the carnival.
○ The carnival was not a success.

Bank Robbers Caught
○ Five bank robbers got away.
● Two bank robbers were caught.

CLASSIFIEDS For Sale 3 black kittens 2 brown puppies Call 555-4109
○ Someone wants to buy kittens and puppies.
● Someone wants to sell kittens and puppies.

Garden Club to Meet Wednesday and Thursday This Week
○ The Garden Club will not meet this week.
● The Garden Club will meet two times this week.

Page 295

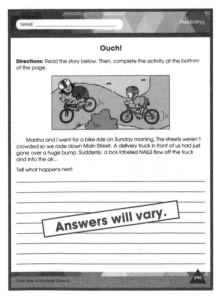

Ouch!

Directions: Read the story below. Then, complete the activity at the bottom of the page.

Marsha and I went for a bike ride on Sunday morning. The streets weren't crowded so we rode down Main Street. A delivery truck in front of us had just gone over a huge bump. Suddenly, a box labeled NAILS flew off the truck and into the air...

Tell what happens next:

Answers will vary.

Page 296

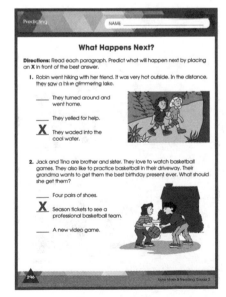

What Happens Next?

Directions: Read each paragraph. Predict what will happen next by placing an X in front of the best answer.

1. Robin went hiking with her friend. It was very hot outside. In the distance, they saw a blue glimmering lake.

___ They turned around and went home.

___ They yelled for help.

X They waded into the cool water.

2. Jack and Tina are brother and sister. They love to watch basketball games. They also like to practice basketball in their driveway. Their grandma wants to get them the best birthday present ever. What should she get them?

___ Four pairs of shoes.

X Season tickets to see a professional basketball team.

___ A new video game.

Page 297

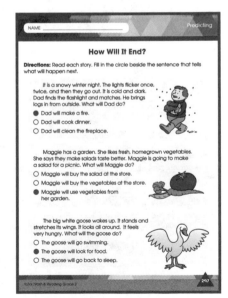

How Will It End?

Directions: Read each story. Fill in the circle beside the sentence that tells what will happen next.

It is a snowy winter night. The lights flicker once, twice, and then they go out. It is cold and dark. Dad finds the flashlight and matches. He brings logs in from outside. What will Dad do?

● Dad will make a fire.
○ Dad will cook dinner.
○ Dad will clean the fireplace.

Maggie has a garden. She likes fresh, homegrown vegetables. She says they make salads taste better. Maggie is going to make a salad for a picnic. What will Maggie do?

○ Maggie will buy the salad at the store.
○ Maggie will buy the vegetables at the store.
● Maggie will use vegetables from her garden.

The big white goose wakes up. It stands and stretches its wings. It looks all around. It feels very hungry. What will the goose do?

○ The goose will go swimming.
● The goose will look for food.
○ The goose will go back to sleep.

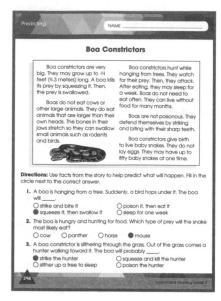

Page 298

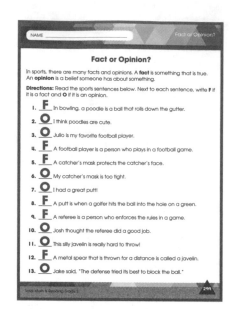

Page 299

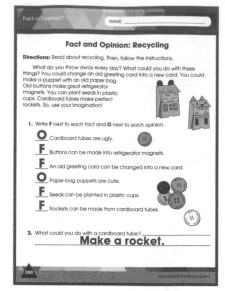

Page 300

Page 301

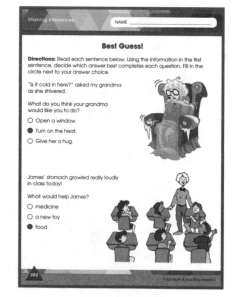

Page 302

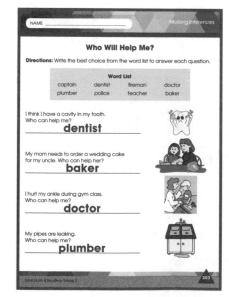

Page 303

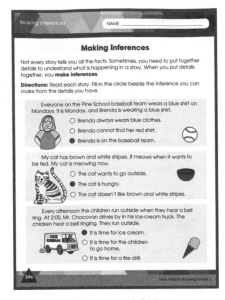

Page 304

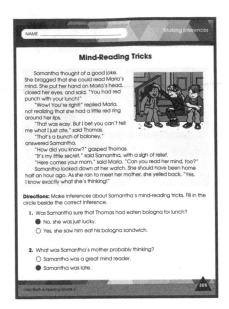

Page 305

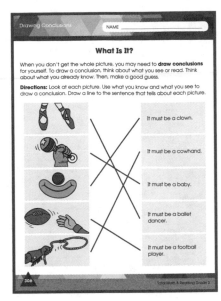

Page 306

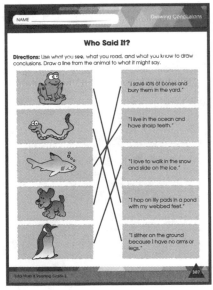

Page 307

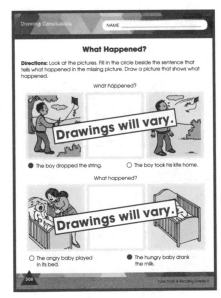

Page 308

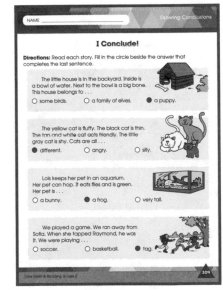

Page 309

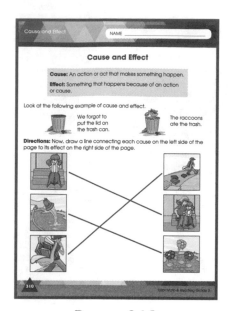

Page 310

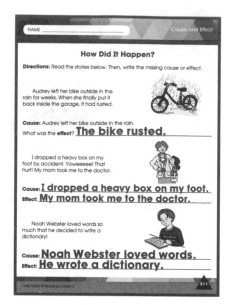

Page 311

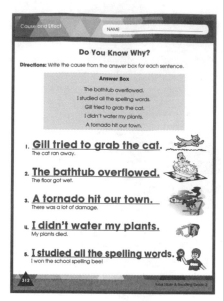

Page 312

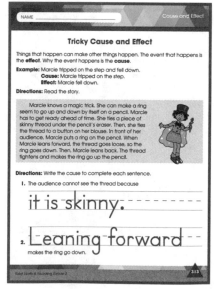

Page 313

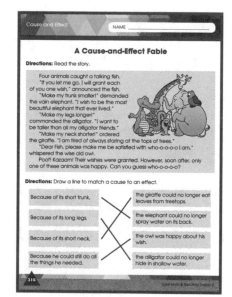

Page 314

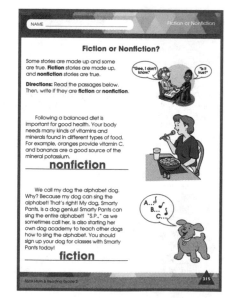

Page 315

Page 316

Fiction or Nonfiction? NAME _____

Nonfiction: Tornado Tips

Directions: Read about tornadoes. Then, follow the instructions.

A tornado begins over land with strong winds and thunderstorms. The spinning air becomes a funnel. It can cause damage. If you are inside, go to the lowest floor of the building. A basement is a safe place. A bathroom or closet in the middle of a building can be a safe place, too. If you are outside, lie in a ditch. Remember, tornadoes are dangerous.

Write five facts about tornadoes.

1. **A tornado begins over land.**
2. **Spinning air becomes a funnel.**
3. **Tornadoes can cause damage.**
4. **A basement is a safe place to be in a tornado.**
5. **If you are outside during a tornado, you should lie in a ditch.**

Page 317

NAME _____ Fiction or Nonfiction?

Fiction: Hercules

The **setting** is where a story takes place. The **characters** are the people in a story or play.

Directions: Read about Hercules. Then, answer the questions.

Hercules was born in the warm Atlantic Ocean. He was a very small and weak baby. He wanted to be the strongest hurricane in the world. But he had one problem. He couldn't blow 75-mile-per-hour winds. Hercules blew and blew in the ocean, until one day, his sister, Hola, told him it would be more fun to be a breeze than a hurricane. Hercules agreed. It was a breeze to be a breeze!

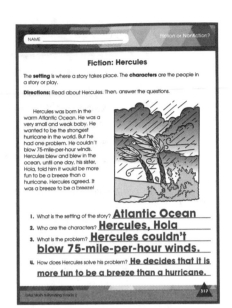

1. What is the setting of the story? **Atlantic Ocean**
2. Who are the characters? **Hercules, Hola**
3. What is the problem? **Hercules couldn't blow 75-mile-per-hour winds.**
4. How does Hercules solve his problem? **He decides that it is more fun to be a breeze than a hurricane.**

Page 318

Fiction or Nonfiction NAME _____

Fiction/Nonfiction: The Fourth of July

Directions: Read each story. Then, write whether it is fiction or nonfiction.

One sunny day in July, a dog named Stan ran away from home. He went up one street and down the other looking for fun, but all the yards were empty. Where was everybody? Stan kept walking until he heard the sound of band music and happy people. Stan walked faster until he got to Central Street. There he saw men, women, children, and dogs getting ready to walk in a parade. It was the Fourth of July!

Fiction or nonfiction? **Fiction**

Americans celebrate the Fourth of July every year, because it is the birthday of the United States of America. On July 4, 1776, the United States got its independence from Great Britain. Today, Americans celebrate this holiday with parades, picnics, and fireworks as they proudly wave the red, white, and blue American flag.

Fiction or nonfiction? **Nonfiction**

Page 319

NAME _____ Fiction or Nonfiction

Fiction and Nonfiction: Which Is It?

Directions: Read about fiction and nonfiction books. Then, follow the instructions.

There are many kinds of books. Some books have make-believe stories about princesses and dragons. Some books contain poetry and rhymes, like Mother Goose. These are fiction.

Some books contain facts about space and plants. And still other books have stories about famous people in history, like Abraham Lincoln. These are nonfiction.

Write **F** for **fiction** and **NF** for **nonfiction**.

F 1. nursery rhyme
F 2. fairy tale
NF 3. true life story of a famous athlete
F 4. Aesop's fables
NF 5. dictionary entry about foxes
NF 6. weather report
F 7. story about a talking tree
NF 8. text about how a tadpole becomes a frog
NF 9. text about animal habitats
F 10. riddles and jokes

Page 321

NAME _____ Story Elements

Character, cont.

First, authors must decide who their main character is going to be. Next, they decide what their main character looks like. Then, they reveal the character's personality by:

what the character does

what the character says

Directions: Answer the questions about the story you just read.

Who is the main character in "Adventurous Alenna"?

Alenna is the main character.

What does Alenna look like? Describe her appearance on the line below:

Alenna had long, blond hair and sea-green eyes.

Give two examples of what Alenna **does** that shows that she is adventurous:

1. **She goes on long bike rides.**
2. **She water-skis.**

Give an example of what Alenna **says** that reveals she is adventurous.

She wants to go snorkeling.

Page 322

Story Elements NAME _____

Character Interview—Lights! Camera! Action!

An **interview** takes place between two people, usually a reporter and another person. The interviewer asks questions for the person to answer.

Directions: Pretend that you are a reporter. Choose a character from a book you read. If you could ask the character anything you wanted to, what would you ask?

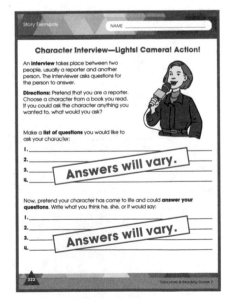

Make a **list of questions** you would like to ask your character:

1.
2.
3. **Answers will vary.**
4.

Now, pretend your character has come to life and could **answer your questions**. Write what you think he, she, or it would say:

1.
2.
3. **Answers will vary.**
4.

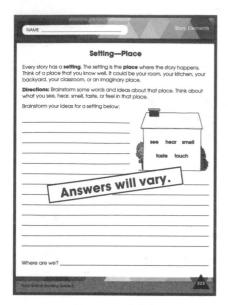

Page 323

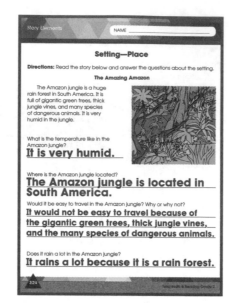

Page 324

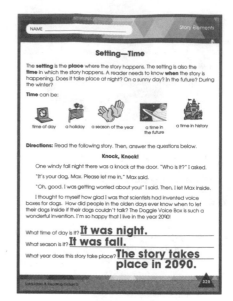

Page 325

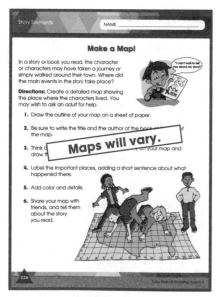

Page 326

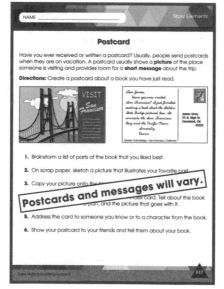

Page 327

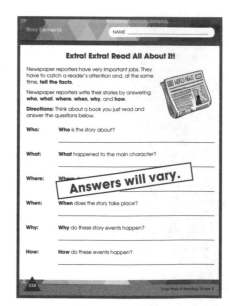

Page 328

Page 329

NAME _____   Story Elements

Extra! Extra! Read All About It!

Directions: Use your answers on page 328 to write a newspaper article about the book you read.

BIG CITY TIMES

Title

(Write a catchy title for your article.)

Articles will vary.

Page 330

Nouns   NAME _____

Common Nouns

A **common noun** names a person, place, or thing.

Example: The **boy** had several **chores** to do.

Directions: Fill in the circle below each common noun.

1. First, the boy had to feed his puppy.
2. He got fresh water for his pet.
3. Next, the boy poured some dry food into a bowl.
4. He set the dish on the floor in the kitchen.
5. Then, he called his dog to come to dinner.
6. The boy and his dad worked in the garden.
7. The father turned the dirt with a shovel.
8. The boy carefully dropped seeds into little holes.
9. Soon, tiny plants would sprout from the soil.
10. Sunshine and showers would help the radishes grow.

Page 331

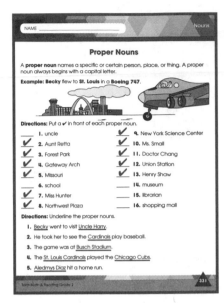

NAME _____   Nouns

Proper Nouns

A **proper noun** names a specific or certain person, place, or thing. A proper noun always begins with a capital letter.

Example: **Becky** flew to **St. Louis** in a **Boeing 747**.

Directions: Put a ✔ in front of each proper noun.

1. uncle
✔ 2. Aunt Retta
✔ 3. Forest Park
✔ 4. Gateway Arch
✔ 5. Missouri
___ 6. school
✔ 7. Miss Hunter
✔ 8. Northwest Plaza
✔ 9. New York Science Center
✔ 10. Ms. Small
___ 11. Doctor Chang
✔ 12. Union Station
✔ 13. Henry Shaw
___ 14. museum
___ 15. librarian
___ 16. shopping mall

Directions: Underline the proper nouns.

1. <u>Becky</u> went to visit <u>Uncle Harry</u>.
2. He took her to see the <u>Cardinals</u> play baseball.
3. The game was at <u>Busch Stadium</u>.
4. The <u>St. Louis Cardinals</u> played the <u>Chicago Cubs</u>.
5. <u>Aledmys Díaz</u> hit a home run.

Page 332

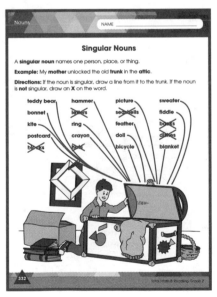

Nouns   NAME _____

Singular Nouns

A **singular noun** names one person, place, or thing.

Example: My **mother** unlocked the old **trunk** in the **attic**.

Directions: If the noun is singular, draw a line from it to the trunk. If the noun is **not** singular, draw an **X** on the word.

teddy bear   hammer   picture   sweater
bonnet   letters   seashells   fiddle
kite   ring   feather   boots
postcard   crayon   doll   dishes
bikes   hat   bicycle   blanket

Page 333

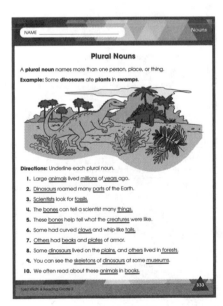

NAME _____   Nouns

Plural Nouns

A **plural noun** names more than one person, place, or thing.

Example: Some **dinosaurs** ate **plants** in **swamps**.

Directions: Underline each plural noun.

1. Large <u>animals</u> lived <u>millions</u> of <u>years</u> ago.
2. <u>Dinosaurs</u> roamed many <u>parts</u> of the Earth.
3. <u>Scientists</u> look for <u>fossils</u>.
4. The <u>bones</u> can tell a scientist many <u>things</u>.
5. These <u>bones</u> help tell what the <u>creatures</u> were like.
6. Some had curved <u>claws</u> and whip-like <u>tails</u>.
7. <u>Others</u> had <u>beaks</u> and <u>plates</u> of armor.
8. Some <u>dinosaurs</u> lived on the plains, and <u>others</u> lived in <u>forests</u>.
9. You can see the <u>skeletons</u> of <u>dinosaurs</u> at some <u>museums</u>.
10. We often read about these <u>animals</u> in <u>books</u>.

Page 334

Verbs   NAME _____

Action Verbs

A **verb** is a word that can show action.

Example: I **jump**.   He **kicks**.   He **walked**.

Directions: Underline the verb in each sentence. Write it on the line.

1. Our school <u>plays</u> games on Field Day.   **plays**
2. Juan <u>runs</u> 50 yards.   **runs**
3. Carmen <u>hops</u> in a sack race.   **hops**
4. Paula <u>tosses</u> a ball through a hoop.   **tosses**
5. One girl <u>carries</u> a jellybean on a spoon.   **carries**
6. Lola <u>bounces</u> the ball.   **bounces**
7. Some boys <u>chase</u> after balloons.   **chase**
8. Mark <u>chooses</u> me for his team.   **chooses**
9. The children <u>cheer</u> for the winners.   **cheer**
10. Everyone <u>enjoys</u> Field Day.   **enjoys**

Answer Key

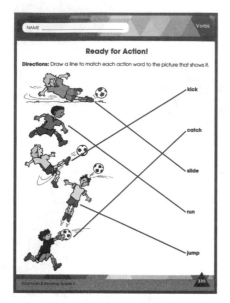

Page 335

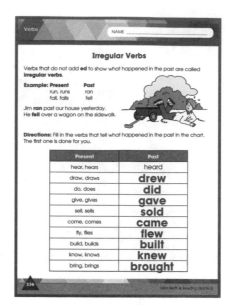

Page 336

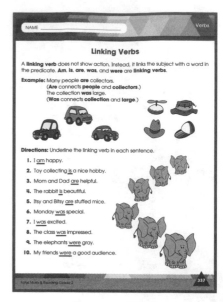

Page 337

Page 338

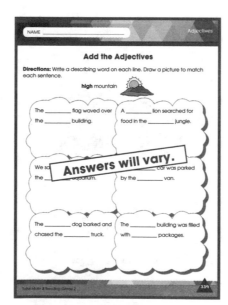

Page 339

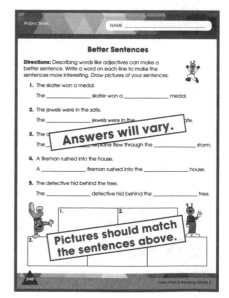

Page 340

Page 341

NAME _____ Adjectives

Describing People

Directions: Choose two words from the box that describe each character. Then, complete each sentence to tell why you chose those words.

understanding spoiled responsible lazy helpful upset happy
busy caring kind mean confused unhappy patient nice

Answers may include: happy and kind because she likes to help people and makes a lot of friends that way.

Mother is _____ and _____ because she _____

Answers will vary.

Father is _____ and _____ because he _____

Page 342

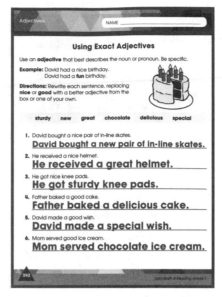

Adjectives **NAME** _____

Using Exact Adjectives

Use an **adjective** that best describes the noun or pronoun. Be specific.

Example: David had a nice birthday.
David had a **fun** birthday.

Directions: Rewrite each sentence, replacing **nice** or **good** with a better adjective from the box or one of your own.

sturdy new great chocolate delicious special

1. David bought a nice pair of in-line skates.
David bought a new pair of in-line skates.

2. He received a nice helmet.
He received a great helmet.

3. He got nice knee pads.
He got sturdy knee pads.

4. Father baked a good cake.
Father baked a delicious cake.

5. David made a good wish.
David made a special wish.

6. Mom served good ice cream.
Mom served chocolate ice cream.

Page 343

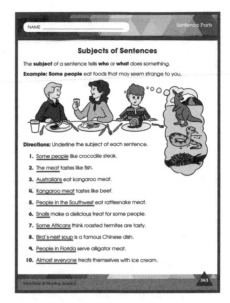

NAME _____ Sentence Parts

Subjects of Sentences

The **subject** of a sentence tells **who** or **what** does something.

Example: Some people eat foods that may seem strange to you.

Directions: Underline the subject of each sentence.

1. Some people like crocodile steak.
2. The meat tastes like fish.
3. Australians eat kangaroo meat.
4. Kangaroo meat tastes like beef.
5. People in the Southwest eat rattlesnake meat.
6. Snails make a delicious treat for some people.
7. Some Africans think roasted termites are tasty.
8. Bird's-nest soup is a famous Chinese dish.
9. People in Florida serve alligator meat.
10. Almost everyone treats themselves with ice cream.

Page 344

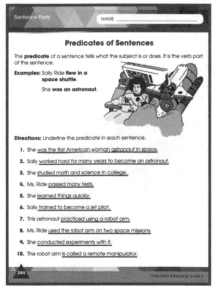

Sentence Parts **NAME** _____

Predicates of Sentences

The **predicate** of a sentence tells what the subject is or does. It is the verb part of the sentence.

Examples: Sally Ride **flew in a space shuttle.**
She **was an astronaut.**

Directions: Underline the predicate in each sentence.

1. She was the first American woman astronaut in space.
2. Sally worked hard for many years to become an astronaut.
3. She studied math and science in college.
4. Ms. Ride passed many tests.
5. She learned things quickly.
6. Sally trained to become a jet pilot.
7. This astronaut practiced using a robot arm.
8. Ms. Ride used the robot arm on two space missions.
9. She conducted experiments with it.
10. The robot arm is called a remote manipulator.

Page 345

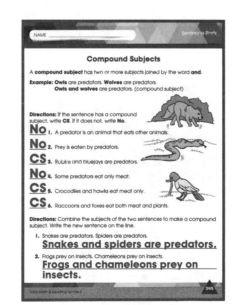

NAME _____ Sentence Parts

Compound Subjects

A **compound subject** has two or more subjects joined by the word **and.**

Example: Owls are predators. **Wolves** are predators.
Owls and wolves are predators. (compound subject)

Directions: If the sentence has a compound subject, write **CS.** If it does not, write **No.**

No 1. A predator is an animal that eats other animals.
No 2. Prey is eaten by predators.
CS 3. Robins and bluejays are predators.
No 4. Some predators eat only meat.
CS 5. Crocodiles and hawks eat meat only.
CS 6. Raccoons and foxes eat both meat and plants.

Directions: Combine the subjects of the two sentences to make a compound subject. Write the new sentence on the line.

1. Snakes are predators. Spiders are predators.
Snakes and spiders are predators.

2. Frogs prey on insects. Chameleons prey on insects.
Frogs and chameleons prey on insects.

Page 346

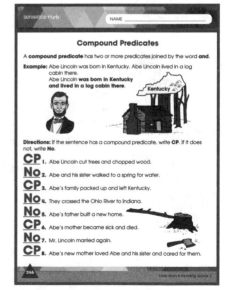

Sentence Parts **NAME** _____

Compound Predicates

A **compound predicate** has two or more predicates joined by the word **and.**

Example: Abe Lincoln was born in Kentucky. Abe Lincoln lived in a log cabin there.
Abe Lincoln **was born in Kentucky and lived in a log cabin there.**

Kentucky

Directions: If the sentence has a compound predicate, write **CP.** If it does not, write **No.**

CP 1. Abe Lincoln cut trees and chopped wood.
No 2. Abe and his sister walked to a spring for water.
CP 3. Abe's family packed up and left Kentucky.
No 4. They crossed the Ohio River to Indiana.
No 5. Abe's father built a new home.
CP 6. Abe's mother became sick and died.
No 7. Mr. Lincoln married again.
CP 8. Abe's new mother loved Abe and his sister and cared for them.

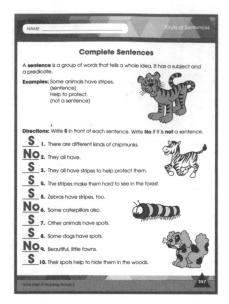

Page 347

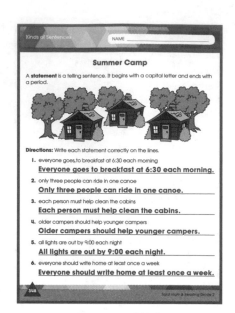

Page 348

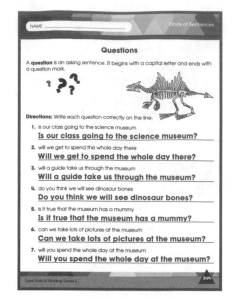

Page 349

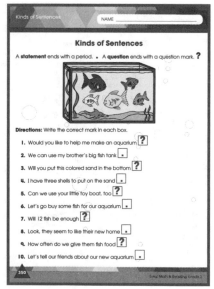

Page 350

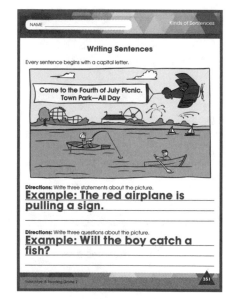

Page 351

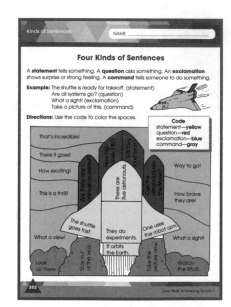

Page 352

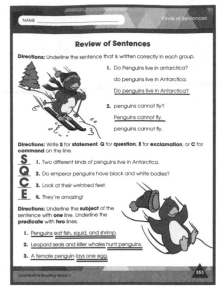

Review of Sentences

Directions: Underline the sentence that is written correctly in each group.

1. Do Penguins live in antarctica?
   do penguins live in Antarctica.
   <u>Do Penguins live in Antarctica?</u>

2. penguins cannot fly?
   <u>Penguins cannot fly.</u>
   penguins cannot fly.

Directions: Write **S** for **statement**, **Q** for **question**, **E** for **exclamation**, or **C** for **command** on the line.

S 1. Two different kinds of penguins live in Antarctica.
Q 2. Do emperor penguins have black and white bodies?
C 3. Look at their webbed feet.
E 4. They're amazing!

Directions: Underline the **subject** of the sentence with **one** line. Underline the **predicate** with **two** lines.

1. Penguins eat fish, squid, and shrimp.
2. Leopard seals and killer whales hunt penguins.
3. A female penguin lays one egg.

Page 353

My Bag's Ready!

The first letter of a word is used to put words in alphabetical (ABC) order.
Directions: Write the golf words below in ABC order. If two or more words begin with the same letter, go to the next letter to put them in ABC order.

club   tee   bag   ball   scorecard   cart   towel

1. **bag**
2. **ball**
3. **cart**
4. **club**
5. **scorecard**
6. **tee**
7. **towel**

Page 354

Slam Dunk!

Directions: Put the words in the box in ABC order.

coach   points   team   hoop
player   game   score   dunk

1. **coach**
2. **dunk**
3. **game**
4. **hoop**
5. **player**
6. **points**
7. **score**
8. **team**

Page 355

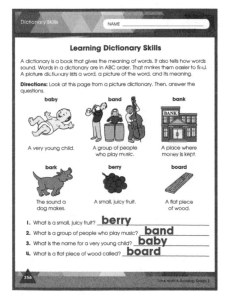

Learning Dictionary Skills

A dictionary is a book that gives the meaning of words. It also tells how words sound. Words in a dictionary are in ABC order. That makes them easier to find. A picture dictionary lists a word, a picture of the word, and its meaning.

Directions: Look at this page from a picture dictionary. Then, answer the questions.

baby — A very young child.
band — A group of people who play music.
bank — A place where money is kept.
bark — The sound a dog makes.
berry — A small, juicy fruit.
board — A flat piece of wood.

1. What is a small, juicy fruit? **berry**
2. What is a group of people who play music? **band**
3. What is the name for a very young child? **baby**
4. What is a flat piece of wood called? **board**

Page 356

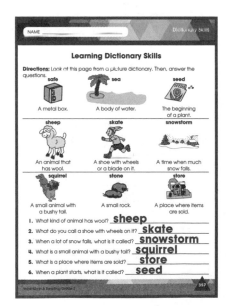

Learning Dictionary Skills

Directions: Look at this page from a picture dictionary. Then, answer the questions.

safe — A metal box.
sea — A body of water.
seed — The beginning of a plant.
sheep — An animal that has wool.
skate — A shoe with wheels or a blade on it.
snowstorm — A time when much snow falls.
squirrel — A small animal with a bushy tail.
stone — A small rock.
store — A place where items are sold.

1. What kind of animal has wool? **sheep**
2. What do you call a shoe with wheels on it? **skate**
3. When a lot of snow falls, what is it called? **snowstorm**
4. What is a small animal with a bushy tail? **squirrel**
5. What is a place where items are sold? **store**
6. When a plant starts, what is it called? **seed**

Page 357

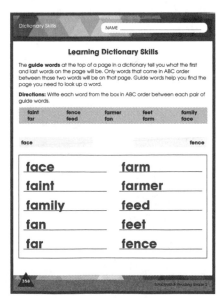

Learning Dictionary Skills

The **guide words** at the top of a page in a dictionary tell you what the first and last words on the page will be. Only words that come in ABC order between those two words will be on that page. Guide words help you find the page you need to look up a word.

Directions: Write each word from the box in ABC order between each pair of guide words.

faint   fence   farmer   feet   family
far   feed   fan   farm   face

face   fence

face	**farm**
faint	**farmer**
family	**feed**
fan	**feet**
far	**fence**

Page 358
